WEST ACADEMIC PUBLISHING'S LAW SCHOOL ADVISORY BOARD

GLOBAL ENERGY JUSTICE

Law and Policy

LAKSHMAN GURUSWAMY
Nicholas Doman Professor of Law
University of Colorado at Boulder

WEST ACADEMIC PUBLISHING

444 Cedar Street, Suite 700
St. Paul, MN 55101
1-877-888-1330

Printed in the United States of America

ISBN: 978-0-314-29161-5

DEDICATION

This book is dedicated to Judge C.G. Weeramantry, the Sri Lankan born judge, professor, and scholar. His awe-inspiring life and work is an indelible testament to the universality of law in global society. His cascade of books, spanning an astonishing array of subjects, demonstrate why law is a universal global phenomenon that should shape societal mores. His works include those on human rights within countries and across traditional cultural divides, the concepts and international lineages of justice, the human and bio-physical environment, nuclear power, technology, and comparative religious perspectives spanning Christianity, Buddhism, Hinduism and Islam.

Judge Weeramantry was a Judge of the Supreme Court of Sri Lanka, a Distinguished Professor at the University of Monash, and a Judge and Vice President of the International Court of Justice (ICJ) in the Hague. His contribution to the jurisprudence of the ICJ is unmatched. He brought unparalleled erudition, extraordinary passion, inimitable wisdom, and peerless vision to his role as an international judge. His great and enduring legacy spans the entire compass of international law.

It has been my privilege to know and treasure Christie as a mentor, philosopher, and friend. I am humbled by his friendship, and it is an honor to dedicate this book to him.

ACKNOWLEDGMENTS

I am indebted to a number of people who have made this offering possible. They have helped in different ways. In particular, my colleague Professor Audrey Huang at the University of Colorado, School of Law, creatively and diligently encouraged and supervised the valuable work of writing and editing the Model Laws on Lighting for Developing countries. The two law students directed by her: Ugyen Tshering and Mahir Haque did commendable and exemplary work. Jason Aamodt, Assistant Dean, University of Tulsa, supervised the work of drafting the Model Law on Lighting for Developed countries with the assistance of law students from the University of Denver, School of Law. He did so assiduously, and with characteristic diligence and skill.

Nasratuliah Shazad Sahak, and Cassidy Woodard reviewed and edited different chapters of this book with skill and expertise, As always, the assistance given by Jane Thompson, the Research and Reference librarian at the School of Law was nothing short of outstanding. The ever obliging Diana Avelis, Faculty Assistant, provided invaluable help at different stages of the MS.

SUMMARY OF CONTENTS

TABLE OF CONTENTS

GLOBAL ENERGY JUSTICE

Law and Policy

Chapter 1

ENERGY AND SOCIETY

We will be explaining the meaning of what may be an unfamiliar concept: "the energy poor." The term conjugates a difficult abstraction: energy, with an elusive social construct: the poor. We will try to obtain a practical and functional, as distinct from a theoretical, understanding of the two parts of this term. The purpose of our endeavor is to appreciate the primary role of energy in society, and how it affects the energy poor. The objective of our book is to explore what can be done to address the energy poor within the frameworks of justice, law and policy.

I. The Concept of Energy

Defining what we mean by energy offers one way of demonstrating its importance. A definition tells you what something is and points to the fact that the word "energy" describes a particular phenomenon. A typical definition of energy, therefore, must offer hard verifiable facts that can be discovered by scientific investigation. But such a single, objective definition may not be possible for a number of reasons. First, definitions may vary according to who is seeking to define the phenomenon of energy.

For example, while they purport to define what they see as datum, physicists—who do not see energy through the same lens as chemists or biologists—may define energy in one way. Energy, as defined by the physicist, is an abstraction of the raw materials of the universe.[1] On the other hand, the definition offered by the chemist is based on what the chemist sees about the interactions and composition of matter.[2] The biologist by contrast sees energy through the prism of living organisms.[3] Each of these definitions may be verifiable and accurate as far as the physicist or chemist or biologist is concerned. None of them can be accused of a wrong definition, nor can one claim that only their definition is true while those of the others is false.

Second, the difficulties of definition are compounded by the fact that the phenomenon of energy can be categorized as *potential* and

---

[1] This may lead the physicist to define energy as the ability to do work. Rachel Scherr, Hunter Close & Sarah McKagan, *Intuitive Ontologies for Energy in Physics*, 1413 AM. INST. PHYSICS 343 (2011).

[2] Leading to a definition of energy as the power created by the reaction of two substances.

[3] This may lead the biologist to define energy as the transformations taking place in plants and animals when they collect energy from the sun and use carbon dioxide and water in the process called photosynthesis to produce sugars.

kinetic, and each of these categories may take differing forms.[4] For example, *potential energy* is stored energy. Chemical energy is stored in the bonds between atoms and molecules. Mechanical energy is stored in objects by tension. Gravitational energy is stored in an object's height. Electrical energy is stored in a battery, and nuclear energy is stored in the nucleus of an atom.

The second category, *kinetic energy*, is the energy of motion. It too is expressed in different forms, such as radiant energy (e.g., sunshine), thermal (heat) energy caused by the vibration of atoms or molecules within substances, and motion energy from the movement of wind, water, or any other object. Both potential and kinetic energy need to be converted in order to do work. Consequently, the extent and use of energy found either in potential or kinetic energy depends on how it is converted. Moreover, given the categories and forms of energy referred to, it is difficult to offer one comprehensive definition that covers all these energy forms.

But, the inability to offer one true, accurate, objective, or comprehensive *definition* of energy does not preclude us from trying to understand the *concept* of energy. It is possible to begin with a "primitive notion" about the concept of energy as found in mathematics and logic that could lead us toward a working definition.[5]

Although "definitions" and "concepts" are usually situated within mathematics and formal systems[6] of logic or mathematics, they also apply to all kinds of other phenomena and social systems, like law. In fact, the evolution of definitions and concepts of law are analogous to those that apply to energy and shed light on how we can understand what we mean by energy. For example, a number of leading legal philosophers have refrained from defining law, but have thought it more useful to explain the concept of law.[7] Similarly, scientists have defined energy as the capacity for doing work or, in other words, the capacity to move an object into or out of some position.[8] While this definition may be criticized as a description of what energy does rather than what it is, it is nonetheless a working and functional definition. Given that the readers of this book are

---

[4] *Kinetic and Potential Energy*, DIFFEN, http://www.diffen.com/difference/Kinetic_Energy_vs_Potential_Energy (last visited Nov. 22, 2015).

[5] Alfred Tarski, *Introduction to Logic: And to the Methodology of Deductive Sciences* 118 (Oxford Univ. Press 1946).

[6] The Editors of Encyclopedia Britannica, *Formal System: Logic,* ENCYCLOPEDIA BRITANNICA, http://www.britannica.com/topic/formal-system (last visited Nov. 29, 2015).

[7] H.L.A. Hart, *The Concept of Law* 14–17 (2d ed. 1994); Richard Posner, *Overcoming Law* vii (reprt. ed. 1996); Ronald Dworkin, *Law's Empire* 104 (1986).

[8] Harold H. Schobert, *Energy and Society: An Introduction* 13 (2d ed. 2014).

predominantly law students or lawyers, we will compare the concept of energy to law.[9]

II. Comparing the Concepts of Law & Energy

Neither energy nor law offer conclusive definitions that encompasses all attributes of those terms. Nonetheless, energy, like law, is both real and universally used. They function as critical determinants in shaping society. Both energy and law are constantly employed to construct and fashion the essential socio-economic, political, and ecological fabric of societies the world over.

The lack of an authoritative canonical definition of law does not prevent us from studying specific branches of law, such as constitutional, criminal, contract, tort, property, environmental, and commercial law. From our study of these subjects, we begin to understand that law is a ubiquitous, yet complex, socio-political phenomenon. It creates the foundations of the economic, political, and social structures of a state and governs the manner in which society regulates and mediates relationships between people.

Notwithstanding the immense power asserted by law, legal philosophers across the centuries have differed over the definition of law—not unlike scientists who have differed over the definition of energy. Some legal philosophers like the English jurist John Austin (1790–1859) defined law as the general command of a sovereign backed by force.[10] His followers are called analytical jurists or legal positivists. Others have disagreed on whether command and force are essential and necessary attributes of law. Historical jurists like Sir Fredrick Pollock pointed to the villages in India governed by customary laws that were not created by a sovereign or backed by force.[11]

Ronald Dworkin argued that, in deciding hard cases, judges often invoke legal principles that do not derive their authority from an official act of promulgation. These principles must be characterized as law because judges are bound to consider them when relevant.[12] This contradicts Austin's pedigree thesis that a proposition of law is valid only by virtue of having been formally promulgated by a sovereign. H.L.A, Hart offered the most compelling

---

9 What we are trying to do is to explain the concept of energy by analogizing energy to law. The law referred to is national, not international, law. As we have noted above, this book makes the case for global energy justice to be institutionalized as international law, but that is not what we are attempting to do at this point.

10 John Austin, *The Province of Jurisprudence Determined* (Wilfrid E. Rumble ed., Cambridge Univ. Press ed. 1995).

11 Fredrick Pollock, *Law and Command*, 1 LAW MAG. & REV. 189, 194–95 (1892).

12 Ronald M. Dworkin, *Taking Rights Seriously*, 40 (Harvard Univ. Press 1977).

criticism of Austin's thesis relating to the use of force. He argued that the command of a gunman ordering someone to hand over her money was not a law just because it was backed by force. According to Hart, legal rules are obligatory because people accept them as standards, and in limited cases, punish deviations.[13] It is this internal point of view, and not force, that creates a sense of obligation, and gives law its legitimacy.[14]

But whatever their differences about the definition of law, all these theorists agreed on the fact and importance of law in society. Their theoretical disharmony does not affect their view that the legal system is in fact a recognizable social phenomenon that governs society. Similarly, whatever the theoretical differences about the definition of energy, it is a reality in every aspect of our lives from food and clothing to shelter, transportation, communication, and medicine. It is a ubiquitous biophysical phenomenon, or fact of life and human history, analogous to the socio-political phenomena of law.

III. A Brief History of Human Energy Use

Humans are endlessly engaged in transforming or converting energy found in the environment into energy useful for human purposes. Such energy can be classified as either endosomatic or exosomatic. Transforming food energy into muscular power is endosomatic (or metabolic) energy. Transforming energy outside the human body into useful energy is exosomatic energy. Exosomatic energy is an essential element of societal development,[15] and some scholars conclude that all civilizations are founded upon, and determined by, the sources of energy they control.[16]

The hominid family of primates emerged about 5 million years ago, with modern humans (*homo sapiens*) appearing around 240,000 B.P. (before the present).[17] Throughout history, humans have focused on controlling the energy flows and stores inherent in the natural world.[18] For the vast majority of this time, humans relied solely on endosomatic energy in the form of chemical (caloric) energy obtained from food that produced the mechanical (kinetic) energy of working

---

[13] Hart, *supra* note 7, at 80.

[14] *Id.* at 56.

[15] Mario Giampietro, Kozo Mayumi, & Alevgul H. Sorman, *Energy Analysis for a Sustainable Future* 27 (Routledge 2013).

[16] E.g., Leslie A. White, *Energy and the Evolution of Culture,* 45 AM. ANTHROPOLOGIST, 335–56, 345 (1943).

[17] Schobert, *supra* note 8, at 18.

[18] James C. Williams, Ph.D., *History of Energy*, THE FRANKLIN INST. (Apr. 25, 2006), http://www.academia.edu/170347/_History_of_Energy_Scientists_and_the_Franklin_Institute_Making_Their_Cases_Philadelphia_PA_The_Franklin_Institute_2006.

muscles. Eventually tools, such as axes, oars, grindstones, spears, and arrows, were developed to make more efficient use of endosomatic energy in the procurement and processing of foodstuffs.[19]

Archaeological evidence suggests that while humans have been making use of fire for at least 500,000 years, the ability to start a fire at will and control the fire as desired only emerged around 9,000 B.P. Domestication of animals began more than 10,000 B.P., but the use of draft animals to do work for humans was more recent, probably arising about 7,000 B.P. Thus, for 97 percent of human history, we have relied solely on muscle power to do work.[20] A breakthrough in human development occurred 3,000 B.P. with the development of the waterwheel, which was probably used to grind grains. This marked the first time that humans had mastered a source of energy to do work that was not based on human or animal muscle power.[21] Windmills were developed much more recently, about 900 B.P.

The development of the steam engine in the early eighteenth century represented a true revolution in energy technology[22] and also "permanently established the link between fossil energy resources and industrialization."[23] Steam engines combine heat and water to convert thermal energy into mechanical energy, and this new technology was eagerly put to use in the early stages of the industrial revolution. Importantly, steam engines gave manufacturers the freedom to build facilities in locations without ready sources of flowing water or wind power. Moreover, steam engines provided the power for locomotives and ships to move goods and people. However, steam power came with significant and immediate environmental costs, most notably widespread deforestation in Europe. As a result, coal became the fuel of choice among the early industrialized nations, eventually to be unseated by oil during the first half of the twentieth century.

By the late nineteenth century, energy demand in industrialized countries had grown considerably.[24] This demand was met by the development of electric energy, an incredibly versatile energy source that can be transmitted over vast distances and put to a wide variety of uses. The first electric power plants were hydroelectric facilities relying on flowing water as their energy source, converting mechanical energy to electrical energy. Subsequent power plants

---

[19] White, *supra* note 16, at 337.

[20] Schobert, *supra* note 8, at 19.

[21] *Id.* at 18–19.

[22] John Fanchi, *Energy in the 21st Century* 149–51 (3d ed. 2013).

[23] Williams, *supra* note 18.

[24] Fanchi, *supra* note 22, at 151.

have employed fossil fuels, and more recently nuclear fission, geothermal, wind, and solar power, to produce electricity. The development of alternating current technology allowed the transmission of electricity over long distances, enabling the development of regional power transmission grids to distribute the electricity generated at a network of large-scale power plants.[25] By the early twentieth century, electricity had emerged as the favored method for transmitting energy, and researchers responded with a range of products that extended the ways in which humankind could apply this electricity.[26]

In the 1950s and 1960s, nuclear power emerged as a widely touted solution to the world's energy problems.[27] Physicist Marie Curie's work on uranium compounds in the nineteenth century set the stage for subsequent discoveries regarding the intrinsic power of the atom. This sparked intense research in atomic physics in Europe in the early decades of the twentieth century, resulting in the understanding that a uranium atom, when split with a neutron, would cause a self-perpetuating chain reaction of atom splitting, releasing tremendous amounts of energy in the process. As World War II broke out, the United States became particularly interested in possible military applications of nuclear fission, leading to the development of the atomic bomb. The United States also created the Atomic Energy Commission to oversee nuclear weapons development and to promote nonmilitary applications of nuclear energy. Other nations were also interested in mastering nuclear technology, both to further their national security interests as well as to provide inexpensive electricity for industrial and domestic use. The world's first civilian nuclear power plant began operations in 1954 in the Soviet Union, and industrialized nations rushed to construct nuclear plants to meet the seemingly ever-growing demand for electric power. Moreover, nuclear power, although environmentally problematic in its own right, was not associated with acid rain and some of the other environmental impacts of fossil fuels that had been identified by the nascent environmental movement, and many of the dangers of nuclear power were not yet fully appreciated. However, the 1979 Three Mile Island nuclear plant accident in Pennsylvania, followed by the catastrophic nuclear reactor meltdowns at Chernobyl, Ukraine, in 1986 and Fukushima, Japan, in 2011, raised serious questions regarding the safety of nuclear power plants and galvanized nuclear power opponents. These incidents, coupled with the unresolved problem of the long-term disposal of nuclear waste, have dramatically slowed the expansion of nuclear power.

---

[25] *Id.* at 152–54.

[26] Williams, *supra* note 18.

[27] *Id.*

Since the late 1990s, renewable energy technologies have blossomed into a rapidly growing segment of the industrialized world's energy mix, thus emerging "as a key solution to the triple challenges of energy supply, security, and climate change."[28] "Renewables" are generally defined as energy sources that use fuel available at no cost or that can be continually replenished, and the term thus encompasses a series of disparate technologies:

1. *Wind*—the fastest growing, which powers technologically sophisticated machines, clustered in "farms," that generate electricity.

2. *Direct sunlight*—captured either by photovoltaic cells (PVs) or by mirrors or other technologies that concentrate the light and transform its energy into electric current.

3. *Biofuels*—ethanol, biodiesel, and advanced biofuels (made of algae, cellulose, or other feedstock), all of which substitute for gasoline, diesel, or potentially, jet fuel.

4. *Biomass*—wood or other plant materials pelletized or otherwise treated and burned in a power plant; also wood or dung that people in developing countries burn for heating and cooking.

5. *Geothermal*—either hot water or hot steam pumped from beneath the ground to the surface to drive an electricity-producing turbine.

6. *Hydropower*—falling or pressurized water that drives turbines; dams are increasingly criticized on environmental grounds and thus are hard to build in many countries.

7. *Passive solar*—now also known as green buildings, which take advantage of the natural habitat to reduce energy consumption, and which often overlaps with energy efficiency.[29]

Critically, these technologies are not based on finite resources and have the added benefit of much lower carbon footprints than conventional energy sources. However, renewables remain a small part of the world's energy mix, and their development to date has often relied on government subsidies. Therefore, the role of renewable energy technologies in the coming decades is not yet clear

---

[28] Daniel Yergin, *The Quest: Energy, Security, and the Remaking of the Modern World* 528 (rev. ed. 2012).

[29] *Id.* at 529–30.

and will be determined by the ongoing interplay of policy, economics, and innovation.[30]

IV. The Importance and Limitations of Energy

As we have seen from its brief history, energy's presence and influence in the human and social world is essentially ubiquitous.[31] While energy is a fundamental human need and the driving determinant of human progress,[32] humans must constantly engage in energy conversions—processes that transform one form of energy into another, more useful form.

A rich, albeit neglected seam of writers and thinkers spanning the life sciences, mathematics, sociology, anthropology, engineering, and philosophy have explained the central role played by energy in the development of society. They have illustrated how societies have used energy, and have elucidated the interface between the physical or natural phenomena of exosomatic energy, and how technology was used to convert such natural resources to energy, as well as the impact of energy on human social systems. A number of them founded their theories on the existence of physical laws of nature that objectively governed an orderly world independent of human actions. These laws were analogous to the laws of motion discovered by Newton.

Some of the most important of these laws are the laws of thermodynamics. They are essential in understanding the limitations inherent in converting some forms of exosomatic energy such as fossil fuels (or hydrocarbons) for human use. Consequently, a grasp of some of the fundamental laws of thermodynamics is critical to a proper understanding of the relationship between modern civilizations and energy resources.[33] Indeed, as observed by Nobel Prize chemist Fredrick Soddy, "[t]he laws of thermodynamics control the rise and fall of political systems, the freedom or bondage of nations, the movements of commerce and industry, the origins of wealth and poverty, and the general physical welfare of the human race."[34]

The first law of thermodynamics is often called the "Law of Conservation of Energy." It posits that while energy can be transferred from one system to another in many forms, it cannot be created or destroyed. Thus, the total amount or quantity of energy

---

[30] *Id.* at 550–52.

[31] Eugene A. Rosa, Gary E. Machlis & Kenneth M. Keating, *Energy and Society*, 14 ANN. REV. SOCIOLOGY 149, 149 (1988).

[32] Leslie A. White, *The Evolution of Culture: The Development of Civilization To The Fall of Rome* 33–57 (McGraw-Hill Book Co., Inc. 1959).

[33] This discussion of thermodynamics is based on G. Tyler Miller Jr. & Scott Spoolman, *Environmental Science* 20–24, 45–55 (15th ed. 2015).

[34] *Id.* at 20.

available in the universe is constant. But that does not mean that the quality of energy remains unchanged. The second law of thermodynamics, identified by Nicolas Léonard Sadi Carnot (1796–1832), considered to be the founder of thermodynamics,[35] significantly modifies the first law by demonstrating that once used, the quality of energy is changed even though its quantity remains constant.

The second law postulates that energy deteriorates when employed to do useful work and that it necessarily flows from a level of high-quality (more concentrated) energy to a level of lower quality (less concentrated) energy. When it reaches the lower level, the energy is still in existence, but is no longer capable of doing work. This is because the transfer of energy to useful work is subject to "entropy" that irretrievably alters the original character of energy by dispersing it, and thereby diminishing its subsequent use. Because of entropy, what remains after the high quality energy is converted or used to perform jobs is an inferior, more dispersed and diffused form of energy that cannot be reused or recycled.[36]

Humans, particularly those living in high-energy civilizations, rely on flows of high-quality energy for their survival and, in the process, generate outputs of degraded energy (heat) and waste matter. The second law states that both energy and matter in the universe are degraded into heat and waste after they are converted. Therefore, post conversion energy will always be inferior to that of the initial state.[37] The cornucopian assumption that the continuous and unrestricted use of coal would generate almost perpetual economic growth was questioned by the discovery of the second law of thermodynamics.

Internal combustion engines, such as those commonly used in automobiles, clearly demonstrate the implications of the laws of thermodynamics. Energy-dense gasoline is put in the tank and combusted in the engine to create energy that is used to turn the wheels. Useful work is done as the vehicle's occupants and cargo are transported from point A to point B. However, the energy-dense gasoline is lost forever, and much energy is dissipated in the form of

---

35 Herman Erlichson, *Sadi Carnot, 'Founder of the Second Law of Thermodynamics'* 20 EUR. J. PHYSICS 183, 183–192 (1992).

36 Michael Pidwimy, *Fundamentals of Physical Geography* Ch. 6 (e) (2006), available at http://www.physicalgeography.net/fundamentals/6e.html (last visited Dec. 6, 2015).

37 The forgoing is based inter-alia on: John E.J. Schmitz, *Approaching the World's Environmental Problems Through the Second Law (Entropy Law) of Thermodynamics*, (2012), available at http://www.eoearth.org/view/article/150152 (last visited Dec. 6, 2015).

heat generated by the vehicle's mechanical processes—energy that is ultimately dispersed into the air and is thus "wasted."

Prior to the industrial revolution, agriculture was the primary method of human development. Agriculture involved the cultivation and use of land for raising plants and animals. The knowledge, skill, and learning devoted to care of the soil and growth of plants advanced the development of human society and has been an important aspect of economic and social growth. Agriculture was, however, dependent upon the energy derived from photosynthesis in plants for its productivity. Photosynthesis is a process used by plants and other organisms to convert light energy, normally from the sun, into chemical energy that fuels the organisms' activities. The quantity of energy that reaches the surface of the earth each year from the sun is vast, but photosynthesis captures less than 0.5 percent of the energy in sunlight.

Mechanical energy derived predominantly from human and animal muscle power was used to grow food and fodder that relied on photosynthesis. Wind and water power were of comparatively minor importance. Photosynthesis was also the source of all heat energy used in production processes since the heat came from burning wood. Furthermore, it required land to grow crops, and the availability of productive land was a severe impediment to growth.[38]

The Physiocrats of the mid eighteenth century understood that agricultural land was the source of material wealth and concluded that agricultural productivity was governed by physical or natural laws, including photosynthesis, which determined climate, rainfall, and the fertility of soil.[39] The extent to which humans recognized and acted upon these laws would increase agricultural productivity. While they saw the importance of the laws of nature, the Physiocrats did not understand the extent to which one form of energy could be transformed into another in order to increase productivity.

The hypothesis that a society's ability to harness energy defines what it can produce was initially articulated by the polymath Herbert Spencer (1820–1903), a philosopher, sociologist, biologist, and political theorist. Spencer compared the evolutionary development of human societies, which he termed "supra-biological" organisms to biological organisms in nature. He argued that the ability of societies to harness energy defines what they can produce; and thus the ability to control and use energy is the basis of both

---

[38] Tony Wrigley, *Opening Pandora's Box: A New Look at the Industrial Revolution*, VOX: CEPR'S POLICY PORTAL (July 22, 2011) http://www.voxeu.org/article/industrial-revolution-energy-revolution.

[39] T.F. Neill, *The Physiocrats Concept of Economics* 63 Q. J. ECON. 532, 532–553 (1949).

social progress and disparities among societies. "Human progress," he explains, "is measured by the degree to which simple acquisition is replaced by production—achieved first by manual power, then by animal power, and finally by machine power."[40] Even though he did not pursue the fuller implications of using nonhuman (fossil fuels) as energy, and concentrated instead on human energy, his thesis that energy was a central component of social organization set the stage for a fuller understanding of the role of energy in society.[41]

In the 1950s, the anthropologist Leslie White refined Spencer's ideas by conceptualizing cultural evolution as movement along a "continuum," where progress is defined in terms of a linear path from "poor" to "advanced" energy use. White posited that societies' ability to exploit new, better forms of energy drives development, and that access to energy dictates the progress of peoples: "Culture evolves as the amount of energy harnessed per capita per year is increased, or as the efficiency of the instrumental means, or the efficiency of conversions which put the energy to work, is improved."[42]

After describing the rise of agriculture and animals to provide energy that facilitated cultural growth from around the sixth to the tenth century BC, he asserted that culture had developed about as far as it could upon the basis of an agricultural-animal husbandry economy. "We may conclude there was little cultural growth until the nineteenth century and the discovery of fossil fuels. The invention of the steam engine and of all subsequent engines that derive power from fuels inaugurated a new era in culture history. When man learned to harness energy in the form of fuel he opened the door of a vast treasure house of energy. Fuels and engines tremendously increased the amount of energy under man's control and at his disposal for culture-building."[43] Leslie White further believed that energy is also inextricably linked with cultural development and the shape of modern society, based on who has access to energy and control over its production.[44]

But what if social systems were unprepared or unready to use fossil fuels and technology that converted them into energy? Here, White had a clear answer: "A social system may so condition the operation of a technological system as to impose a limit upon the extent to which it can expand and develop. When this occurs, cultural evolution ceases."[45] White clearly believed in technological

---

40 Herbert Spencer, *The Principles of Sociology*, Vol. 3, 356 (1898).

41 Andrew McKinnon, *Energy and Society: Herbert Spencer's Energetic Sociology' of Social Evolution and Beyond,* 10 J. CLASSICAL SOC. 439 (2010).

42 White, *supra* note 16.

43 *Id.* at 344–45.

44 White, *supra* note 32.

45 *Id.* at 348.

determinism and the linear progression of society and culture. He did so despite the fact that twentieth century anthropologists generally did not believe in the kind of cultural evolution propounded by him.[46]

The sociologist Fred Cottrell further developed and built upon the theories of Spencer and White by considering energy as a limiting factor. According to him, the ability (or inability) to harness energy equates to human capacity for growth.[47] But unlike White, he recognized that the natural world places a limit, in the form of the second law of thermodynamics, on the amount of energy that can ultimately be harnessed for human use.[48] More recently, the economists Nicholas Georgescu-Roegen[49] and Herman Daly,[50] in the late twentieth century, advanced this theme and challenged economic orthodoxy by emphasizing that the second law of thermodynamics dictates limits to economic growth. The physicist Amory Lovins has suggested that this necessitates shifting to a "soft energy path" emphasizing energy efficiency and renewable energy resources.[51] Moreover, modern empirical studies have demonstrated that the relationship between energy consumption and wellbeing is not, as White postulated, entirely linear. Rather, as pointed out by other commentators, "while a threshold level of high energy consumption is probably necessary for a society to achieve industrialization and modernity, once achieved, there is wide latitude in the amount of energy needed to sustain a high standard of living."[52]

Applying these insights within a modern milieu reveals that access to energy is essential to development. Moreover, the inability to access energy within low energy civilizations can both cause and perpetuate poverty. This occurs where those without access to modern forms of energy are forced to rely on the inefficient conversion of biomass and human muscle power to complete the daily tasks necessary for their livelihood and well-being.

---

[46] *Id.*

[47] Fred Cottrell, *Energy And Society (Revised): The Relation Between Energy, Social Change, And Economic Development* 7 (rev. ed. 2009).

[48] Rosa et al., *supra* note 31, at 153.

[49] Nicholas Georgescue-Roegen, *The Entrophy Law and the Economic Process* (1999).

[50] Herman E. Daly, *Beyond Growth: The Economics of Sustainable Development* (1997).

[51] Rosa et al., *supra* note 31, at 153–54 (citing Amory B. Lovins, *Soft Energy Paths: Toward a Durable Peace* (Penguin Books 1977)).

[52] Rosa et al., *supra* note 31, at 159.

V. Modern High-Energy Civilizations and Fossil Fuels

In modern high-energy (fossil fuel based) societies, energy is critical for maintaining innumerable vital life support systems spanning domestic, commercial, and industrial uses: transportation, food production, information technology, national security, health care, cooking, lighting, mechanical power, chemical production, and general economic growth. To meet these requirements, the high-energy world relies primarily on combustion of hydrocarbons (fossil fuels). However, as discussed later in this chapter, problems with this system have emerged as hydrocarbon combustion is implicated as a key driver of anthropogenic climate change. Moreover, supplies of the primary hydrocarbon energy source—oil—has become increasingly embroiled in geopolitics, and increasing demand, gives rise to national security concerns. Fossil fuels are the dominant energy source in the modern world and its high-energy civilizations. Fossil fuels include energy sources such as coal, oil, and natural gas, which are alternatively referred to as hydrocarbons because they are composed entirely of hydrogen and oxygen atoms.

The most prominent hydrocarbons are petroleum fluids, including oil and gas that are mixtures of hydrocarbons and inorganic impurities.[53] The biochemical process begins with the death of microscopic organisms such as algae and bacteria that settle into sediments at the bottom of water bodies. As this organic debris is buried by further sedimentation, it is subject to increasing temperature and pressure and is transformed by bacterial action into oil and gas. These hydrocarbons may accumulate in a geologic trap, such as the pore space of sedimentary rock, forming a petroleum reservoir. Similarly, coal is formed by a process known as coalification where vegetation dies and decays in aqueous environments like swamps and is buried by subsequent geological activity.[54]

Fossil fuels offer much higher energy density than wood and are thus generally preferable as fuels for high-energy processes. As the technology for extracting fossil fuels from the earth and processing them into more useful forms, such as gasoline, diesel, and kerosene, has advanced, fossil fuels have become firmly entrenched at the heart of economic and social activity in the modern world.

Of course, the dependence of high-energy societies on fossil fuels is not without its problems. Despite significant doubts about the extent of damage caused by global warming, global reliance on

---

[53] Fanchi, *supra* note 22, at 26–27, 35–37.

[54] *Id.* at 25, 30–32.

hydrocarbons is implicated, by climate scientists and policy makers, as a primary driver of anthropogenic climate change that causes global warming and results in dire consequences for many areas of the world.[55] There is now a high degree of certainty among the international scientific community that humans are the primary cause of global warming.[56] Human activities, most importantly fossil fuel combustion and deforestation that result in the release of greenhouse gases (GHGs) such as CO_2, are upsetting the delicate balance of atmospheric gases. GHGs, as their name implies, essentially trap outgoing radiation (i.e., heat) in the earth's atmosphere, thereby increasing the earth's temperature through the "greenhouse effect." While much uncertainty is inherent in long-term climatological predications, there is a widespread consensus that anthropogenic climate change is likely to result in a number of adverse environmental impacts, including rising temperatures, changes in precipitation and water stress, sea level rise, ice melt, and ocean acidification.

Human activities continue to result in the discharge of vast amounts of GHGs. As many GHGs are long-lived in the atmosphere, this has resulted in ever-increasing atmospheric GHG concentrations that will continue to affect the climate even if all anthropogenic emissions were to cease immediately. The fact that developing country emissions now exceed those of developed countries and are expected to continue to grow rapidly[57] contributes to the complexities inherent in addressing the climate change problem.

VI. Low Energy Civilizations and the Energy Poor

Because energy is necessary for meeting basic needs of all humankind, including cooking, sanitation, water access, lighting, heating, and motive or mechanical power, effective energy conversion depends on efficient human organization in the development and exploitation of energy resources. Technological innovations are also critical in converting fossil fuels, solar radiation, nuclear fuels, and moving water or wind into other, more useful energy forms, such as electricity, mechanical energy, or heat.

The modern fossil-fuel-based civilization of the more prosperous two-thirds of the world population has literally fueled its development by exploiting the rich energy endowment embodied in

---

[55] *See, e.g.*, Lakshman D. Guruswamy & Mariah Zebrowski Leach, *International Environmental Law in a Nutshell* 204–14 (4th ed. 2012).

[56] Intergovernmental Panel on Climate Change, *Summary for Policymakers, in* IPCC FOURTH ASSESSMENT REPORT, CLIMATE CHANGE 2007: THE PHYSICAL SCIENCE BASIS 10 (2007) [hereinafter IPCC FOURTH ASSESSMENT REPORT: THE PHYSICAL SCIENCE BASIS].

[57] Intergovernmental Panel on Climate Change, *Summary for Policymakers, in* IPCC FOURTH ASSESSMENT REPORT, CLIMATE CHANGE 2007: MITIGATION 3 (2007).

fossil hydrocarbons. The very high energy density of these sources, along with the technological systems that have been fashioned to harness them, has created an enormously effective engine for ongoing economic development by the affluent. Regrettably, at least one-third of the world's population has not benefitted from these developments and still lacks access to appropriate forms of energy adequate to meet their basic needs.

A disturbingly large swath of humanity is caught in a time warp. Between 2 to 2.5 billion people (the "other third")—nearly a third of the world's population—rely upon biomass-generated fire as their principal source of energy. These fires are made by burning animal dung, waste, crop residues, rotted wood, raw coal, and other forms of biomass. Moreover, the biomass-generated fire they rely upon is an inadequate source of energy. It does not provide the kind of exogenous energy required for sustainable human development. Fire can be used for cooking and heating, but fails to serve most other basic energy needs. Fire does not, for example, power water pumps, grinding mills, vehicles, or agricultural equipment. Further, it does not provide clean lighting, water filtration, or more generally aid in the procurement of food, clothing, and shelter. Furthermore, unlike the high-energy world, the "other third" live without access to safe and reliable lighting, space heating, cooking, sanitation, and mechanical power. They suffer from grinding poverty, serious diseases, lack of safe drinking water and sanitation, and restricted access to education—all of which hinder economic and social development.

Source: *Helping the World's Least Developed Countries*, MAKING IT MAGAZINE, http://www.makingitmagazine.net/wp-content/uploads/2010/11/bhattacharya_LDCs.jpg (last visited Nov. 23, 2015).

These energy poor (EP) peoples, as identified in the graphic, mostly reside in least developed countries (LDCs) concentrated along the low latitudes in Africa, Asia, and the Pacific. LDCs are defined as "low-income countries suffering from structural impediments to sustainable development. These handicaps are manifested in a low level of human resource development and a high level of structural economic vulnerability."[58] Although all developing countries tend to be conceptualized within a single typology based on the binary division of the world into developing and developed countries (sometimes euphemistically referred to as the "north" and "south," respectively), the fallacy of doing so is underlined by an authoritative joint report of the UNDP and World Health Organization (WHO) emphasizing the plight of the LDCs.[59] While 28 percent of people in developing countries lack access to electricity, in the LDCs that number is 79 percent.[60] Clearly, the differences between the LDCs, located primarily in sub-Saharan Africa and parts of Asia, in contrast to the advanced developing countries (ADCs) like China, India, the

---

58 U.N. Development Policy & Analysis Division, *LDC Criteria* (Oct. 2014), http://www.un.org/en/development/desa/policy/cdp/ldc/ldc_criteria.shtml (last visited Dec. 5, 2015).

59 Gwenaelle Legros et al., *The Energy Access Situation in Developing Countries* 1–4 (WORLD HEALTH ORG. & U.N. DEV. PROGRAMME 2009), available at http://content.undp.org/go/cms-service/stream/asset/?asset_id=2205620 [hereinafter LEGROS ET AL.] (last visited Nov. 27, 2015).

60 *Id.* at 1.

Asian Tigers, and Brazil, must be recognized. It is therefore necessary at the outset to acknowledge at least two major categories among the developing countries: LDCs and ADCs. Obviously, there are no cookie cutter solutions, and the variegated energy needs and social objectives of ADCs and LDCs call for complex, nuanced, and demanding responses that must be tailored on a case-by-case basis.

In order to do so, it is important, as noted above, to situate the LDCs, ADCs and energy poor within a geopolitical context. In what amounts to a vast and detrimental oversimplification, the 192 countries of the world were, and to some degree continue to be subject to a binary system of classification as either "developed" or "developing."[61] Developed countries are characterized by their relatively high levels of economic development, with per capita gross national product (GDP) generally in excess of $15,000 and with advanced infrastructure. The service sector tends to be economically more significant than the industrial sector in developed economies today.

The binary system has been modified, and while precise classifications vary according to the metrics adopted, some analysts have found three kinds of countries: advanced economies, countries in transition, and developing countries.[62] Advanced economies are found in The Organisation for Economic Co-operation and Development (OECD), comprised of 34 of the world's wealthiest market-oriented countries, mostly from Europe and North America. Transition economies are those moving from a centrally planned to a market-oriented economy.[63] Developing countries have a low GNP.[64]

Moreover, a number of "developing" countries have made tremendous economic strides in recent decades and are now

---

[61] *World Trade Organization (WTO). Who are the developing countries in the WTO?* https://www.wto.org/english/tratop_e/devel_e/d1who_e.htm (last visited Jan. 2, 2016).

[62] E.g., U.S. Central Intelligence Agency, *The World Factbook Appendix B: International Organizations & Groups*, https://www.cia.gov/library/publications/the-world-factbook/appendix/appendix-b.html#D (listing 34 developed countries) (last visited Nov. 23, 2015); Int'l Monetary Fund, *World Economic Outlook, October 2012: Coping With High Debt and Sluggish Growth* 180 (2012), available at http://www.imf.org/external/pubs/ft/weo/2012/02/pdf/text.pdf (listing 35 "advanced economies," including Taiwan and Hong Kong) (last visited Nov. 23, 2015).

[63] Edgar L. Feige, *The Transition to a Market Economy in Russia: Property Rights, Mass Privatization, and Stabilization, in* Gregory S. Alexander & Grazyna Skapska, *A Fourth Way?: Privatization, Property, and the Emergence of New Market Economics* 57–78 (Routledge 1994).

[64] The United Nations Development Programme (UNDP) takes a more expansive approach. The UNDP calculates a Human Development Index (HDI) for each country, which accounts for income, education, and life expectancy, and classifies the top quartile (47 countries with HDIs above 0.8) as possessing "very high human development." U.N. Development Programme, *United Nations Human Development Report 2013* 144 (2013).

recognized as "newly industrializing" or "advanced developing" countries (ADCs). This category includes the BRIC countries of Brazil, Russia, India, and China,[65] South Africa; and the "Asian Tigers" of Taiwan, Singapore, Hong Kong, and South Korea.[66] They have been emulated by Thailand, Indonesia, Malaysia, and the Philippines, which are following the trajectory of exceptional economic growth and rapid industrialization of the Asian Tigers and have consequently been dubbed "Tiger Cub Economies."[67] Significant segments of these ADCs are in fact high-energy users. In fact, the industrial prosperity of these ADCs has been built upon and depends on high energy generated by fossil fuels. The following figures illustrate the extent to which energy consumption by the OECD, comprised of the older industrial developed countries of the world, has been overtaken by the newer industrializing or advanced developing countries.

WORLD ENERGY CONSUMPTION 1990–2040

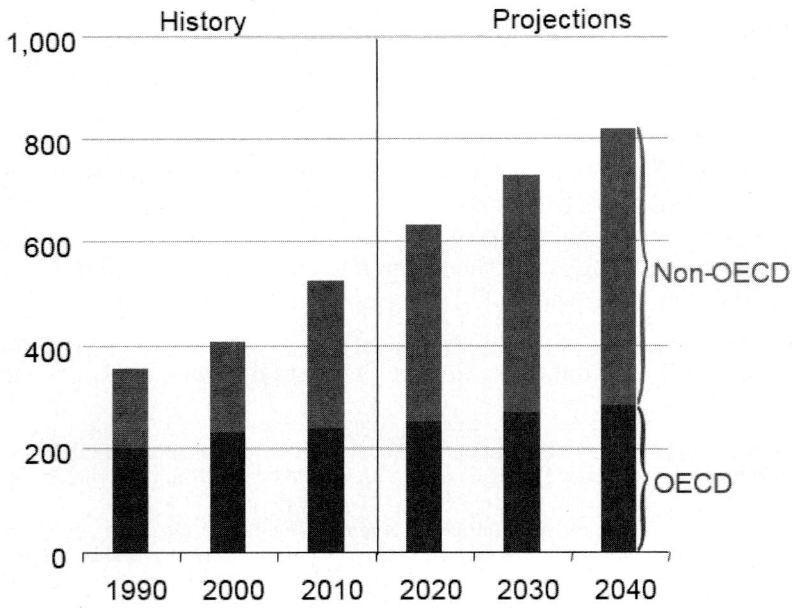

Energy Information Agency, International Energy Outlook, 2013

Sources of Energy 1990–2014

---

[65] Jean Folger, *What is a BRIC Nation?*, INVESTOPEDIA, http://www.investopedia.com/ask/answers/13/what-is-bric-nation.asp (last visited Nov. 23, 2015).

[66] *Four Asian Tigers*, INVESTOPEDIA, http://www.investopedia.com/terms/f/four-asian-tigers.asp (visited Nov. 23, 2015).

[67] *Tiger Cub Economies*, INVESTOPEDIA, http://www.investopedia.com/terms/t/tiger-cub-economies.asp?layout=orig (visited Nov. 23, 2015).

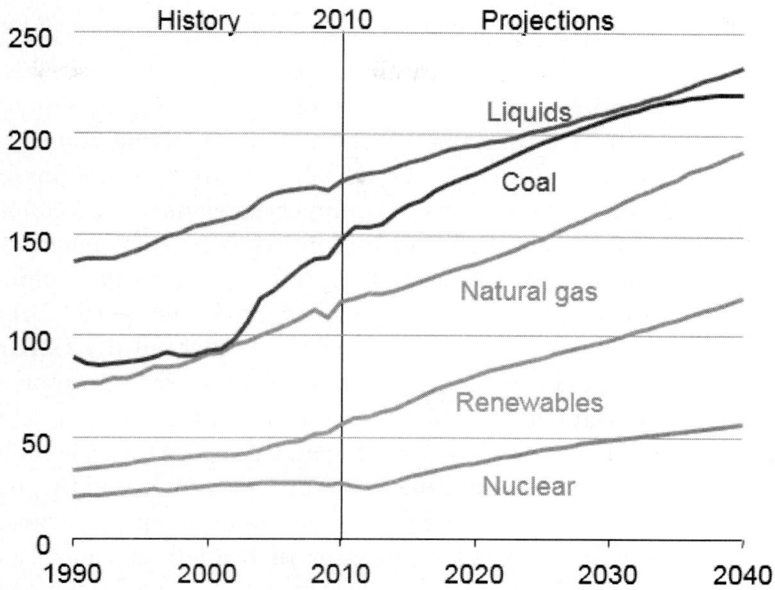

Energy Information Agency, International Energy Outlook, 2013

By contrast, the LDCs consist of 49 countries and 844 million people located largely in Africa and Asia.[68] The LDCs have been officially identified by the UN as "least developed" in the light of their low income (GDP of less than $7,500), weak human assets (low nutrition, high mortality, lack of school enrollment, and high illiteracy), high economic vulnerability, exposure to natural shocks and disasters, prevalence of trade shocks, small economies, and economic remoteness.[69] In other words, they do not share the economic or technological strengths of the ADCs. It is worth noting in this context that the push for more energy, and specifically for coal-powered energy, arises from the rapidly industrializing ADCs, not the LDCs. The problems facing the LDCs and the predominantly rural EP located within them, unlike those of ADCs, arise from their woeful lack of energy and suboptimal energy conversions. In

[68] U.N. Office of the High Representative for the Least Developed Countries, Landlocked Developing Countries and Small Island Developing States *Factsheet—Least Developed Countries (LDCs),* (May 28, 2013), http://www.unohrlls.org/docs/ohrlls/ldcs/UN_LDC_Factsheet_130517.pdf.

[69] Committee For Development U.N. Dep't Of Econ. & Soc. Affairs, *Handbook On The Least Developed Country Category: Inclusion, Graduation And Special Support Measures* (Nov. 2008), http://www.un.org/en/development/desa/policy/cdp/cdp_publications/2008cdphandbook.pdf.

contrast, most ADCs use fossil fuel energy and hunger for more of it to satisfy their industrial appetite.

Geopolitically, the differences between the high-energy users, and the low-energy users or EP in ADCs have not been satisfactorily recognized. The fact that the EPs reside in the same country as others with access to energy should not obscure the monumental disparities between them. While the upper echelons of the economic pyramid in ADCs are inhabited by high-energy users, the much more numerous EP—who have no access to power or electricity—populate the lower parts of the economic pyramid. The substance of these realties is echoed by a recent report of the WHO and the UNDP.[70] Indeed, as the middle classes of China and India rapidly approach lifestyles comparable to the middle classes in OECD member states, the predicament of the EPs in these countries is often glossed over as they are cut off from the attention of their governments and the wider world. To the extent that the EPs in many developing countries are not stakeholders in the government or in the political machinery exercising control over the areas that they inhabit, such societies are most accurately perceived when considered apart from the geopolitical entities in which they reside.

ADCs, like China and India, have been treated as monoliths when, in reality, those who inhabit the developed parts of these countries live dramatically different lives from the rural and urban EPs. Such mega-sovereign states may count as single nations under international laws and relations, but in fact they consist of a plurality of socio-political, economic, cultural, and geographical entities. To illustrate this dynamic, India rose in the annual rankings of billionaires by country while simultaneously slipping in the UN's HDI.[71] Although the socioeconomic condition and lack of technological knowledge among the approximately 500 million EP in China and India are analogous to the 844 million EP in the LDCs, the similarity between the EP in LDCs and the EP in ADCs has

---

70 Legros et al., *supra* note 63, at 1–4; U.N. Development Programme, *Human Development Report 2007–2008*, 355–57 (2007), available at http://hdr.undp.org/en/media/HDR_20072008_EN_Complete.pdf.

71 *See* P. Sainath, *India 2007: High Growth, Low Development*, THE HINDU (Dec. 26, 2007), http://www.indiatogether.org/2007/dec/psa-i2007.htm (last visited Nov. 25, 2015) The HDI is from the Human Development Report (HDR) of the UNDP that has been published annually since 1990. This index looks beyond gross domestic product (GDP) to a broader definition of "well-being." The HDI seeks to capture three dimensions of human development: a long and healthy life (measured by life expectancy at birth), being educated (measured by adult literacy and enrollment in primary, secondary, and tertiary education), and GDP per capita measured in U.S. dollars at Purchasing Power Parity (PPP).

generally been ignored. Justice, however, calls for these EP to be recognized and treated as distinct, burdened societies.

In developing countries, a large and growing proportion of the population lives in or around large cities, "including the zone termed the 'peri-urban interface' where their livelihoods depend to some extent on natural resources such as land for food, water and fuel, and space for living."[72] Rapid population growth means that such zones are often overcrowded and resources overexploited. This is primarily due to the inability of cities to plan for and develop proper housing and infrastructure to accommodate large numbers of additional low-income residents. Many impoverished inhabitants of the peri-urban interface are particularly vulnerable to impacts associated with both rural and urban systems, including lack of access to energy, clean water, and basic sanitation, poor housing, and risks to health and life related to occupation of unsuitable sites.[73] Such slums and squatter settlements are home to one billion people.[74]

The prevalence of energy poverty today points to the fact that the provision of energy services could save millions of lives among the EPs in any type of developing country. Energy services could supply safer drinking water and help provide sanitation to reduce water-borne diseases by powering pumps and filters. Cooking devices powered by any of a number of fuels would minimize the indoor pollution that is presently responsible for millions of premature deaths among the EP due to pulmonary diseases—primarily among women and children—caused by the indoor use of wood and other biomass in open fires for cooking and heating. As the drudgery of chores like fuel and water collection generally falls on young girls, access to energy services would free them from this burden, thereby enabling them to go to school. Energy is the key component of a functional health system, providing lights for operating rooms, refrigeration for life-saving vaccines and medications, and power for communication systems.[75] Cheap, accessible energy would also decrease environmental degradation, particularly deforestation and desertification arising from the pursuit for fuel, food, and water in arid climates.

---

[72] Robert M. Brook & Julio Davila, *The Peri-Urban Interface: A Tale of Two Cities* 1 (2000).

[73] *Id.*

[74] Giok Ling Ooi & Kai Hong Phua, *Urbanization and Slum Formation*, 84 J. URBAN HEALTH: BULLETIN N.Y. ACAD. MED. i27, i29 (2007), available at http://www.ncbi.nlm.nih.gov/pmc/articles/PMC1891640/pdf/11524_2007_Article_9167.pdf (last visited Nov. 27, 2015).

[75] Vijay Modi, Susan McDade, Dominique Lallement & Jamal Saghir, *Energy Services For The Millennium Development Goals, The U.N. Millennium Project* 29 (2005).

The availability of modern energy services also has the potential to promote income generation and economic development in developing countries. Electricity can provide illumination to permit longer working, studying, and shopping hours. Irrigation pumps and other powered tools can help yield high-value crops. The use of process heat for food processing can create value-added products from raw agricultural commodities. Similarly, refrigeration can extend shelf life and enable sales to higher-value markets. Computers, Internet, and telephones can provide access to information and markets, thereby facilitating increased trade.[76] But, as noted above, modern fossil fuel energy does not provide a path to sustainable development, and when all externalities are considered, its true costs of outweighs its benefits. Consequently, appropriate sustainable energy technologies (ASETs) should be employed to produce energy that satisfies the energy needs of the EP while avoiding the problems associated with fossil fuels.

VII. The Millennium Development Goals

As we shall see in Chapter 3, over the course of three decades, the United Nations and its member states strove for a rational and integrated application of sustainable development encompassing economic development, environmental protection, and social development. One of the most important outcomes of these efforts was the UN Millennium Declaration, resulting from the September 2000 Millennium Summit. It expresses the collective commitment of the world to achieving eight major development goals by 2015.[77] These goals, which became known as the Millennium Development Goals (MDGs), seek to: (1) eradicate extreme poverty and hunger; (2) achieve universal primary education; (3) promote gender equality and empower women; (4) reduce child mortality; (5) improve maternal health; (6) combat HIV/AIDS, malaria, and other diseases; (7) ensure environmental sustainability; and (8) develop a global partnership for development.[78] Although no MDG is expressly dedicated to providing access to energy services, satisfying the MDGs necessitates improved access to energy. The following is a broad overview of how energy relates to each of the MDGs.[79]

---

[76] *See* Global Network On Energy For Sustainable Development, *Reaching The Millennium Development Goals And Beyond: Access To Modern Forms Of Energy As A Prerequisite 5* (2007).

[77] *United Nations Millennium Declaration*, U.N. Doc. A/RES/55/2 (2000), available at http://www.un.org/millennium/declaration/ares552e.pdf.

[78] U.N. Dep't of Econ. And Soc. Affairs, *The Millennium Development Goals Report (2006)*, available at http://mdgs.un.org/unsd/mdg/Resources/Static/Products/Progress2006/MDGReport2006.pdf].

[79] This subsection is based on: Lakshman Guruswamy, *Energy Poverty*, 36 ANN. REV. ENV'T & RESOURCES 139, 153–57 (2011).

At this juncture it is necessary to delineate the relevance of the MDGs from an energy perspective, even though they have now been replaced by 17 Sustainable Development Goals (SDGs)[80] and 169 targets.[81] Chapter 3 contains a broad and quantitative evaluation of the MDGs, that traverses the broader socio-economic and developmental goals of the MDGs, and the extent to which they have been met. The analysis in this chapter focuses on the unarticulated energy dimensions of the MDGs, and deals with the extent to which energy is necessary to achieve the MDGs.

A very important reason for assessing the importance of energy for the MDGs lies in the fact that no MDG dealt explicitly and directly with energy. The energy shortcomings of the MDGs were apparently remedied by SDG 7. The objective of SDG 7 is to: "Ensure access to affordable, reliable, sustainable and modern energy for all." The explanation of the goal states that: "Energy is central to nearly every major challenge and opportunity the world faces today. Be it for jobs, security, climate change, food production, or increasing incomes, access to sustainable energy for all is essential."[82] This chapter explains how the importance of access to energy became evident, in the implementation of the MDGs, and led to this conclusion. Chapter 3 analyzes how and why the resources necessary to achieve SDG 7, are being diverted to meet other SDGs like climate action.

Goal 1: Eradicate Extreme Poverty and Hunger

As established above, access to electricity, mechanical energy, and fuels for cooking is critical to development. Specifically, access to energy can reduce hunger by employing electric or mechanical energy to improve food production and storage. Access to modern fuels for cooking would also increase agricultural yields, as more of the nutrient-rich crop residues remain on the land rather than being burned as biomass for cooking, thereby improving food security.

Access to energy can reduce poverty by providing families with a greater number of productive hours for work by illuminating their homes after dark and by cutting travel and production time with nonhuman mechanical energy. Energy services can provide jobs by enabling communities to develop small industries and can give local

---

[80] United Nations, *Sustainable Development Goals*, http://www.un.org/sustainabledevelopment/sustainable-development-goals (last visited Nov. 23, 2015).

[81] Int'l Council For Sci. & Int'l Soc., *Review Of Targets For The Sustainable Development Goals: The Science Perspective (2015)*, available at http://www.icsu.org/publications/reports-and-reviews/review-of-targets-for-the-sustainable-development-goals-the-science-perspective–2015/SDG–Report.pdf (last visited Nov. 25, 2015).

[82] U.N. Found., *Achieving Universal Energy Access*, http://www.unfoundation.org/what-we-do/issues/energy-and-climate/clean-energy-development.html (last visited Nov. 27, 2015).

economies better access to markets through improved communication and more efficient transportation.[83] Furthermore, with better access to more efficient and sustainable forms of energy, indigent families will spend less of their time and money on procuring energy and energy services. For example, a 10-country study in East Africa showed that 80 percent of urban households lacked a piped (i.e., pumped) water supply and were thus forced to spend over 20 percent of their income purchasing water at prices 10 times the normal utility water supply rate.[84] With access to a treadle pump (which can pump up to 130 litersper-minute without causing fatigue) or wind pump, money previously devoted to the purchase of water owing to lack of access to energy services would be liberated to promote growth.

Goal 2: Achieve Universal Primary Education

Worldwide, over 115 million children were not enrolled in school.[85] The poorest are disproportionately affected, as demonstrated by the fact that in sub-Saharan Africa, children from the richest 20 percent of households are three to four times more likely to attend school than those from the poorest quintile.[86] This phenomenon is largely attributable to lack of access to energy. First, EP families often must rely on children to meet the physical workload necessary to achieve sustenance without access to energy services, such as collecting fuel and water and processing food. For desperately poor families, these life-sustaining activities take priority over a child's education. Second, children are unable to study at night in homes without illumination. This hinders their ability to complete assignments and is a significant impediment to educational achievement. Finally, there is a huge problem in securing and retaining qualified teachers in the most remote and impoverished regions of the world. In addition to enabling students, improved energy services can help attract more qualified teachers to such areas by improving the area's standard of living and by providing technologies that enable access to educational materials, distance learning, and continued education for teachers.[87]

"Reducing drudgery in women's lives by providing clean, affordable fuels for food grinding, water pumping, cooking, and

---

[83] Francis X. Johnson & Fiona Lambe, *Energy Access,* in *Climate And Development, Commission On Climate Change And Development* (2009).

[84] Liz Bates, Steven Hunt, Smail Khennas & Nararya Sastrawinata, *Expanding Energy Access In Developing Countries: The Role Of Mechanical Power 11* (Practical Action Publishing Ltd. 2009).

[85] U.N. Development Programme, *Energizing The Millennium Development Goals: A Guide To Energy's Role In Reducing Poverty* 10 (2005).

[86] Bates et al., *supra* note 84.

[87] Modi et al., *supra* note 75, at 24–25.

transportation is one of the most important challenges to achieving universal primary education and gender equality."[88] One example of how improved access to energy can increase primary education in schools can be seen in Mali, where a Multifunctional Platform (MFP) project was implemented beginning in the late 1990s. MFPs provide mechanical and electrical energy from small diesel engines (which can also be fueled by biomass-derived fuel without any drop in power) that are mounted on chassis that enables them to power a variety of modular components. The platforms are configured based on local demand, but may consist of food processers (grinding mills or oil pressers), battery chargers, water pumps, lighting, or power tools (welding and carpentry). Much of the work done by MFPs was traditionally carried out by women and girls. Appropriately, the program required female ownership and operation of the MFPs, facilitated by training and financing from project partners. Research based on the first 500 MFP installations showed that the project saved women about 2.5 hours per day of labor on daily chores and resulted in an average income increase of about 56 percent per woman.[89] This increased access to energy also correlated with an increased level in girls' attendance in primary school, an increase in the proportion of children completing primary school, and improvements in girls' scholastic achievements.[90]

Goal 3: Promote Gender Equality and Empowerment of Women

As noted above, lack of access to energy services disproportionately affects women (and children) in multiple ways. These include the time spent in securing daily needs, adverse health effects caused by inefficient combustion of biomass for cooking, and the burdens of domestic labor Access to energy services, and in particular dissemination of ASETs such as the MPF in Mali, water pumps, or cookstoves, invariably saves precious time and reduces physical stress and illness, thus enabling the empowerment of women. Indeed, simply reducing the amount of time devoted to water and fuel collection can free up the time and energy essential for women to engage in income-generating and educational activities[91] as well as in cultural pursuits or leisure.

Goal 4: Reduce Child Mortality

In 1990, almost 11 million children under the age of five died every year from preventable causes—19 percent resulting from acute

---

[88] Energizing The Millennium Development Goals, *supra* note 85, at 10 (quoting Susan McDade, Manager, UNDP Sustainable Energy Programme).

[89] Bates et al., *supra* note 84, at 25–26.

[90] Modi et al., *supra* note 75, at 59; Energizing The Millennium Development Goals, *supra* note 85, at 8, 10.

[91] Johnson & Lambe, *supra* note 83, at 3.

respiratory infections (ARIs), 18 percent from diarrhea, and 37 percent from neonatal conditions.[92] Improved access to energy services can help combat each of these conditions. First, access to clean-burning cookstoves directly reduces the amount of particulate pollution young children are exposed to while their mother is cooking. For example, in western Kenya more than 16,000 improved cookstoves have been installed in rural households as part of a project aimed at improving conditions in rural households. These cookstoves have produced a 60 percent reduction in indoor smoke, which has resulted in a 65 percent reduction in ARIs among mothers and a 70 percent reduction of conjunctivitis among children under five years old.[93] Second, pumped water and latrines would reduce the propensity of contracting various enteric infections through contaminated drinking water or generally poor sanitary conditions. Finally, access to energy services would improve health care infrastructure in general, as clinics could see children after dark and would have access to medications and vaccines that require refrigeration.[94]

Goal 5: Improve Maternal Health

Again, women carry the majority of the burden of securing energy services by traditional means. This responsibility does not stop during pregnancy and indeed is amplified by the physical burden of carrying a child coupled with the increased difficulty of securing adequate nutrient. Poor nutrition during pregnancy causes anemia, among other things, which is known to augment the risk of maternal deaths, stillbirths, and low birth-weight babies.[95] Furthermore, energy projects aimed at improving health care infrastructure have been directly linked to improvements in maternal health. A statistical analysis was conducted in 15,000 townships in the Philippines where a rural electrification campaign had been recently launched. The National Demographic Health Survey showed that women with access to electricity were 17 percent more likely to have a doctor-assisted birth than those without access after income and other demographic variables were accounted for.[96]

Goal 6: Combat HIV/AIDS, Malaria, and Other Diseases

The global campaign to combat disease, particularly with respect to HIV/AIDS and malaria, is connected in various ways to the availability of energy. First, as indicated above, access to electricity and mechanical energy helps improve sanitation and is vital for

---

92 Bates et al., *supra* note 84, at 12.

93 Energizing The Millennium Development Goals, *supra* note 85, at 12.

94 Modi et al., *supra* note 75, at 29.

95 Bates et al., *supra* note 84, at 12.

96 Energizing The Millennium Development Goals, *supra* note 85, at 12.

health care infrastructure. Better hygiene reduces the incidence of secondary opportunistic infections that can be deadly to immunocompromised individuals such as HIV/AIDS patients, while better clinics can house and refrigerate vaccines, antivirals, and other medications. Second, education and awareness campaigns are essential to disease prevention, especially for HIV/AIDS. These campaigns are generally conducted using radio and television and, therefore, require access to energy services among at-risk communities to reach their intended audience.[97]

Finally, just as energy infrastructure can help to attract better teachers, it can also provide indigent communities better access to doctors, nurses, midwives, and healthcare workers.[98] One relatively new application of this idea is telemedicine: "the use of information and communications technology to provide health care services to individuals who are some distance from the health care provider."[99] Although there are few successful case studies of dissemination of this idea in the developing world to date, it has the potential to dramatically improve global health care. For example, MIT and the Costa Rica Foundation for Sustainable Development are currently working on the Little Intelligent Communities (LINCOS) project to bring telemedicine to remote indigent communities in Costa Rica and the Dominican Republic.[100] To maximize economic efficiency, the project develops town centers equipped with communication technologies including telemedicine consultation rooms. This has had the dramatic result of bringing doctors to rural villages previously without healthcare.[101] Another example comes from rural India, where Aravind has provided an invaluable service by employing a telemedicine model to become "the largest and most productive eye care facility in the world."[102] Telemedicine, however, requires modern energy services. Providing mini-grid electricity generation, for example, could increase the potential for telemedicine, thereby helping to combat disease worldwide.

---

[97] Modi et al., *supra* note 75, at 29.

[98] Bates et al., *supra* note 84, at 13.

[99] Risto Rione, Arto Ohinmaa & David Hailey, *Assessing Telemedicine: A Systematic Review of the Literature* 165 CAN. MED. ASS'N J. 765 (2001).

[100] Ari T. Adler, *A Cost-Effective Portable Telemedicine Kit for Use in Developing Countries* (2000) (unpublished Master's thesis, Mass. Inst. Tech.), available at http://dspace.mit.edu/handle/1721.1/9304 (last visited Nov. 28, 2015).

[101] The LINCOS project and other telemedicine projects in developing countries have been criticized for cultural insensitivity and potentially high costs. However, given that telemedicine is still in its infancy, such criticisms should not be regarded as fatal.

[102] Anant Saxena & Neeraj Awasthy, *Telemedicine: A Ray of Hope for Rural Healthcare System, in* SUSTAINABILITY AND DEVELOPMENT: PARADIGM SHIFT IN KNOWLEDGE CREATION AND INNOVATION 834, 838 (Ajay Singh, Jay Mitra & Neeraj Awasthy eds., 2013).

Goal 7: Ensure Environmental Sustainability

Addressing energy poverty contributes to ensuring environmental sustainability on a number of levels. As discussed above, lack of access to modern fuels for cooking forces the EP to harvest and burn biomass. Burning biomass results in the emission of black carbon into the atmosphere, reducing the albedo effect and thus contributing to global climate change. In addition, harvesting wood for fuel leads to deforestation and contributes to land degradation, erosion, desertification, depletion of water resources, and greenhouse gas emissions resulting from land cover change. Improving access to energy services, such as clean fuels and more efficient cookstoves, will mitigate these negative environmental outcomes while improving the daily lives of the EP. For example, the Senegalese government embarked on a reform and subsidy program in the 1970s aimed at helping EP households' transition from using traditional biomass, such as charcoal, to liquefied petroleum gas (LPG) for cooking that has resulted in tangible environmental benefits. In 2002, the people of Senegal consumed more than 100,000 metric tons of LPG, which equates to the avoidance of 40,500 hectares of deforestation and the production of 337,500 tons of charcoal.[103]

Furthermore, increasing access to energy for the EP by using ASETs, which are by definition inherently environmentally sustainable, provides a unique and important opportunity to reduce global reliance on fossil fuels. "Accelerated use of renewable and more energy efficient technologies can provide 'win-win' options to tackle global and local development challenges."[104] For example, since 2001, the Himalayan Environmental Studies and Conservation Organization (HESCO) has worked to update the nearly 200,000 traditional watermills, some hundreds of years old, existing in rural communities throughout the Himalaya region. While each community's watermill is unique, basic watermill design entails diverting stream water to turn a turbine. The shaft of the turbine is attached to and drives a rectangular metal key that turns the top stone of a pair of grinding stones. HESCO has developed a model for upgrading these traditional watermills with modern multipurpose technology at a cost of several hundred dollars per mill. Each upgraded mill provides both mechanical power for grinding grains and electrical power by harnessing the kinetic energy of the stream. Some upgraded watermills can return up to $135 per month from faster and better grinding of grains such as wheat, corn or rice, and have increased both power use and efficiency by 90 percent,

---

[103] Johnson & Lambe, *supra* note 83, at 4–5.

[104] Energizing the Millennium Development Goals, *supra* note 85, at 15.

spawning a number of small enterprises.[105] These watermills exemplify a locally maintained and environmentally sustainable technology that addresses the needs of the EP while contributing to economic development.

Goal 8: Develop a Global Partnership for Development

Finally, the energy sector presents significant prospects for potential for synergies across markets, regions, and financial resources. "Energy is a cross-cutting issue by its very nature and thus requires participation from all development sectors in order to maximize its impact on development."[106] Thus, addressing the energy access problem can help to develop and realize global partnerships by providing a unique opportunity for collaboration.

Consider, for instance, the Global Village Energy Partnership (GVEP). GVEP is a collaboration of governments from developing and developed countries, public and private organizations, businesses, and consumers that aim to address the energy needs of the EP.[107] GVEP objectives center on capacity building and technology transfer as a means to improve access to energy services. While it boasts more than 700 partners from the energy, agriculture, education, environment, health, water, and development sectors, there has not been an assessment of GEVP's impact on the actual problem of energy poverty. Thus, although GVEP remains a promising example of global partnerships, as envisioned by MDG Goal 8, the extent of its success remains to be evaluated.

Clearly, satisfying the MDGs requires improved access to energy. The environmental and global warming implications of the MDGs are equally apparent. Addressing poverty and access to energy empowers and enables healthier, more educated peoples, including women, to adapt to and mitigate global warming. Healthier, better-educated peoples are undoubtedly in a better position to confront global warming compared to an inadequately educated population experiencing mortality from illness, disease, hunger, malnutrition, and burdensome opportunity costs associated with access to traditional energy sources. SDG Goal 7 now expresses this conclusion. Chapter 3 will discuss the MDGs and SDGs within the framework of sustainable development (SD).

---

105 Bates et al., *supra* note 84, at 33.

106 Energizing the Millennium Development Goals, *supra* note 85, at 16.

107 *Id.* at 17.

Chapter 2

GLOBAL JURISPRUDENTIAL LINEAGES OF LAW AND JUSTICE

I. Introduction

This chapter is not intended as a comprehensive survey of global jurisprudential thought (that would be an entirely different book), nor is it meant to suggest that the jurisprudential and philosophical lineages discussed are the sole schools of thought that matter. Rather, it is intended as a simple survey of some of the fundamental concepts underpinning various approaches to law and justice from around the world.

Law, however it is defined, is globally and inextricably related to the concept of justice. Defining the concept of justice requires moral reasoning. That is to say, in a society without a differentiation between morality and immorality, there is no such thing as a just or unjust decision. This is vitally important in understanding the very real and apparent differences in which legal outcomes are considered just among varying jurisprudential theories. Thus, a consideration of justice in a global sense must also consider theories of morality.

The most basic conception of morality is the distinction between "good" and "evil." This idea is exemplified in the natural law tradition conceptualized by Thomas Aquinas:

> All those things to which man has a natural inclination are naturally apprehended by reason as being good and, consequently, as objects of pursuit, and their contraries as evil and objects of avoidance. [. . .] Wherefore the order of the precepts of the natural law is according to the order of natural inclinations.[1]

In the Islamic tradition, the concept of Istislah (استصلاح)—literally "proper behavior"—also exemplifies this idea. Under Istislah, what is "good" must be connected to one of five "basic goods." These basic goods were abstracted from the five legal precepts in the Quran and Sunnah: religion, life, reason (al-aql), family (an-nasab), and wealth (al-mal).[2]

---

[1] Thomas Aquinas, *Summa Theologicae, Part II, I, Q. 94 The Natural Law*, (Fathers of the English Dominican Province eds., Benziger Bros. 1947) (1485), http://web.mnstate.edu/gracyk/courses/web%20publishing/aquinas-Natural-Law.htm (last visited Dec. 3, 2015).

[2] Gender And Equality In Muslim Family Law 142 (Ziba Mir-Hosseini, et al. eds., 2013), *referencing* Abu Hamid al-Gazali, b. 1111 A.D.

The question of what is just may produce different answers in these traditions on metaphysical and empirical grounds. For example, the utilitarian approach and its corollary, the "the greatest happiness for the greatest number of people," may be challenged as unjust because something that results in "the greatest happiness" may not be a "natural inclination" or align with the five "basic goods."

The relationship between law and justice is most readily visible by examining an unjust law. Let us consider Article 1 of the Law for the Protection of German Blood and German Honour:

> Marriages between Jews and citizens of German or kindred blood are forbidden. Marriages concluded in defiance of this law are void, even if, for the purpose of evading this law, they were concluded abroad.[3]

Is this "law?" This question can be answered easily. This law was promulgated and passed correctly according to the applicable procedures in Germany at the time, making it law. But, does this law represent justice? Is it "moral?"

In examining this law utilizing the concept of Istislah, it is clear that it is not a just law. The basic good of family can be considered as establishing a fundamental right to social bonds between individuals, and this law clearly infringes on that right. The same result is obtained utilizing the concepts of natural law, which dictate that what is good follows what is moral. This is not to suggest that all questions result in the same answers. In any society, justice results from the interaction between the morality and laws of that society. One very tangible ramification of this relationship is that law can shape morality and morality can shape law.

The broader purpose of contemplating the various lineages of justice is to ascertain if there exists jurisprudence calling for justice regarding the energy poor of the world. Doing so requires consciousness of a globalized world that is narrowing the differences between national and international laws. Nonetheless, the world is still comprised of sovereign nation states embodying differing and variegated nationalities and peoples governed by national or municipal laws. In addition, where applicable, nation states may be subject to international laws, which they are required to implement. These international laws include "general principles of law"[4] that govern all nations. If the evidence so warrants, it may be possible to

---

[3] Holocaust Memorial Museum: *Holocaust Encyclopedia, Nuremburg Race Laws: Translation, Reich Citizenship Law of September 15, 1935*, http://www.ushmm.org/wlc/en/article.php?ModuleId=10007903 (last visited Dec. 2, 2015).

[4] Article 38, section (1)(c) of the Statute of the International Court of Justice lists "general principles of law" as a primary source of law to be applied by the Court. Statute of the International Court of Justice, 1945 I.C.J. 59 Stat. 1031 at art. 38(1)(c).

identify concepts of justice, located within analogous jurisprudential lineages from different parts of the world, resulting in "general principles of law recognized by civilized nations."[5]

It is important also to note that this chapter traverses legal philosophy (sometimes called the "philosophy of law," or simply jurisprudence), which interfaces with, but cannot be equated with, the broader realm of philosophy in general. It has discerningly been observed by Julius Stone that the phrase *philosophy of law* may be a misnomer because philosophy of law is not based upon, and may remain untouched by, and indifferent to, the conflicts of different philosophical schools. Consequently, legal philosophers may, without constraint, draw on different and diverse philosophical perspectives that do not allow for the fragmented or piecemeal adoption of their closely knit and structured thesis. This may result in legal concepts that are philosophically stranded, fragmented, and unsystematic, and led Stone to conclude that it is not possible to treat philosophy of law as a specialized branch of philosophy such as ethics, political philosophy, epistemology, or logic. Philosophy of law is an eclectic collation of different disciplines, and ideas that may illumine jurisprudential problems found not only in philosophy, but in all systematic bodies of thought.[6] This chapter also discusses a related modern phenomenon: the unfortunate chasm separating moral and political philosophy from the jurisprudence of contemporary international law.

II. Jurisprudential Roots

Law, simply defined as "the body of rules, whether proceeding from formal enactment or from custom, which a particular state or community recognizes as binding on its members or subjects,"[7] is a universal concept that is part of the socio-political structure of all countries. The term "law" refers to a concept that embraces national (municipal) laws, and the law of nations, called public international law, as well as transnational laws, based on contract or custom, that govern transactions between corporations, civil society entities, and individuals belonging to different nation states. In this general sense, law arises from normal human and societal interaction. The specifics vary, changing greatly across time and culture, as do the theories that embody the justice behind law. This variance is significant for any project of law aimed at a global goal. However, in contrast to this

---

5 *Id.*

6 Julius Stone, *Philosophy of Law*, ENCYCLOPEDIA BRITANNICA ONLINE, http://www.britannica.com/EBchecked/topic/332775/philosophy-of-law (last visited Dec. 5, 2015).

7 Oxford English Dictionary Online, *Law, n.1.* Oxford University Press. http://www.oed.com/view/Entry/106405?rskey=32NFQd&result=2&isAdvanced=false (last visited Oct. 8, 2015).

variance, there are also powerful parallels that may not be obvious at first glance. To begin our project, we will consider first the concepts of law and then the theories of justice embodied within four jurisprudential lineages: Western, Islamic, Buddhist, and Confucian. The extent to which justice permeates the law applicable to all nations is examined in section III of this chapter dealing with International law and moral philosophy.

A. Western Jurisprudence

Western jurisprudence has two classical schools of thought: natural law and legal positivism. Natural law, as expounded by its most authoritative expositor, Thomas Aquinas,[8] assumes one of four forms: eternal law, referring to divine reason, known only to God as His plan for the universe; divine law, which is revealed in the scriptures and is God's positive law for mankind; natural law, which is the eternal law as it applies to humans, which through reason enables them to naturally understand how the good should be pursued, and evil eschewed in law; and human law, created for the purpose of implementing natural law. Only two of these are of relevance for our purposes: natural law and human law. Human law is, as defined by Aquinas, "an ordinance of reason for the common good, made by him who has care of the community, and promulgated."[9] It is predicated on the premise that the law that "is" enacted by the law-maker expresses law that "ought" to be enacted under principles of natural law.

In contrast, legal positivism refutes the conflation of "is" and "ought" and recognizes duly enacted legislation or case law as law, even if it conflicts with principles of natural law. If the law that "is" so enacted is substantively flawed, it "ought" to be changed. However, the law that is enacted is valid, even if it violates natural law, until and unless it is changed. Legal positivism has given rise to analytical jurisprudence, a method of legal study that concentrates on the logical structure of law, the meanings and uses of its concepts, and the formal terms and the modes of its operation.[10]

According to noted British jurist John Austin's (1790–1859)[11] classic definition, law is the command of a sovereign backed by

---

[8] The fundamentals of Aquinas's natural law doctrine are contained in the so-called Treatise on Law in Thomas's masterwork, the *Summa Theologiae*, comprising Questions 90 to 108 in the first part of the second part of the three-part *Summa*. Thomas Aquinas, *Summa Theologicae* (Fathers of the English Dominican Province eds., Benziger Bros. 1947) (1485).

[9] *Id.*, at *Summa* I–II, question 90, answer 4.

[10] Blackwell Reference Online, *Analytical Jurisprudence,* http://www.blackwellreference.com/public/tocnode?id=g9781405106795_chunk_g97814051067952_ss1-123 (last visited Dec. 5, 2015).

[11] Much of John Austin's work did not become famous until after his death.

force.[12] The "sovereign" is interpreted to include a democratic legislature. While agreeing on the separation of law and morals, or distinguishing "is" from "ought" in law, legal positivists have delineated their positions from different conceptual predicates. In his famous book, *The Concept of Law*,[13] the great legal philosopher H.L.A. Hart (1907–92) restated the positivist case within a framework of descriptive sociology and analytical jurisprudence, and he defined a legal system as a combination of primary and secondary rules.[14] By contrast Hans Kelsen (1881–1973), another great legal philosopher, advanced a pure theory of law.[15] According to Kelsen, the traditional legal philosophies at the time were hopelessly contaminated with political ideology and moralizing on the one hand, or, on the other hand, with attempts to reduce the law to natural or social sciences. He rejected both of these reductionist endeavors and suggested a "pure" theory of law that avoided reductionism of any kind.[16]

Many influential strands of modern and contemporary Western jurisprudence have moved from an analytical and philosophical, to more sociological and empirical approaches demonstrated, for example, by legal realism,[17] critical legal theory,[18] and pragmatic instrumentalism.[19] These schools of thought are mostly concerned

---

[12] John Austin, *The Province Of Jurisprudence Determined* (W. Rumble ed., Cambridge University Press 1995) (1832).

[13] H. L. A. Hart, *The Concept Of Law* (Oxford University Press, 1961).

[14] According to Hart, "primary" rules are rules of obligation which impose duties, *i.e.*, require people to do or abstain from certain actions, whether they wish to or not. Such rules are to be contrasted with secondary rules under which human beings "may by doing or saying certain things introduce new rules of the primary type, extinguish or modify old ones, or in various ways determine their incidence or control their operations." *Id.*, at 79. There are several types of secondary rules in Hart's scheme: rules specifying criteria for identification of valid rules of the legal system, rules empowering legislators and courts to legislate and adjudicate, and rules specifying sanctions. In essence, primary rules impose duties while secondary rules "confer powers, public or private." *Id.*

[15] M. Knight, *Pure Theory Of Law*, (Max Knight Trans, University of California Press, 1967).

[16] Kelsen characterized laws as rules or interlinked norms. A norm was a valid norm if a higher norm authorized the making of the lower norm and it had been made in accordance with the higher authorizing law. He explained that the chain of validity will ultimately run out of higher authorizing valid norms, a point where it was not possible to proceed further. The validity of law (norm) would then rest on a "grundnorm," which is sometimes translated as "basic norm." Kelsen described the grundnorm as the fundamental assumption made by people in society about what would be treated as law. *Id.*

[17] Horwitz, Morton J., *The Transformation Of American Law, 1870–1960: The Crisis Of Legal Orthodoxy* 193 (Oxford University Press, 1992).

[18] Roberto Mangabeira Unger, *The Critical Legal Studies Movement* (Harvard University Press, 1983); Mark Kelman, *A Guide To Critical Legal Studies* (Harvard University Press, 1987).

[19] Robert Summers, *Instrumentalism and American Legal Theory* 20 (Cornell University Press, 1982).

with the relationship between the law and the real-world outcomes of the law as experiments in social engineering and the testing grounds for social and economic policies. Long before these twentieth century developments, Jeremy Bentham (1748–1832), an English jurist, re-drew the contours of law, which had hitherto been based on case law, and recreated a vastly expanded domain of law in a way that had not hitherto been done. He called for a complete, comprehensive, and integrated re-envisioning of the existing system of law and government focused on legislation and its implementation.[20]

Any discussion about justice and law must include John Rawls, whose book *A Theory of Justice*[21] is the most influential exposition of justice in the twentieth century. He is a political philosopher rather than a legal philosopher and he does not bridge the perplexing separation of political and legal philosophy; indeed, he hardly mentions the word "law."[22] Despite this, his enormous importance requires that we clarify and situate Rawls' conception of justice within the legal context and traditions of natural law and positivism. Section III of this chapter will attempt to do so.

B. Islamic Jurisprudence

Jurisprudence in the Islamic tradition has a somewhat different, but not entirely dissimilar, rendition to that of Western jurisprudence. The Arabic term commonly translated as jurisprudence, *usul al-fiqh* (أصول الفقه), is not a literal translation. A more nuanced translation requires breaking down the Arabic and attempting to understand the term as an Arabic speaker would. The first word of the term, *usul*, in a general sense, means foundations. Its specific meaning varies depending on context—for instance it signifies "basic principles" when used in the context of science, and it means "assets" in the context of finance. It implies something which is firmly rooted, established, or of noble origin.[23] The second part of the term, *fiqh,* in its most general sense signifies understanding, comprehension, knowledge, and insight.[24] It implies what a prudent person would discern from the obvious. However, in the technical sense, *fiqh* signifies understanding of Islamic law. Taken together, in the general sense, the term *usul al-fiqh* means the foundations of understanding. In the specific sense, it refers to the foundations of Islamic law. There are four such foundations : the *Quran* (القرآن)—the

---

20 David Lieberman, *The Province of Legislation Determined* 286 (1989).

21 John Rawls, *A Theory of Justice* (Belknap Press, 1971, rev'd 1975, 1999).

22 Harold J. Berman, *Faith And Order: The Reconciliation Of Law And Religion* 296 (Wm. B. Eerdmans Publishing Co., 1993).

23 *The Hans Wehr Dictionary Of Modern Written Arabic* (J.M. Cowan ed., Spoken Language Services, 1993).

24 *Id.*

holy book of Islam; *Sunnah* (سنة)—the record of the teachings, deeds and sayings of Muhammad; *Qiyas* (قياس)—the process of deductive analogy; and *Ijma'* (إجماع)—the consensus of Islamic scholars. Of these, the Quran and Sunnah are primary sources. These two are primary because they represent divine law as revealed to Muhammad, whereas the other two are derived from human understanding of that law.

There is a strong parallel here to Aquinas's conceptions of law. The revealed divine law of the Quran and Sunnah may be equated with Aquinas's concept of eternal and divine law. Qiyas and Ijma' seem remarkably close to Aquinas's natural law, discerned through human reason that is able to differentiate between good and evil. Simply put, in both the Islamic tradition and the Natural Law tradition there is an eternal law, discovered through reasoning, which is the ultimate source of all law. Indeed, one of the names of Allah is hakim (حكيم)—most commonly translated as "the wise." But, it is also the title used for judges, and it is closely related to the words signifying the authority to determine what is right and what is wrong.[25]

C. Buddhist Jurisprudence

Recent studies have challenged the popular conception of Buddhism as an apolitical religion without implication for law.[26] A notable example of the legal and political dimension of Buddhism is demonstrated by the rule of Emperor Ashoka, the Mauryan king of India from 269 BCE to 232 BCE. His vast empire extended from Iran in the west to Bangladesh in the east and to all of present-day India except for Kerala and Tamil Nadu. His empire was multiracial, multireligious and multicultural; it included Greeks, the Kambojas, the Nabhakas, the Nabhapamkits, the Bhojas, the Pitinikas, the Andhras and the Palidas professing differing faiths. Ashoka governed this vast empire according to principles of justice rooted in Buddhism which he enshrined in a collection of 33 inscriptions found on the Pillars of Ashoka as well as on boulders and cave walls throughout his empire.[27]

The contents and quality of Asoka's edicts identify him as one of the greatest rulers of the world.[28] Jurisprudentially his edicts differentiated between binding state law and aspirational private or individual morality. In some respects, this differentiation can be

---

25 *Id.*

26 *See* Rebecca Redwood French And Mark A. Nathan, *Buddhism And Law: An Introduction* (Cambridge University Press, 2014).

27 Ven. S. Dhammika, *The Edicts Of King Ashoka* (Buddhist Publication Society, 1993), Dharma Net version available at http://www.cs.colostate.edu/~malaiya/ashoka.html (last visited Nov. 25, 2015).

28 H.G. Wells, *The Outline Of History* (George Newnes, 1919–20).

equated to the distinction that legal positivism makes between what is law and what ought to be law. From a different perspective, the edicts of Ashoka embody the political reality that ruling a heterogeneous society requires the consent of the governed. Accordingly, his laws were based on consensus that appealed to an universal sense of justice.

Ashoka derived his laws from Buddhist principles and was careful to distinguish the edicts of the state from private morality and behavior.[29] His edicts, or laws, as distinct from his exhortations persuading his subjects to behave differently, were binding on all the people. These edicts were not based on his whim or command as an Emperor. Instead Ashoka's edicts and laws were founded and justified on Buddhist principles. From one perspective, it is a kind of non-Thomian natural law. But, as enacted by Ashoka, the edicts enshrined Buddhist law derived from principles of Buddhism. Regardless of how they are characterized, Ashok's edicts resonated in justice.

Ashoka's edicts laying out state duties, which formed the law and administration of his empire, were directed toward creating a more just and spiritually inclined society. The protection of all religions, their promotion, and the fostering of harmony between them, were also seen as duties of the state.[30] The judicial system was reformed in order to make it more fair, less harsh, and less open to abuse, while those sentenced to death were given a stay of execution to prepare appeals, and regular amnesties were given to prisoners. State resources were used for useful public works like the importation and cultivation of medical herbs, the building of rest houses, the digging of wells at regular intervals along main roads, and the planting of fruit and shade trees.[31]

Under these edicts, the state had a responsibility not just to protect and promote the welfare of its people, but also its wildlife. Hunting certain species of wild animals was banned, forest and wildlife reserves were established, and cruelty to domestic and wild animals was prohibited. The Ashokan state also gave up the

---

[29] Ashoka's exhortations on private morality recommended and exhorted individuals to practice and become imbued with the Buddhist values of compassion, moderation, tolerance and respect for all life. The individual morality that Asoka hoped to foster included respect (susrusa) towards parents, elders, teachers, friends, servants, ascetics and brahmins—behavior that accords with the advice given to Sigala by the Buddha in Digha Nikaya, (Discourse No. 31). He encouraged generosity (dana) to the poor (kapana valaka), to ascetics and brahmins, and to friends and relatives.

[30] *Ven. S. Dhammika,* fn. 27 *supra.*

[31] *Id.*

predatory foreign policy that had characterized the prior Mauryan empire and replaced it with a policy of peaceful coexistence.

D. Confucian Jurisprudence

Confucianism is an all-encompassing way of thinking and living, propagated by the Chinese philosopher Confucius in the 6th to 5th century BCE. It is a worldview regarded sometimes as a philosophy and sometimes as a religion, and it has been followed by the Chinese people for more than two millennia. Confucianism spread to other East Asian countries under the influence of Chinese culture and has greatly influenced spiritual and political life. The theory and practice of Confucianism have undeniably shaped the systems of government, society, education, and family in East Asia. Commentators have pointed out that East Asians may profess themselves to be Shintōists, Daoists, Buddhists, Muslims, or Christians, but regardless of their religious affiliations, seldom do they cease to be Confucians.[32]

The *Lunyu* (*Analects*) the most revered sacred scripture in the Confucian tradition, was most likely compiled by generations of Confucius' disciples.[33] Much the same as the Platonic dialogues embody Socratic pedagogy, it captures the Confucian spirit in form and content.[34]

The Confucian conception of law is embodied by the Second Analect:

> The Master said: "If you govern with the power of your virtue, you will be like the North Star. . . . If you govern the people legalistically and control them by punishment, they will avoid crime, but have no personal sense of shame. If you govern them by means of virtue and control them with propriety, they will gain their own sense of shame, and thus correct themselves."[35]

Virtue (self-improvement) is the ultimate goal of laws in Confucian jurisprudential thought. The opposition to this school of thought was legalism, the school of Chinese philosophy that attained prominence during the turbulent Warring States era (475–221 BCE) and, through the influence of the philosophers Shang Yang, Li Si, and Hanfeizi, formed the ideological basis of China's first imperial dynasty, the Qin (221–207 BCE).

---

[32] Tu Weiming, *Confucianism*, ENCYCLOPEDIA BRITANNICA ONLINE, http://www.britannica.com/topic/Confucianism (last visited Dec. 5, 2015).

[33] *Id.*

[34] *Id.*

[35] *Analects of Confucius*, translated by A. Charles Muller (1990, rev'd 2015), http://www.acmuller.net/con-dao/analects.html (last visited Dec. 3, 2015).

Legalist philosophers abided by three main precepts: the strict application of widely publicized laws (*fa*), the application of such management techniques (*shu*) as accountability (*xingming*) and "showing nothing" (*wuxian*), and the manipulation of political purchase (*shi*). The legalists believed that political institutions should be modeled in response to the realities of human behavior, primarily in recognition of their belief that human beings are inherently short-sighted and selfish. Thus, the legalists believed that social harmony could only be achieved through strong state control and absolute obedience to authority. The legalists advocated for a government that comprised of a system of laws that rigidly prescribed punishments and rewards for behaviors. The ultimate goal of legalists was to increase the power of the ruler and the state. The brutal implementation of this policy by the authoritarian Qin dynasty led to that dynasty's overthrow, and it ultimately cause the widespread discrediting of legalist philosophy in China.[36]

In the early years of the Western Han (206 BCE–25 CE), however, the legalist practice of absolute power of the emperor, complete subjugation of the peripheral states to the central government, total uniformity of thought, and ruthless enforcement of law were replaced by the Daoist practice of reconciliation and noninterference. This practice is commonly known in history as the Huang-Lao method, referring to the art of rulership attributed to the Yellow Emperor (Huangdi) and the mysterious founder of Daoism, Lao-Tzu. Although a few Confucian thinkers, such as Lu Jia and Jia Yi, made important policy recommendations, Confucianism, before the emergence of Dong Zhongshu (*c.* 179–*c.* 104 BCE), was not particularly influential.

Nonetheless, the gradual Confucianization of Han politics began soon after the founding of the dynasty.[37] Although Confucian thought accepted the social hierarchy of its time, this existed side-by-side with the view that the basic tasks of government were to relieve people's suffering[38] and promote economic well-being.[39] The basic ideas embodied in these views are not foreign to the other jurisprudential lineages discussed. Unique to Confucian thought (at the time) however, was the idea that these basic tasks were to be achieved by ensuring that the government was run by the virtuous,

---

[36] *Legalism*, ENCYCLOPEDIA BRITANNICA ONLINE, http://www.britannica.com/topic/Legalism (last visited Dec. 5, 2015).

[37] *Tu Weiming*, fn. 32 *supra*.

[38] Mencius, Book I, B: 5 (D.C. Lau trans., Penguin Books, 1970).

[39] Confucius, *The Analects*: 13.9. *The Analects Of Confucius: A Philosophical Translation* (Roger T. Ames and Henry Rosemont, Jr. trans., Ballantine Books, 1998).

who obtained their position based on merit rather than birth.[40] This is the origin of the traditional Chinese competitive examination system for civil service.

III. International Law and Moral Philosophy

In discussing law and justice, it is unfortunate that Western theorizing on global justice is found within political and moral philosophy and not within what Steven Ratner calls the "thin justice" of international law or jurisprudence.[41] Ratner has exposed the unbridged chasm between the jurisprudence of international law and philosophical ethics.[42] In a world made up of sovereign states governed by international law, political and moral philosophers, who have systematically probed issues of global justice, have inexplicably avoided the implications of their theorizing on international law. They appear impervious to the fact that theories of international justice and international ethics float in a cloud of ideas unless they are anchored within the existing international legal order. The manner in which political and moral philosophers have left the premises of international law unarticulated and unexplored is both puzzling and disconcerting.

For their part, international lawyers who study the existing international order have been equally oblivious to the moral foundations of justice rooted in philosophy. Moral philosophy and justice have been treated as falling outside the compass of law, and generally ignored.[43] Contemporary international law needs to fill in the lacunae between law and justice. When doing so, the interface of politics and law raise important questions, which we will examine through the historical lens of western jurisprudence.

It has been pointed out that "(I)f the rules of law concern good order, and if politics aims at good order in a polity, law must be a crucial part of politics."[44] Politics is about power, law is about the shaping and the limiting of power-structures, and the concept of justice is central to this function of law. In "The Republic"[45] Plato

---

[40] Xunzi: Knoblock, John, *A Translation And Study Of The Complete Works, Vol. Ii, Ch. 9, "On The Regulations Of A King," at 9.1, 9.4* (Stanford University Press, 1998).

[41] Steven Ratner, *The Thin Justice Of International Law* 1–2, 27–28 (Oxford University Press, 2015).

[42] *Id.* 1–2, 20–41.

[43] *Id.*

[44] Beverly Brown and Neil MacCormick, *Law, philosophy of'*, ROUTLEDGE ENCYCLOPEDIA OF PHILOSOPHY, https://www.rep.routledge.com/articles/law-philosophy-of/v–1/ (last visited Dec. 5, 2015).

[45] Thomas Brickhouse and Nicholas D. Smith, *Plato (c.427–347 BC),* THE INTERNET ENCYCLOPEDIA OF PHILOSOPHY, UNIVERSITY OF TENNESSEE, http://www.iep.utm.edu/plato/#SH3b (last visited Dec. 5, 2015).

(428–348 BCE) demonstrates how Thrasymachus, a proponent of the thesis that justice is the will of the powerful, was convincingly refuted by Socrates. In his refutation, Socrates postulates a human capability to discern principles of right societal conduct independently of any formal enactment or legislative decision made by those exercising authority and power. These principles in their very nature are normative, not descriptive.[46]

Aristotle (384–322 BCE) devotes Book V of the *Nicomachean Ethics* to justice.[47] He articulates the same general idea by noticing that while much that is observed as law is locally variable and arbitrary, there appear to be fundamental common principles across different polities. Some principles may then become legal simply "by enactment," but others seem to be so "by nature." For Aristotle, understanding the nature of humans as rational and political animals helps in discovering what is "right" by nature.[48]

The Stoics (3rd century BCE) extended the domain of common principles based on what is right "by nature" universally. They reasoned that individuals should, by way of rational argument, extend and expand concern beyond themselves in concentric circles until all humankind, meaning the entire human race, is eventually included. "This attitude of the mind, which allots to each their own, and maintains this community of human association . . . is called justice."[49]

Roman jurists adapted some of the Stoic ideas of natural law in their codification of the civil law by Justinian (482–565) in the Corpus Juris Civlis. For medieval and early modern Europe, the existence of the Justinianic compilation of the whole body of Roman law was held by many thinkers to embody in large measure the promise of law as written reason.[50]

The applicability of law to all nations, as distinct from that which prevailed within a nation or state or polity, is canvased by a rich lineage of philosophers. The origins of the idea of the law of

---

46 Brown and MacCormick, *supra* note 44.

47 *Nicomachean Ethics* (T.H. Irwin trans., Hackett Publishing Company, 1999).

48 Brown and MacCormick, *supra* note 44.

49 Cicero, *De Finibus* V 65, *cited in* Julia Annas, *The Morality of Happiness* 316–317 (Oxford University Press, 1993).

50 *The Corpus Juris Civilis* contained the *Digest*, also known as the *Pandects*, a compilation ordered by the emperor Justinian I in the 6th century (AD 530–533). It spans 50 volumes, and represented a reduction and codification of all *Roman laws* up to that time. The other two parts of the civil law were the *Institutes of Justinian*, and the *Codex Justinianus*. A fourth part, the Novels (or *Novellae Constitutiones*), was added later. Tony Honoré, "Justinian's Codification" in THE OXFORD CLASSICAL DICTIONARY 803–804 (Simon Hornblower and Antony Spawforth eds., 3rd rev. ed., 2003).

nations—the *ius gentium*—was first articulated In the *Institutes* of the Roman jurist Gaius (130–180). The *ius gentium* is closely associated with the *ius naturale*.[51] According to Aquinas (1225–1274), the *ius gentium* was that aspect of positive law that was immediately derived by deduction from the natural law and was universally applicable across jurisdictional boundaries. Francisco Suárez (1548–1617) divided *ius gentium* into two groups. The first group comprised those laws that were part of the domestic law of most commonwealths, such as laws governing property and domestic commerce. The second group comprised those laws that were common in the way they coordinated relationships between peoples and commonwealths (laws *inter nationes*). Examples included the laws governing war, international commercial interactions, and the treatment of diplomats.[52] It was the almost completely universal character of the *ius gentium*, Suárez held, that invested it with a moral status more authoritative than other positive laws.[53]

Hugo Grotius (1583–1645), often known as the father of international law, developed his theory of natural law and natural rights from the Roman Law found in the Digest, and he concluded that this law was binding internationally.[54] Thomas Hobbes (1588–1679) perceived the law of nature as the law which all rational humans follow in order to survive and prosper. He divided the law of nature into the laws of man and that of states; the latter being, according to Hobbes, the law of nations.[55] Vattel (1714–1767) redefined the applicability of natural law internationally by clarifying that the laws of nature had to be specifically adapted to the law of nations because the law of nations dealt with different legal problems to those found within a country. He called for the use of "right reason" in adapting and formulating the laws of nature to the law of nations.[56]

John Rawls' theory of justice is predicated on what society "ought" to be. He makes the normative case for a society based on justice as fairness; a necessary corollary of his theory is that laws must reflect justice, and they cannot just express the will of the

---

[51] Samuel Gregg, *Natural Law and the Law of Nations*, THE WITHERSPOON INSTITUTE, http://www.nlnrac.org/earlymodern/law-of-nations (last visited Dec. 5, 2015).

[52] Francisco Suárez, S.J., *Selections From Three Works Of Francisco Suárez, S.J: De Legibus, Ac Deo Legislatore, 1612; Defensio Fidei Catholicae, Et Apostolicae Adversus Anglicanae . . . Theologica, Fide, Spe, Et Charitate*, 1621, *at De Legibus*, II.17.1 (W.S. Hein, 1995).

[53] Samuel Gregg, note 51, *supra*.

[54] Benjamin Straumann, *Roman Law In The State Of Nature: The Classical Foundations Of Hugo Grotius' Natural Law* 4–5 (Cambridge University Press, 2015).

[55] Thomas Hobbes, *De Cive* 28 (H. Warrender ed., Clarendon Press, 1983).

[56] Emer De Vattel, *Les Droits Des Gens* 9 (Béla Kapossy and Richard Whatmore eds., Liberty Fund, 2008).

sovereign or lawmaker. Based on his conclusion that laws should reflect more than the will of the sovereign, some writers view Rawls as articulating a nonThomian species of natural law.[57] Others, who take a more traditional and conservative view of natural law, dismiss any such connection. According to them, a "minimalist natural law" falls outside the traditional scholastic tradition of commentators, and casuists, who situate natural law within a rich, and highly determinate, theory of nature, human nature, and finality.[58] For the purposes of this chapter, it is more important to understand what he says than to classify him under any predetermined taxonomy.

In *The Law of Peoples*,[59] John Rawls's lays the foundations for his concept of international justice based on a "realistic utopia" grounded in socio-political, institutional, and psychological reality.[60] Rawls expands on his "original position," a thought experiment expounded in *A Theory of Justice*,[61] and developed in numerous other works. In *A Theory of Justice*, Rawls envisioned a collection of negotiators from liberal democratic societies assembled behind a veil of ignorance, shorn of any knowledge that might be the basis of self-interested bias—such as knowledge of their gender, wealth, race, ethnicity, abilities, and general social circumstances. Rawls explains that the purpose of such a negotiation was to arrive at legitimate principles of justice under fair conditions—hence "justice as fairness."[62]

In *The Law of Peoples*, Rawls addresses justice in the international context. In doing so, he extends his theories from liberal democratic states to "decent" peoples living in nondemocratic international societies. Rawls envisions such "well-ordered hierarchical societies" to be "nonliberal societies whose basic institutions meet specified conditions of political right and justice (including the right of citizens to play a substantial role, such as participating in associations and groups making political decisions) and lead their citizens to honor a reasonably just law for the Society of Peoples."[63] Well-ordered societies must satisfy a number of

---

[57] Lloyd Weinreb, *Natural Law and Justice* (Harvard University Press, 1987), *especially* chapter four, "Natural Law without Nature."

[58] Russell Hittinger, *Liberalism and the American Natural Law Tradition*, 25 Wake Forest L. Rev. 429 (1990); *see also* Russell Hittinger, *Varieties of Minimalist Natural Law Theories*, 34 Am. J. of Juris. 133 (1989).

[59] John Rawls, *The Law Of Peoples* 106 (Harvard University Press, 2001). The following sections on Rawls are based on and reproduce, Lakshman Guruswamy, *Global Energy Justice,* 55 in *International Energy and Poverty: The emerging frontiers* Lakshman Guruswamy, ed. (Routledge, 2015).

[60] *Id.*

[61] John Rawls note 21, *supra.*

[62] John Rawls, note 59, *supra.*

[63] *Id.* at 106.

criteria: they must eschew aggressive aims as a means of achieving their objectives, honor basic human rights dealing with life, liberty, and freedom, and possess a system of law imposing bona fide moral duties and obligations, as distinct from human rights. Moreover, they must have law and judges to uphold common ideas of justice.[64]

Rawls demonstrated how the law of peoples may be developed out of liberal ideas of justice similar to, but more general than, the idea of "justice as fairness" presented in *A Theory of Justice*.[65] Just as individuals in the first original position were shorn of knowledge about their attributes and placed behind a veil of ignorance to create principles for a just domestic society, the bargainers in the so-called second original position are representatives of peoples who are shorn of knowledge about their people's resources, wealth, power, and the like. Behind the veil of ignorance, the representatives of peoples—not states, as states lack moral capacity—develop the principles of justice that will govern relations between them: "the law of peoples."

It should be noted at this juncture that there is a difference between John Rawls' theories of domestic and international justice. The principles of domestic distributive justice espoused by Rawls in *A Theory of Justice* are not applied to the international sphere. A pivotal reason for this is that the international community does not possess the basic institutions of a liberal democratic society necessary to institute and implement distributive justice. The machinery of government, consisting of a legislature that can make laws, an executive branch that implements such laws, and courts with compulsory jurisdiction that interpret and apply the laws of the state, does not exist on a global level. These factors were among the reasons that his book is titled "The Law of Peoples" rather than "the law of nations" or "the law of states."

Rawls emphasized the need for global order and stability over global distributive justice. Once the duty to assist burdened peoples is satisfied, there are no further requirements on economic distribution within Rawls' *The Law of Peoples*; inequalities across national borders are of no political concern as such. Individuals around the world may suffer greatly from bad luck, and they may be haunted by spiritual emptiness. The practical goal of *The Law of Peoples* is the elimination of the great evils of human history: unjust war and oppression, religious persecution, the denial of liberty of conscience, starvation and poverty, genocide, and mass murder. The

---

[64] *Id.* at 3.

[65] *Id.*

limits of this ambition mean that there will be much in the world to which Rawls's political philosophy offers no reconciliation.[66]

Rawls seeks to determine the principles of cooperation for such "well-ordered peoples." Rawls posits that non-ideal conditions cannot adequately be addressed unless principles of justice are determined for ideal conditions. Otherwise, it is impossible to know what kind of just society to aim to establish and the necessary means to do so.[67] A "realistic utopia," as Rawls prefers to call his theory, is an aspiration that does not reflect the existing reality of international law and relations.

Rawls emphasizes the crucial importance of peoples rather than states because of a people's capacity for "moral motives" that is lacking in the bureaucratic machinery of a state.[68] Noah Feldman correctly observes that a "people" for Rawls is a philosophical construct. It is an abstract conception needed to work out principles of justice for a particular subject—in this case, relations among different, well-ordered liberal and "decent" societies.[69] The acceptance of sustainable development may suggest the functional confluence of peoples and nations. Moreover, Rawls remains trenchant when it comes to the application of sustainable development. Rawls is not talking then about a people regarded as an ethnic or religious group (e.g. Slavs, Jews, Kurds) who are not members of the same society. Rather, a "people" consists of members of the same well-ordered society who are united under, and whose relations are governed by, a political constitution and basic structure. Comprised of members of a well-ordered society, a people is envisioned as having effective political control over a territory that its members govern and within which their basic social institutions take root. In contrast to a state, however, a people possesses a "moral nature" that stems from the effective sense of justice for its individual members. A peoples' members may have "common sympathies" for any number of non-requisite reasons, including shared language, ethnic roots, or religion. The most basic reason for members' common sympathies, however, lies in their shared history as members of the same society and consequent shared conception of justice and the common good.

---

66 L. Wenar, "John Rawls," in THE STANFORD ENCYCLOPEDIA OF PHILOSOPHY (E. N. Zalta ed., 2008) (visited Nov. 26, 2015).

67 John Rawls, note 59 *supra*, at 3.

68 *Id.*

69 N. Feldman, *Cosmopolitan Law?* 116 YALE L. J. 1022 at 1038 (2007).

Rawls's concept of "peoples" has been criticized. Among his more cogent critics, Pogge[70] and Nussbaum[71] question the validity of the distinction between peoples and states and the difficulties of defining peoples. They claim their criticisms assume importance in any attempt to realize the "Society of Peoples" Rawls envisions as his realistic utopia. Such criticisms have actually been anticipated by Rawls, who pointed out that he eschewed the "state" as a polity because of its historical Hobbesian connotations in "realist" international political theory, which suggests that the power of states can be limited only by the states, and not by moral or legal constraints.[72]

IV. Interim Conclusions

First, the conclusion most pertinent to our discussion of justice is that Rawls elucidates the duty of liberal democratic and decent hierarchical peoples to assist "burdened societies" to the point where burdened societies are enabled to join the "Society of Peoples." It is of particular pertinence that Rawls's duty of assistance does not absolve developing country governments of their obligation to take appropriate action.

Second, in ascertaining the jurisprudential basis for applying Rawls, it is important that we do not ignore natural law. Within legal theory, the application of natural law to the law of nations has become attenuated, even though natural law is embodied in the Statue of the International Court of Justice, which stipulates that the International Court of Justice (ICJ) apply "the general principles of law recognized by civilized nations" as a primary source of law.[73]

Third, our brief survey suggests that the general principles of law referred to in the Statute of the ICJ, are based on concepts of justice, applicable to global energy poverty. They may be found within Islamic, Buddhist, and Confucian global jurisprudential lineages, outside western natural law. Consequently, it is possible to discover general principles of law and justice within the world's jurisprudential heritage. These general principles of law and justice should form part of the legal response to global energy poverty. Chapter 4 describes how sustainable development law, and principles of energy justice, might respond to the global challenge of energy poverty.

---

[70] T. W. Pogge, *The Incoherence BetweenRawls's Theories of Justice* 72 FORDHAM L. REV. 1739 at 1743 (2004).

[71] M. C. Nussbaum, *Frontiers of Justice: Disabilities, Nationality, Species Membership* 236–244 (Harvard University Press, 2006).

[72] John Rawls, *supra*, note 59, at n.88.

[73] 1945 I.C.J. 59 Stat. 1031 at art. 38(1)(c).

Chapter 3

SUSTAINABLE DEVELOPMENT & THE SUSTAINABLE DEVELOPMENT GOALS (SDGs)

The concepts of justice, emerging from their jurisprudential lineages discussed in Chapter 2, are playing an important role in today's international society of nations and peoples. Concepts of international justice provide a moral foundation, and should continue to shape and govern the future trajectory of Sustainable Development (SD), and the Sustainable Development Goals (SDGs). This chapter will examine how SD has evolved, and delineate where and how it is expressed in international laws, principles, and policies.

I. The Evolution of Sustainable Development

A. The Stockholm Conference on the Human Environment

Over a period stretching nearly half a century, an important segment of laws and policies governing international society have crystalized into the concept of SD. The 1972 Stockholm Conference on the Human Environment[1] primarily intended as a conference about the international environment, may well have been the chrysalis from which SD emerged as an international concept.

The themes articulated in Rachel Carson's book, *Silent Spring* (1962), Barry Commoner's book, *The Closing Circle* (1971), and Kenneth Boulding's *Spaceship Earth* (1966) resonated from the US into the thinking of other industrial nations.[2] Many of these and other themes were melded and expressed with crusading cogency in an international context in *Limits to Growth*,[3] a computer modeled study sponsored by the Club of Rome, a private group of industrialists and world leaders. *Limits to Growth* painted an apocalyptic picture of the growth of population, pollution, and the exhaustion of natural resources, leading to a breakdown of the carrying capacity of the earth. Along with a growing awareness of environmental phenomena, such as acid rain and the poisoning of

---

[1] United Nations Conference on the Human Environment, Stockholm, Swed., June 5–16, 1972, *Report of the United Nations Conference on the Human Environment*, U.N. Doc. A/CONF.48/14/Rev.1 (1973) [hereinafter *Report of the United Nations Conference on the Human Environment*].

[2] *See generally* Kenneth Boulding, *The Economics of the Coming Spaceship Earth*, in *Environmental Quality in a Growing Economy* 3 (H. Jarret ed., 1966).

[3] Donella H. Meadows Et Al., *Limits To Growth* (1972).

Japanese fisherman in Minamata Bay, these publications led to a realization of the frailty of the planet earth and created a ferment of apprehension among a cross section of common people, influential elites, and decision makers in the industrial world.

In the face of these concerns, the UN moved to convene a special international environmental conference to discuss the human environment in 1972. Sweden, which had begun to experience transboundary acid rain, volunteered to host the conference in Stockholm. The overall sense of crisis crying out for global action was brilliantly captured in the book by Rene Dubos and Barbara Ward, specially commissioned for the Stockholm Conference[4]

While concern about the environment motivated many rich, industrialized countries, the poor, developing countries did not share the view that environmental degradation was the biggest threat facing the planet. For developing countries, poverty and the alleviation of misery remained a more poignant and real problem. In the preparatory meetings leading to the Stockholm Conference, the developing countries—which called themselves the Group of 77 (their original number)—sharply and forcefully articulated the view that the worst pollution was caused by poverty.

Developing countries believed that greater development leading to material prosperity far outweighed any damage that might be caused by resource use and pollution. They were particularly scornful of the claim that industrialized countries were genuinely trying to steer them away from pitfalls into which the industrialized countries had already fallen. Developing countries also expressed resentment over the fact that industrialized countries—whose drive toward wealth had already consumed a great part of the earth's resources and led to devastating pollution—were now asking the developing countries to remain poor, and, more gallingly, to pay for the clean up, restoration, and conservation of the earth. Moreover, many developing countries feared that new environmental standards adopted by industrialized countries would effectively bar the entry of their goods into industrial markets.

This ideological impasse presented a formidable challenge to international environmental diplomacy. Consequently, nearly all the regional seminars and special meetings convened prior to the conference were focused on the interrelationship between development and the environment.[5] The question was resolved, as best it might be, by way of a compromise worked out in a meeting at

---

[4] See generally, Rene Dubos & Barbara Ward, *Only One Earth: The Care and Maintenance Of A Small Planet* (1972).

[5] Report of the United Nations Conference on the Human Environment, *supra* note 1 at 38.

Founex, near Geneva, Switzerland, in 1971. The compromise held that economic development was not necessarily incompatible with environmental protection and that environmental considerations should be an integral part of the development process. The essence of that understanding was summed up in the Preamble to the Stockholm Declaration of the UN Conference on the Environment (Stockholm Declaration),[6] It stated "[i]n the developing countries most of the environmental problems are caused by under-development" and that industrialized countries must "direct their efforts to development, bearing in mind their priorities and the need to safeguard and improve the environment."[7] Similarly, the industrialized countries were exhorted to make efforts to reduce the developmental gap between themselves and the developing countries.

In sum, the developing countries successfully thwarted potential environmental laws and policies from damaging their efforts to develop and grow economically, whether by industrial progress or trade. The developing countries did not, however, obtain substantial bankrolling for environmentally conscious development nor did they pledge to protect the global environment. This early declaration also did not meaningfully advance the doctrine of "common but differentiated responsibility" later accepted at the 1992 Earth Summit as a means of recognizing the different needs of developing and industrialized countries.

However, for a number of other reasons, the Stockholm Declaration may also be considered the cocoon of SD. First, the biosphere, or the planet, was identified as a subject and placed on the agenda of national and international policy and law in a way that had never been done before. Second, the conference was widely attended, with 114 of the then 131 UN members participating (the Soviet bloc abstained from attending, not because it rejected the purpose or mission of the conference, but because of the status accorded to East Germany). Third, the Stockholm Conference resulted in the creation of the United Nations Environment Programme (UNEP) the first international organization with an exclusively environmental mandate. Fourth, it produced the Stockholm Declaration; which sought to strike a balance between economic and social development and the improvement of the environment. The Stockholm Conference also created an action plan containing recommendations for future implementation.[8]

---

[6] Stockholm Declaration of the United Nations Conference on the Environment, Jun. 16, 1972, 11 I.L.M 1416.

[7] *Id.* ¶ 4.

[8] Report of the United Nations Conference on the Human Environment, *supra* note 1 at 67.

The nature of the balance struck at Stockholm was weighted in favor of the environment. A number of specific principles of the Stockholm Declaration bear mention. Principles 1, 2, and 5, dealing with responsibilities to future generations, were undergirded by an obligation to conserve. Principle 1, albeit counterbalanced by Principle 11, recognized a nascent right to " . . . an environment of a quality that permits a life of dignity and well-being . . . " Principle 21 referred to the right of a state to exploit its resources pursuant to its environmental (not developmental) policies, and affirmed its obligation not to cause transboundary injury. By holding states responsible for their transnational damage, Principle 21 may have crystallized or generated customary law. Lastly, Principle 22 posited that states should cooperate to develop international law regarding liability and compensation for transboundary harm.

These Principles have been re-institutionalized in many post-Stockholm agreements. For example, Principle 21 has been incorporated in a wide range of treaties including the United Nations Framework Convention on Climate Change,[9] Convention on Biological Diversity,[10] The Vienna Convention for the Protection of the Ozone Layer,[11] the Convention on Long-Range Transboundary Air Pollution[12] and the United Nations Convention on the Law of the Sea.[13] Furthermore, the post-Stockholm world has spawned a prolific number of environmental treaties. Over 150 post-Stockholm treaties mirror almost every concern that has been the subject of national laws or regulations including acid rain, hazardous waste, ozone depletion, sea pollution from land and vessels, toxics, resource conservation, and climate change.

B. 1982 United Nations Convention on the Law of the Sea (UNCLOS)

Negotiations about the law of the sea had commenced even before the Stockholm Conference. Those negotiations lasted until 1982, when the UN Convention on the Law of the Sea (UNCLOS) was opened for signature. UNCLOS finally came into force on November 16, 1994. It is the strongest comprehensive environmental treaty now

---

[9] United Nations Framework Convention on Climate Change, June 9, 1992, 31,ILM 849 (1992) [hereinafter UNFCCC].

[10] Convention on Biological Diversity, art. 3, June 5, 1992 31, I.L.M. 818 (1992) [hereinafter CBD].

[11] Vienna Convention for the Protection of the Ozone Layer, art. 2, Mar. 22 1985, 26 I.L.M. 1529 (1987) [hereinafter Vienna Convention on the Ozone Layer].

[12] Convention on Long-Range Transboundary Air Pollution, arts. 1 and 2 Nov. 13, 1979, 18 I.L.M. 1442.

[13] United Nations Convention on the Law of the Sea, 1982, arts 1(4), Part X11, 194 (2) Dec.10, 1982, 21 I.L.M. 1261 (1982) [hereinafter UNCLOS].

in existence or likely to emerge for quite some time.[14] It may be seen as a constitution for the oceans. The character and reach of its 59 provisions obligating environmental protection and conservation, out of 320 provisions in all, arguably possess such a fundamental and overarching character. Moreover, UNCLOS functions not only as a treaty, but as a codification and articulation of customary international rules applicable to oceans. It is therefore binding on its parties as a treaty, while nonparties are bound by it because it is a codification of customary law.[15]

It is worth remembering, in this context, that the oceans occupy over 70 percent of the landmass of the earth and are, in many ways, a proxy for the global environment. Most pollution released into the environment from land-based sources is eventually deposited into the oceans through direct and indirect pathways. Moreover, notable areas of oceanic governance, such as conservation of wetlands, coastal areas, and biodiversity, are of critical significance to international environmental protection in general.

UNCLOS contains at least 59 environmental provisions, ranging from the global to the specific, spread out over several parts of the text including: The Territorial Sea and Contiguous Zone (Part II), Exclusive Economic Zone (Part V), High Seas (Part VII), Enclosed or Semi-Enclosed Areas (Part IX), The Area (Part XI), Protection and Preservation of the Marine Environment (Part XII), and Marine Scientific Research (Part XIII). The environmental provisions deal with: the conservation and management of living resources; pollution prevention, reduction, and control; vessel pollution; and environmental management.

As an umbrella convention, UNCLOS brings other international rules, regulations, and implementing bodies within its canopy. At the substantive level of obligation and implementation, many of its provisions are of a constitutional or general character and must be augmented and supplemented by specific regulations, rules, and implementing procedures formulated by other international agreements and states.

While UNCLOS does not use the term "sustainable development," the two elements of SD (as then conceived) dealing with economic development, and environmental protection or conservation, are embodied in it. Within their 200-mile exclusive

---

[14] Letter of Submittal of the Secretary of State to the President of the United States, Sept. 23, 1994. reprinted in *Special Supplement: Message from the President of the United States and Commentary Accompanying the United Nations Convention on the Law of the* Sea,7 GEO. INT'L ENVT'L L. REV. 77 (1994).

[15] Jonathan I. Charney, *Entry Into Force of the 1982 Convention on the Law of the Sea,* 35 VA. J. INT'L. L. 381 (1995); Louis Sohn & Kristen Gustafson, *The Law of the Sea In a Nutshell* (1984).

economic zone (EEZ), UNCLOS confers both rights and duties on states to explore, economically exploit, conserve and manage the natural resources.[16] In the high seas beyond national jurisdiction states are required to maintain or restore harvested species at levels that can produce maximum yield.[17] Moreover part Xll on the Protection and Preservation of the Marine Environment deal with the various ways in which states are obliged to protect and preserve the marine environment.[18] In sum, UNCLOS attempted to balance economic development and environmental protection, and in doing so established the importance of SD as embracing not only the atmosphere and land but also the oceans.

C. 1983 World Commission on Environment and Development (Brundtland Commission)

Despite the uneasy truce at Founex reflected in the Stockholm Declaration, the persistent clash of two world views, one asserting environmental protection and the other economic development, continued to impede the progress of SD. In order to resolve this problem, the World Commission on Environment and Development (also called the Brundtland Commission) was created by the General Assembly of the UN in 1983 and charged with proposing long-term environmental strategies for SD. That elusive term was not defined by the UN. After four years of deliberation and worldwide consultation, the Brundtland Report, *Our Commons* Future,[19] articulated the paradigm on which the Earth Summit, and indeed SD, has since been based. In essence, it rejected the despairing thesis that environmental problems were past repair, spiraling out of control, and could only be averted by arresting development and economic growth resulting in a policy of no growth. Instead, it argued that economic growth was both desirable and possible within a context of SD

Although SD was not clearly defined and continues to elude canonical definition, some of its seminal attributes are identifiable. SD calls for developmental policies and for economic growth that can relieve the great poverty of the developing countries, while simultaneously protecting the environment from further damage. Such development and growth should be based on policies that sustain and expand the environmental resource base in a manner that meets the needs of the present generation without

---

[16] UNCLOS, *supra* note 13, at art. 56(a).

[17] *Id.* at art. 119(1)(a).

[18] *Id.* at arts 192 to 237.

[19] World Comm'n On Env't & Dev., *Our Common Future* (1987), available at http://www.un-documents.net/our-common-future.pdf.

compromising the ability of future generations to meet their own needs.

In order to draw up a global plan for SD, the Brundtland Commission called for an international conference to act as the successor to the Stockholm Conference and carry forward its legacy. The UN General Assembly complied by convening the 1992 Earth Summit and directing it to further develop SD, taking account, *inter alia*, of the Stockholm Declaration. An ambitious agenda was drawn up for the Earth Summit that included the following three endeavors: (1) an Earth Charter that would be the successor to the Stockholm Declaration; (2) an action plan for the planet called Agenda 21; and (3) the ceremonial signing of two conventions on biodiversity and climate change.

D. 1992 United Nations Conference on Environment and Development

The United Nations Conference on Environment and Development (Earth Summit), held in Rio de Janeiro, Brazil, in June 1992, was attended by over 180 countries and 100 heads of state, and heralded as the greatest summit level conference in history. It departed somewhat from its original agenda, but resulted in five international instruments, predicated on SD: (1) the Rio Declaration on Environment and Development.[20] (2) Agenda 21,[21] (3) the Global Consensus on Sustainable Development of Forests (Forestry Declaration),[22] (4) United Nations Convention on Climate Change (UNFCCC).[23] and (5) the Convention on Biological Diversity (CBD).[24]

We very briefly advance some conclusions about the environmental dimensions of the 1992 Earth Summit, dealing first with the legally binding treaties and then moving on to the non-legally binding instruments. To begin, it is worth emphasizing a premise reiterated and reaffirmed in all the documents (legal and otherwise) emerging from the Earth Summit. It is that the right of developing countries to economic advancement cannot be divorced from the pursuit of environmentalism and climate change.

---

[20] *Rio Declaration on Environment and Development,* Rio De Janeiro, 13 June 1992, 31 I.L.M. 874 (1992) [hereinafter Rio Declaration].

[21] United Nations Conference on Environment and Development, Rio de Janeiro, Braz., June 3–14, 1992, *Agenda 21,* June 13, 1992, https://sustainable development.un.org/content/documents/Agenda21.pdf (visited Dec. 21, 2015).

[22] United Nations Conference on Environment and Development, Rio de Janeiro, Braz., June 3–14, 1992, *Non-Legally Binding Authoritative Statement of Principles for a Global Consensus on the Management, Conservation and Sustainable Development of All Types of Forests,* U.N. Doc. A/CONF.151/26 (Vol. III), Annex III (Aug. 14, 1992).

[23] UNFCCC, *supra* note 9.

[24] *CBD, supra* note 10.

We start with the UNFCCC, which is the most important treaty dealing with climate change because it is a treaty to which all nations of the world including the United States is a party. The objective of the UNFCCC is to ". . . prevent dangerous anthropogenic interference with the climate system . . ."[25] The parties make commitments to mitigate climate change by addressing anthropogenic emissions and adapting to the impacts of climate change.[26] It is important to understand the rationale behind this objective.

The mitigation (cutting down or reduction) of carbon dioxide emissions addresses the environmental problems arising from the atmospheric accumulation of carbon dioxide resulting in a global greenhouse effect (GHG). A GHG effect occurs when some of the heat which reaches the earth is trapped in it and cannot get out back into the atmosphere. This results in global climate change that can lead to the melting of ice packs in Greenland, a global rise of sea levels, and alteration in weather patterns.

The UNFCCC is a treaty addressing climate change and lays the foundation for climate action within the framework of SD. Commencing with its Preamble, UNFCCC makes abundantly clear that responses to climate change should be coordinated with social and economic development ". . . taking into full account the legitimate priority needs of developing countries for the achievement of sustained economic growth and the eradication of poverty . . ."[27] Moreover, the UNFCCC stipulates that the parties have a right to and should promote SD policies, taking into account that economic development is an essential component of action against climate change.[28]

Furthermore, the UNFCCC coalesced with the other widely accepted treaty adopted at the Earth Summit, the CBD[29], by forcefully and unequivocally expressing the developmental priority of SD. Article 4(7) of the UNFCCC, and Article 20(4) of the CBD, reaffirm in unison that parties "will take fully into account that economic and social development and poverty eradication are the first and overriding priorities of the developing country Parties."

The importance of economic development and the eradication of poverty are also affirmed in the nonbinding agreements or declarations embodying "soft law" norms. Treaties and custom generally create binding obligations on nations, while soft law

---

25 UNFCCC, *supra* note 9, art. 2.

26 *Id.* arts 4(1)(b) & (e).

27 *Id.* at Preamble.

28 *Id.* at art. 3(4).

29 CBD, *supra* note 10.

sources are largely aspirational. Among the non-binding instruments, the Rio Declaration continues to emphasize the importance of economic development while pursuing environmental protection. For example, the nascent right to a wholesome environment, embodied in the Stockholm Declaration, was replaced by a right to development.[30] The Rio Declaration refers to "developmental and environmental needs of present and future generations."[31] This re-formulation impliedly negates or weakens the obligation to conserve expressed in the Stockholm Declaration. In similar vein, the obligation to *conserve*, implied by the duty to protect the environment for the benefit of future generations, found in the Stockholm Declaration, is displaced in the Rio Declaration by a right to *consume* or develop. Furthermore, the obligation not to cause transboundary damage, contained in Principle 21 of the Stockholm Declaration, was weakened in the Rio Declaration by the addition of crucial language authorizing States "to exploit their own resources pursuant to their own environmental and *developmental* policies."[32] (Emphasis added). Thus, the Rio Declaration incorporated several allowances for nations' developmental needs, perhaps at the expense of more environmentally protective provisions found in the Stockholm Declaration.

Agenda 21 was a second institutional result of Earth Summit. Similar to the Rio Declaration, Agenda 21 was also shaped by the tension between development and environmental protection, and calls for the integration of environment and development concerns.[33] While committing to the conservation and protection of resources, Agenda 21 mirrors the Rio Declaration in acknowledging and affirming the priority of political and social challenges in developing nations.[34] Specifically, Chapter 3.2 gives substantial deference to the use of natural resources to combat poverty. Chapter 39, which deals with the review and development of international environmental policy, stresses the importance of participation by developing countries in drafting new legal instruments, but reaffirms the need to weigh their developmental needs against the obligations that might be imposed by those instruments.

This is not to gloss over the significant environmental dimension of Agenda 21. Chapters 9 through 22 are devoted to and deal, *inter alia*, with the protection of the atmosphere, combating of deforestation, an integrated approach to land management, managing fragile ecosystems, conserving biodiversity, managing

---

[30] Rio Declaration, *supra* note 20, at Principle 2.

[31] *Id.* at Principle 3.

[32] *Id.*

[33] Agenda 21, *supra* note 21, at Chapter 1.1.

[34] *Id.* at Chapter 1.5.

toxic chemicals, and the management of hazardous, solid, and radioactive wastes.

In assessing the individual strands that together comprise the braided rope of SD today, it is important to understand the conceptual evolution of these strands. In 1992, SD remained a syncopated concept consisting of economic development and environmental protection. By contrast, the present concept of SD possesses three elements: economic development, social development and environmental protection. When the various documents emerging from the Earth Summit were being negotiated, the social dimension of SD was in fact recognized and expressly articulated, as we have noted, by Article 4(7) of the UNFCCC, and Article 20(4) of the CBD. Social development was not, however, institutionalized as one of the three formal components of SD until the World Summit on Sustainable Development in 2002.

E. 2000 Millennium Summit and the Millennium Development Goals (MDGs)

The Millennium Summit held in 2000 was the largest gathering of world leaders in history as of that date. The Millennium Summit adopted the UN Millennium Declaration, committing nations to a new global partnership to reduce extreme poverty and setting out a series of time-bound targets, with a deadline of 2015, which become known as the Millennium Development Goals (MDGs).

The MDGs distilled the results of a wide array of global processes involving diverse actors over several years. Apart from conferences on SD and the environment, many international goals and targets were established through a series of other major subject-specific conferences in the 1990s. The agendas spanned education (Jomtien 1990), children (New York 1990), population (Cairo 1994), social development (Copenhagen 1995), and the status of women (Beijing 1995). In 1995 and 1996, the OECD development assistance committee set out to summarize the disparate agreements into a shorthand set of international development goals (IDGs) that could help motivate donors.[35]

The MDGs were time-bound and quantified targets for addressing extreme poverty in its many dimensions, including income poverty, hunger, disease, and lack of adequate shelter, while promoting gender equality, education, environmental sustainability, and social development.[36] They are expressed as individual benefits,

---

[35] John W. McArthur, *The Origins of the Millennium Development Goals,* XXXIV (2) SAIS REVIEW (Summer–Fall 2014). http://johnmcarthur.com/wp-content/uploads/2015/01/SAISreview2014mcarthur.pdf (visited Dec. 8, 2015).

[36] Millennium Project *What They Are,* http://www.unmillenniumproject.org/goals/index.htm (visited Dec. 29, 2015).

granting each person on the planet the right to health, education, shelter, and security.

All 189 United Nations member states at the time (there are 193 currently), and at least 23 international organizations, committed to help achieve the following MDGs by 2015:[37]

1. To eradicate extreme poverty and hunger
2. To achieve universal primary education
3. To promote gender equality
4. To reduce child mortality
5. To improve maternal health
6. To combat HIV/AIDS, malaria, and other diseases
7. To ensure environmental sustainability
8. To develop a global partnership for sustainable development by 2015.

Evaluating the MDGs

An important inter-agency UN evaluation of the MDGs in 2015[38] demonstrates what the MDGs have achieved or failed to deliver. What follows is a progress report of each MDG, as summarized in the report.

Goal 1: Eradicate Extreme Poverty and Hunger.

- Extreme poverty has declined significantly over the last two decades. In 1990, nearly half of the population in the developing world lived on less than $1.25 a day; that proportion dropped to 14 percent in 2015.
- Globally, the number of people living in extreme poverty has declined by more than half, falling from 1.9 billion in 1990 to 836 million in 2015. Most progress has occurred since 2000.
- The proportion of undernourished people in the developing regions has fallen by almost half since 1990, from 23.3 percent in 1990–1992 to 12.9 percent in 2014–2016.

---

[37] *Id.*

[38] United Nations, *The Millennium Development Goals Report* 2015 4–7 (2015), www.un.org/es/millenniumgoals/pdf/2015/mdg_2015_rev(july1).pdf (visited Dec. 10, 2015).

Goal 2: Achieve Universal Primary Education

- The primary school net enrollment rate in the developing regions has reached 91 percent in 2015, up from 83 percent in 2000.
- The number of out-of-school children of primary school age worldwide has fallen by almost half, to an estimated 57 million in 2015, down from 100 million in 2000.
- Sub-Saharan Africa has had the best record of improvement in primary education of any region since the MDGs were established. The region achieved a 20 percent increase in the net enrolment rate from 2000 to 2015, compared to a gain of 8 percentage points between 1990 to 2000.
- The literacy rate among youth aged 15 to 24 has increased globally from 83 percent to 91 percent between 1990 and 2015. The gap between women and men has narrowed.

Goal 3: Promote Gender Equality and Empower Women

- Many more girls are now in school compared to 15 years ago. The developing regions as a whole have achieved the target to eliminate gender disparity in primary, secondary, and tertiary education.
- In Southern Asia, only 74 girls were enrolled in primary school for every 100 boys in 1990. Today, 103 girls are enrolled for every 100 boys.
- Women now make up 41 percent of paid workers outside the agricultural sector, an increase from 35 percent in 1990.
- Between 1991 and 2015, the proportion of women in vulnerable employment as a share of total female employment has declined 13 percentage points. In contrast, vulnerable employment among men fell by 9 percentage points.
- Women have gained ground in parliamentary representation in nearly 90 percent of the 174 countries from data over the past 20 years. The average proportion of women in parliament has nearly doubled during the same period. Still only one in five members are women.

Goal 4: Reduce Child Mortality

- The global under-five mortality rate has declined by more than half, dropping from 90 to 43 deaths per 1,000 live births between 1990 and 2015.
- Despite population growth in the developing regions, the number of deaths of children under five has declined from 12.7 million in 1990 to almost 6 million in 2015 globally. Since the early 1990s, the rate of reduction of under-five mortality has more than tripled globally.
- In sub-Saharan Africa, the annual rate of reduction of under-five mortality was over five times faster during 2005–2013 than it was during 1990–1995.
- Measles vaccination helped prevent nearly 15.6 million deaths between 2000 and 2013. The number of globally reported measles cases declined by 67 percent for the same period.
- About 84 percent of children worldwide received at least one dose of measles-containing vaccine in 2013, up from 73 percent in 2000.

Goal 5: Improve Maternal Health

- Since 1990, the maternal mortality ratio has declined by 45 percent worldwide, and most of the reduction has occurred since 2000.
- In Southern Asia, the maternal mortality ratio declined by 64 percent between1990 and 2013, and in sub-Saharan Africa it fell by 49 percent.
- More than 71 percent of births were assisted by skilled health personnel globally in 2014, an increase from 59 percent in 1990.
- In Northern Africa, the proportion of pregnant women who received four or more antenatal visits increased from 50 percent to 89 percent between 1990 and 2014.
- Contraceptive prevalence among women aged 15 to 49, married or in a union, increased from 55 percent in 1990 worldwide to 64 per cent in 2015.

Goal 6: Combat HIV/AIDS, Malaria and Other Diseases

- New HIV infections fell by approximately 40 percent between 2000 and 2013, from an estimated 3.5 million cases to 2.1 million.

- By June 2014, 13.6 million people living with HIV were receiving antiretroviral therapy (ART) globally, an immense increase from just 800,000 in 2003. ART averted 7.6 million deaths from AIDS between 1995 and 2013.
- Over 6.2 million malaria deaths have been averted between 2000 and 2015, primarily of children under five years of age in sub-Saharan Africa. The global malaria incidence rate has fallen by an estimated 37 percent and the mortality rate by 58 percent.
- More than 900 million insecticide-treated mosquito nets were delivered to malaria-endemic countries in sub-Saharan Africa between 2004 and 2014.
- Between 2000 and 2013, tuberculosis prevention, diagnosis, and treatment interventions saved an estimated 37 million lives. The tuberculosis mortality rate fell by 45 percent and the prevalence rate by 41 percent between 1990 and 2013.

Goal 7: Ensure Environmental Sustainability

- Ozone-depleting substances have been virtually eliminated since 1990, and the ozone layer is expected to recover by the middle of this century.
- Terrestrial and marine-protected areas in many regions have increased substantially since 1990. In Latin America and the Caribbean, coverage of terrestrial protected areas rose from 8.8 percent to 23.4 percent between 1990 and 2014.
- In 2015, 91 percent of the global population is using an improved drinking water source, compared to 76 percent in 1990.
- Of the 2.6 billion people who have gained access to improved drinking water since 1990, 1.9 billion gained access to piped drinking water on premises. More than half the global population (58 percent) now enjoys this higher level of service.
- Globally, 147 countries have met the drinking water target, 95 countries have met the sanitation target, and 77 countries have met both.
- Worldwide, 2.1 billion people have gained access to improved sanitation. The proportion of people practicing open defecation has fallen almost by half since 1990.

- The proportion of urban population living in slums in the developing regions fell from approximately 39.4 percent in 2000, to 29.7 percent in 2014.

Goal 8: Develop a Global Partnership for Development

- Official development assistance from developed countries increased by 66 percent in real terms between 2000 and 2014, reaching $135.2 billion.
- In 2014, Denmark, Luxembourg, Norway, Sweden, and the United Kingdom continued to exceed the United Nations official development assistance target of 0.7 percent of gross national income.
- In 2014, 79 percent of imports from developing to developed countries were admitted duty free, up from 65 percent in 2000.
- The proportion of external debt service to export revenue in developing countries fell from 12 percent in 2000 to 3 percent in 2013.
- As of 2015, 95 percent of the world's population is covered by a mobile-cellular signal.
- The number of mobile-cellular subscriptions has grown almost tenfold in the last 15 years, from 738 million in 2000, to over 7 billion in 2015.
- Internet penetration has grown from just over 6 percent of the world's population in 2000, to 43 percent in 2015. As a result, 3.2 billion people are linked to a global network of content and applications.

The progress appears remarkable, even though some of the claims of this report appear to be inaccurate, self-validating, and even misleading. For example, the claim that the improvement of the Ozone layer resulted from the MDG 7 is misleading. The MDGs are political, not legal, commitments and the improvement in the Ozone layer primarily resulted from the implementation of the legally binding Vienna Convention on the Ozone Layer,[39] the Montreal Protocol,[40] and their various Adjustments and Amendments.[41] Similarly, improvements in terrestrial and marine protection may

---

[39] Vienna Convention for the Protection of the Ozone Layer, *supra* note 11.

[40] Montreal Protocol on Substances that Deplete the Ozone Layer, Sept. 16, 1987, 26 I.L.M. 1550 (1987).

[41] Lakshman Guruswamy, *International Environmental Law*, 275–284 (4th ed. 2012).

more fairly be attributed to the implementation of two legally binding treaties: UNCLOS[42] and the CBD,[43] and not MDG 7.

MDG 4 called for the reduction of child mortality, and the report gives MDG 4 credit for improved child mortality. But, the implementation of another legally binding Convention on the Rights of the Child (CRC),[44] ratified by 192 countries in 2000, may well be the stronger reason for the drop in child mortality. CRC Articles 6 and 24 clearly established a child's right to survival, development, and health. Parties to the CRC are required to implement it, and at least a significant component of the reduction of child mortality should be attributed to the CRC and not merely MDG 4.

With regard to MDG 6, the Gates Foundation, which is not a party to the MDGs, has played a pivotal role in the fight against malaria[45] and HIV/ AIDs.[46] In fact a joint report by the UN and the Gates Foundation showed that global investment in malaria has jumped in recent years by 2,000 percent annually, from just $130 million in 2000 to $2.7 billion in 2013. The extent of the investment by the Gates Foundation, which has committed more than $500 million, fundamentally transformed the fight against the disease.[47] It is, therefore, inaccurate to primarily credit MDG 6 for successes in the fight against malaria. Doubts about this claim are supported by the fact that Overseas Development (ODA) over the period amounted in total to $134 billion for all 8 MDGs. The Gates Foundation alone has invested billions of dollars in arresting malaria and HIV/AIDS, and must lay claim for a significant part of the progress made. Attributing such success to the MDG 6 alone is misleading.

Notwithstanding these caveats, about a few MDGs, the overall progress made by MDGs is very impressive. The fact that the MDGs obtained a large increase in ODA to meet the additional funds

---

[42] UNCLOS, *supra* note 13.

[43] CBD, *supra* note 10.

[44] Convention on the Rights of the Child, Nov. 20, 1989, G.A. Res. 44/25, Annex, U.N. GAOR, 44th Sess., Supp. No. 49, U.N. Doc. A/44/49, at 167 (1989) [hereinafter CRC]. The CRC sets out norms and principles governing the human rights of children under the age of 18. Article 6, establishes every child's inherent right to life, and obligates the state to do so. Article 24 (1) and (2) obliges States parties to recognize the right of the child to the enjoyment of the highest attainable standard of health and to ensure that no child is deprived of his or her right of access to health care services.

[45] Gates Foundation, *Malaria Strategy Overview,* http://www.gatesfoundation.org/What-We-Do/Global-Health/Malaria#OurStrategy (visited Dec. 9, 2015).

[46] Gates Foundation, *HIV Strategy Overview*, http://www.gatesfoundation.org/What-We-Do/Global-Health/HIV (visited Dec. 9, 2015).

[47] *UN News Centre, Report by UN and Gates Foundation Presents Vision for Eradicating Malaria by 2040,* (Sept. 28, 2015), http://www.un.org/apps/news/story.asp?NewsID=52006 (visited Dec. 9, 2015. South China Morning Post, *Gates Foundation To Spend US$500m Stopping Malaria And Other Diseases,* March 4, 2016 http://www.scmp.com/news/world/article/1631289/gates-foundation-spend-us500m-stopping-malaria-and-other-diseases (visited March 5, 2016).

required is particularly significant. It is important in this context to point out that many poverty reduction goals, similar to the MDGs, have been embraced by civil society entities, such as the Gates Foundation. The extent to which civil society groups contribute toward energy justice bears examination.

Civil Society Contributions

The MDGs were adopted and implemented by governments and international inter-governmental organizations. The ODA is an international fund set up under the auspices of the OECD to provide the aid necessary to meet the MDGs. But there are numerous groups outside the government sector that have adopted and worked toward achieving antipoverty objectives similar to the MDGs. Nongovernmental organizations (NGOs), like the Gates Foundation, mentioned above, are one among many civil society groups. They are many other nonprofit associations operating independently of government, working toward worthy social or political objectives. They may provide humanitarian relief and development assistance, like the International Committee of the Red Cross,[48] Oxfam,[49] and CARE,[50] or engage in environmental analysis and advocacy like Greenpeace,[51] World Wildlife Fund (WWF),[52] and the World Conservation Union (IUCN).[53] They may be financed by private donations, international organizations, governments, or charitable foundations. Some, like the Gates Foundation, are privately endowed while others, such as Greenpeace or WWF, depend on grass roots member support.

Partnerships are another kind of civil society entity. Partnerships consist of voluntary multi-stakeholder or multi-institutional initiatives, organized around a common purpose, and administered as their own entity, distinct from their constituent partners. The Renewable Energy and Energy Efficiency Partnership (REEEP)[54] and REN 21[55] are two examples. Partnerships have become a recognized fixture in the international development arena and differ in size, agenda, and organization. They are also

---

[48] INT'L COMM, OF THE RED CROSS, https://www.icrc.org/ (last visited Dec. 29, 2015).

[49] OXFAM INT'L, https://www.oxfam.org/ (last visited Dec. 29, 2015).

[50] CARE INT'L, http://www.care-international.org (last visited Dec. 29, 2015).

[51] GREENPEACE, http://www.greenpeace.org/ (last visited Dec. 29, 2015).

[52] WILDLIFE CONSERVATION SOC'Y, http://www.wcs.org/ (last visited Dec. 29, 2015).

[53] INT'L UNION FOR CONSERVATION OF NATURE, http://www.iucn.org/ (last visited Dec. 29, 2015).

[54] REEEP, http://www.reeep.org/ (visited Dec. 10, 2015).

[55] RENEWABLE ENERGY POLICY NETWORK FOR THE 21ST CENTURY, http://www.ren21.net/ (last visited Dec. 29, 2015).

increasingly recognized as an essential mechanism for promoting and implementing sustainable development in all its dimensions, and as a central element of contemporary sustainability governance.[56]

Private for-profit corporations spanning manufacturers, agribusinesses, mining, banks, hotels, and others have increased their role in international development. It is affirmed that the private sector in industrialized and developing countries has become a key partner in international development.[57]

Faith groups are part of civil society. It has been found that religious leaders and institutions are often the most trusted institutions in developing countries. Faith groups can inspire confidence and trust and are often seen as more embedded in, and committed to, local communities. They are often the first groups that people turn to in times of need and contribute to in times of plenty.[58] For example, Caritas Internationalis is one among several faith groups operating across the world. Caritas follows the mission of the Catholic Church to serve the poor, promote charity and justice throughout the world and act on behalf of the world's most vulnerable people.[59]

The extent to which these civil society groups are inspired and motivated by concepts of justice will be discussed in Chapter 4.

F. 2002 World Summit on Sustainable Development (WSSD)

The first major UN conference on SD, so titled, was organized in 2002, ten years after the Earth Summit. The World Summit on Sustainable Development (WSSD) was held in Johannesburg. As originally envisioned, WSSD was intended primarily to stimulate implementation of the environmental aspects of Agenda 21. The focus of WSSD, however, as reflected in the deliberations and in the two documents produced by it, was more clearly on the problems

---

[56] UN-DESA/DSD, *Multi-Stakeholder Partnerships in the Post-2015 Development Era: Sharing knowledge and expertise to support the achievement of the Sustainable Development Goals.* https://sustainabledevelopment.un.org/content/documents/7366Partnerships_Knowledge_BackgroundPaper_final.pdf (visited Dec. 13, 2015.

[57] Bradford Strickland, *Creative Assocs. Int'l, Survey Of Trends In Private Sector Partnerships For International Development And Modalities For Engagement* (Mar. 2014), http://www.creativeassociatesinternational.com/wp-content/uploads/2014/08/Survey_Of_Trends.pdf (visited Dec. 13, 2015).

[58] DEP'T FOR INT'L DEV., U.K., *Faith Partnership Principles: Working Effectively With Faith Groups To Fight Global Poverty* 3 (2012), https://www.gov.uk/government/publications/faith-partnership-principles-working-effectively-with-faith-groups-to-fight-global-poverty (visited Dec. 13, 2015).

[59] CARITAS INTERNATIONALIS, http://www.caritas.org/ (last visited Dec. 29, 2015).

created by poverty, as distinct from environmental degradation. The conference gave birth to just two documents: a political Declaration[60] and an Implementation Plan.[61]

The Implementation Plan incorporated several important new goals to be reached within the next 20 years, including meeting people's basic sanitation needs, producing and using non-harmful chemicals, restoring the world's fish stocks, and reducing the rate of loss of biodiversity.[62] More importantly, the Declaration articulated a new dimension to SD by affirming "a collective responsibility to advance and strengthen the interdependent and mutually reinforcing pillars of sustainable development—economic development, social development, and environmental protection—at the local, national, regional, and global levels."[63] The same principles were endorsed in the Implementation Plan.[64]

As noted above, this re-statement of SD confirms the third element in the definition of SD introduced at the Millennium Summit.[65] Social development, which hitherto had been subsumed under the rubric of economic development, is now treated as a separate concept. This is a significant development to the extent that SD—which hitherto consisted of two legs (economic development and environmental protection)—has now been given a third (social development). Consequently, environmental protection, which had enjoyed rough parity with economic development, has now been reduced to a third part of a tripartite concept.

WSSD also represented a step forward in implementation of Agenda 21's focus on non-state actors. Section III of Agenda 21 sets forth a novel, hands-on approach with an emphasis on the importance of major social groups in implementing new environmental policies. Unlike previous conferences on SD, in which delegates were exclusively from States, delegates to WSSD included not only 10,000 government delegates, but also some 8,000 delegates from civil society, including representatives from nongovernmental organizations (NGOs), corporate interests, and other areas. In addition, parallel events incorporated conferences between

---

60 *Johannesburg Declaration on Sustainable Development*, U.N. Doc. A/CONF.199/20 (Sept. 4, 2002) [hereinafter Johannesburg Declaration on Sustainable Development].

61 *Plan of Implementation of the World Summit on Sustainable Development*, U.N. Doc. A/CONF.199/20 (Sept. 4, 2002) [hereinafter Plan of Implementation of the World Summit on Sustainable Development].

62 *Id.*

63 Johannesburg Declaration on Sustainable Development, *supra* note 60, at ¶ 5.

64 Plan of Implementation of the World Summit on Sustainable Development, *supra* note 61 ch. 1, at ¶ 2.

65 *Supra,* text accompanying notes 35 to 37.

interested parties representing NGOs: women, indigenous people, youth, farmers, trade unions, business leaders, the scientific and technological community, local authorities, and Chief Justices from various countries.[66]

G. Rio+20 United Nations Conference on Sustainable Development 2012

The Rio+20 United Nations Conference on Sustainable Development, (UNCSD),[67] transpired 20 years after the Earth Summit. The Rio+20 United Nations Conference on Environment and Development, did not result in any treaties or legally binding documents. Instead, it produced a political Outcome Document: *The Future We Want*[68] consisting of 283 paragraphs. This largely hortatory Outcome Document spanned the gamut of international concerns, and contained a long list that traversed:

1. A common vision (discussed more fully below)

2. Re-affirming of the Rio Principles of the 1992 Earth Summit (section D *supra*).

3. Integrating and implementing the conclusions of previous summits on SD.

4. Engaging sub-national and civil society stakeholders, including the private and business sector.

5. Strengthening the three dimensions of SD, through better collaboration between intergovernmental agencies.

6. Replacing the Commission on Sustainable Development with a High Level Political Forum.

7. Buttressing the environmental dimension of SD by strengthening the United Nations Environment Program (UNEP).

---

[66] World Health Organization (WHO), *World Summit on Sustainable Development (WSSD)* http://www.who.int/trade/glossary/story097/en/ (visited Dec. 7, 2015).

[67] United Nations Conference on Sustainable Development, Rio de Janiero, Braz., June 20–22, 2012, *Report of the United Nations Conference on Sustainable Development*, U.N. Doc. A/CONF.216/16 (June 20–22, 2012). (visited Dec. 7, 2015).

[68] The Future We Want, G.A. Res. 66/288, U.N. Doc. A/RES/66/288 (July 27, 2012), https://sustainabledevelopment.un.org/rio20/futurewewant (visited Dec. 7, 2015).

8. Mainstreaming of SD funding in the mandates of international financial institutions.

9. According the "highest Priority" to poverty eradication, while promoting food security, nutrition, and sustainable agriculture and integrating water and sanitation into SD.

10. Recognizing the critical role of energy in development and addressing the challenge of access to sustainable modern energy services for all, in particular for the poor, while improving energy efficiency.

11. Acknowledging the importance of sustainable tourism, sustainable transport and sustainable cities.

12. Promoting full and decent employment for all.

13. Sustaining and preserving the oceanic environment.

14. Protecting the fragility of small island developing states, least developed countries, and landlocked developing states.

15. Underlining importance of Africa's development needs.

16. Reaffirming commitment to disaster risk reduction.

17. Emphasizing that climate change is one of the greatest challenges of our time and expressing profound alarm that emissions of greenhouse gases continue to rise globally.

18. Highlighting the importance of forests and mountains and the protection of global biodiversity.

19. Managing the life cycle of chemicals in a manner avoiding harm to human health and the environment.

20. Better managing the mining sector.

21. Promote universal access to primary education.

22. Prioritizing gender equality.

23. Create new Sustainable Development Goals (SDGs) to succeed the Millennium Development Goals (MDGs) that expire in 2015.

24. Improve technology transfers from developed to developing countries.

25. Enhancing capacity building.

26. Reaffirm that trade is an engine of development.

This smorgasbord of something for everyone was the result of last-minute maneuvering by the host country, Brazil, to obtain consensus on a final document[69] that contrasted with the dissensus that prevailed at the 2009 Copenhagen UN Climate Change Conference.[70] But in order to find the needles buried in the Outcome Document's haystack of aspirations, it is necessary to examine the conference negotiations. The conference negotiations focused on three issues: the green economy, a new iteration of SD in the form of sustainable development goals (SDGs) to replace the MDGs, and better institutional support for the envisioned SDGs.

Discussions about the green economy sought to lay the foundations for an effective transition to a low-carbon economy. A few matters relevant to the green economy are worthy of mention. First, economic and social development had hitherto been premised on conventional economic growth measured by Gross Domestic Product (GDP). A green economy called for broader metrics and measures of progress, and took account of environmental and social considerations not typically included in the GDP. Given that national accounting systems are based on monetary values in dollars, it was sought to give monetary or economic values to environmental and social factors by placing economic or dollar values on environmental services provided by nature. There was some resistance to these ideas by those who felt that such an approach diminished the ethical and aesthetic essence of nature by giving dollar values to qualities that could not be reduced to dollars.[71] But the prevailing wisdom was that a green economy would need to express some environmental and social values in dollars.

Second, it became clear during the conference discussions that the green economy could not be established by governments alone, and required the backing of the private sector. Consequently, the conference saw a need to increase the role of civil society and the

---

[69] Int'l Inst. for Sustainable Dev., *Summary of the United Nations Conference on Sustainable Development: 13–22 June 2012* 27(51) EARTH NEGOTIATIONS BULL. 1 (June 25, 2012), http://www.iisd.ca/download/pdf/enb2751e.pdf (visited Dec. 7, 2015).

[70] Copenhagen Accord, Copenhagen, Den., Dec. 7–19, 2009, *Report of the Conference of the Parties, Part Two: Action Taken by the Conference of the Parties at its Fifteenth Session*, U.N. Doc. FCCC/CP/2009/11/Add.1 (Mar. 30, 2010).

[71] Suan Ee Ong, et al., *Examining Rio+20's Outcome*, COUNCIL ON FOREIGN RELATIONS (July 5, 2012), http://www.cfr.org/world/examining-rio20s-outcome/p28669.

private sector in promoting sustainable development policies. Third, the need for a green economy drew attention to the fact that a green economy must be established at national and local level. Therefore, the responsibility for ushering green economics would need to be shifted primarily to developing countries.

On setting the foundations for an institutional framework for SD, conference negotiations were directed toward the importance of launching a process to develop universal and inclusive SDGs applicable to all countries and to all three dimensions of sustainable development.[72] The envisioned SDG topics would extend momentum in international development work beyond the poverty-eradicating mission of the MDGs, which lapsed in 2015. In order to reinforce governance, it was decided to create a "high-level" political forum that would replace the existing Commission on Sustainable Development.

It is important to emphasize the extent to which the conceptualization of the SDGs and the green economy in the Outcome Document is radically different to SD as hitherto accepted. Up to this time, every formulation of SD in legal and political documents had given primary emphasis to eradicating poverty through economic and social development. A dramatically different picture now emerges. First, there is a new iteration of SD emphasizing global public goals (GPGs), discussed below, as distinct from the eradication of poverty, based on individual economic growth. Second, developing countries, assume greater responsibility for SD. Previously, SD had been premised on the legal and political principle of common but differentiated responsibility—(CBDR), decreed in the UNFCCC. CBDR declared that it was the overriding responsibility of developed countries to help developing countries. The Outcome Document, however, appears to shift the onus by placing significant responsibility for the SDGs, and the green economy, on national states, the large majority of whom are developing countries.

H. The Sustainable Development Goals (SDGs) 2015

Based on the Outcome Document of Rio+20, the 2015 SDGs were developed with input from the UN's 193 member states and an array of nongovernmental organizations. They are embodied in a large document,[73] that consists of 17 goals, including 169 targets and

---

[72] Frederico Ramos de Armas, *Rio+20—Start of a Process*, OUR PLANET, Feb. 2013, at 5–6, available at http://www.unep.org/pdf/OP–FEB–EN–2013.pdf.

[73] *Transforming Our World: the 2030 Agenda for Sustainable Development*, A/RES/70/1, https://sustainabledevelopment.un.org/post2015/transformingourworld (visited Dec. 2, 2015).

indicators.[74] The SDGs will replace the MDGs in January 2016. The SDGs deal with the following:

1. **Poverty**—End poverty in all its forms everywhere
2. **Food**—End hunger, achieve food security and improved nutrition and promote sustainable agriculture
3. **Health**—Ensure healthy lives and promote well-being for all at all ages
4. **Education**—Ensure inclusive and equitable quality education and promote lifelong learning opportunities for all
5. **Women**—Achieve gender equality and empower all women and girls
6. **Water**—Ensure availability and sustainable management of water and sanitation for all
7. **Energy**—Ensure access to affordable, reliable, sustainable and modern energy for all
8. **Economy**—Promote sustained, inclusive and sustainable economic growth, full and productive employment, and decent work for all
9. **Infrastructure**—Build resilient infrastructure, promote inclusive and sustainable industrialization, and foster innovation
10. **Inequality**—Reduce inequality within and among countries
11. **Habitation**—Make cities and human settlements inclusive, safe, resilient, and sustainable
12. **Consumption**—Ensure sustainable consumption and production patterns
13. **Climate**—Take urgent action to combat climate change and its impacts
14. **Marine ecosystems**—Conserve and sustainably use the oceans, seas, and marine resources for sustainable development
15. **Ecosystems**—Protect, restore, and promote sustainable use of terrestrial ecosystems, sustainably

---

[74] *"United Nations General Assembly Draft Outcome Document Of The United Nations Summit For The Adoption Of The Post-2015 Development Agenda"* https://sustainabledevelopment.un.org/post2015/summit (visited Dec. 2, 2015).

manage forests, combat desertification, halt and reverse land degradation, and halt biodiversity loss

16. **Institutions**—Promote peaceful and inclusive societies for sustainable development, provide access to justice for all, and build effective, accountable and inclusive institutions at all levels

17. **Sustainability**—Strengthen the means of implementation and revitalize the global partnership for sustainable development

II. Evaluating SD Today

A. Comparing and Contrasting MDGs and SDGs

The MDGs were written and institutionalized to mobilize support from the donor countries and their citizens, primarily through Official Development Assistance (ODA),[75] which rose to a historic high mark in 2013.[76] The goals, focus largely on the symptoms of underdevelopment and reducing poverty. The MDGs 1 to 7 refer to improvements in private welfare through reduction of poverty and hunger, access to education, improving child mortality, better maternal care, proving safe drinking water and sanitation, and combating diseases such as malaria and HIV/Aids.

Goals are associated with a distinct tradition in ethics and political philosophy called development ethics,[77] which places prime importance on "life-sustenance."[78] The goal of life sustenance is to prolong peoples' lives and render them less afflicted by poverty, hunger, and disease. Because life-sustenance is a value of universal significance, life-sustaining indices are also used as a measurement of development. These goals are distinctly utilitarian, calculated to maximize welfare gains.

Amartya Sen argues that development should not simply be understood as economic growth, but as the expansion of people's valuable capabilities including what people can or cannot do, e.g.,

---

[75] ODA is a term coined by the Development Assistance Committee (DAC) of the OECD to measure aid. The DAC is an international forum of many of the largest funders of aid, including twenty-nine DAC Members. The World Bank, IMF, and UNDP participate as observers. ORG. FOR ECON. CO-OPERATION & DEV.,*Development Assistance Committee (DAC)*, http://www.oecd.org/dac/developmentassistance committeedac.htm (last visited Dec. 29, 2015).

[76] Aid to Developing Countries Rebounds in 2013 to Reach an All-time High, ORG. FOR ECON. CO-OPERATION & DEV., (Apr. 8, 2015), http://www.oecd.org/newsroom/ aid-to-developing-countries-rebounds-in–2013–to-reach-an-all-time-high.htm.

[77] Denis Goulet, *The Cruel Choice: A New Concept In Theory Of Development* (1971).

[78] Denis Goulet, *Development Ethics: A Guide To Theory And Practice* (Zed Books Ltd. ed. 1995).

whether they can live long, escape avoidable morbidity, be well nourished, be able to read and write and communicate, take part in literary and scientific pursuits,[79] His conclusions reinforce the importance of individual welfare gains, and point to how they constitute a first step toward greater human self-realization.

According to the UNDPs Human Development Report of 2005, the MDGs created incentives for donors and governments to favor quick impacts rather than addressing underlying complex social systems. This was advanced in the "quick wins" strategy outlined in the report on investing to advance the MDGs. The strategy calls for funding for "high potential, short-term impact" initiatives that can yield "breathtaking results within three or fewer years . . . " and "start countries on the path to the Goals."[80] These measures include, for example, mosquito bed-nets for malaria protection, MDG model villages, immunizations, school meals, and water purification devices. Such investments have two kinds of payoff: they begin to drive down key indicators for the goals, and they offer the prospect of quick impact that can mobilize donors' aid funds. Most of them deliver individual health and education benefits, rather than systemic change. These "quick win" strategies made them central to its campaign, and to its call for "scaled-up" investment in development assistance. Because MDGs are attractive to donor agencies and their domestic constituencies, they attract aid funds and therefore the attention of poor-country governments. Pragmatically, this feature can be seen as a strength of the MDGs: the goals establish benchmarks with attainable levels of progress, and they rely on interventions that can be accomplished without even attempting to address the thorny social and political causes of inequality and deprivation. Accomplishing the goals would mean real improvement in quality of life for some of the world's poor.

MDG strategies visualize the eradication of poverty and envision development and investment in measures benefitting individuals and households, as a means of supplying material wants from a utilitarian perspective. Poverty is depicted as a multidimensional human material deprivation that arises from lack of income, water, food, education and health services.[81] By contrast, most of the SDGs seek to achieve global public goods (GPGs).

---

[79] Amartya Sen, *Resources, Values And Development* (1st ed. Harvard Univ. Press 1984); Amartya Sen, *Development As Freedom* (Oxford Univ. Press 1999).

[80] UNDP, *Human Development Report, 25* (2005) http://hdr.undp.org/sites/default/files/reports/266/hdr05_complete.pdf.

[81] Sakiko Fukudua-Parr, *Recapturing the Narrative of International Development*, in *The Millennium Development Goals And Beyond: Global Development After 2015*, 42 (Rorden Wilkinson & David Hulme ed., 2012).

B. Global Public Goods (GPGs)

National public goods have been part of the economic theory of government for centuries.[82] The idea that society needs government to overcome the failures of the market in achieving efficiency and equity in the allocation and distribution of resources is well established. It is widely understood that national public goods and services, such as environmental protection, health services, social security, and transportation infrastructure, are fundamental to the well-being of people, and that governments and markets must work together to provide them. Public goods have two key properties: non-rivalry and non-excludability. They are commodities for which the cost of extending the service to an additional person is zero, and for which it is impossible or expensive to exclude individuals from enjoying.[83]

In a globalizing world, problems and solutions reach across national borders, resulting in a growing need for international collective action. Inge Kaul, who pioneered the concept of global public goods (GPGs), extended the concept of "public goods" from the national level to the global level. Her book *Global Public Goods: International Cooperation in the 21st Century*[84] convincingly argues that the two tests of a public goods, non-rivalry and non-excludability, can be applied at the global level to such things as environment, health, culture, and peace. GPGs, are goods whose benefits reach across borders, generations, and population groups, and the concept of GPGs has become an increasingly important part of international policy making. A clean environment, climate stability, health, knowledge, property rights, peace, and security are all examples of public goods that could be made global.

In stark contrast to the MDGs the SDGs decisively address the problems of GPGs. As enumerated in the table below, 9 of the SDGs—Goals 9 to 17—embrace GPGs.

---

[82] William D. Nordhaus, *Paul Samuelson and Global Public Goods,* http://www.econ.yale.edu/~nordhaus/homepage/PASandGPG.pdf (visited Dec. 7, 2015).

[83] *Id.*

[84] *Global Public Goods: International Cooperation in The 21st Century* (Inge Kaul, Isabelle Grunberg, & Marc A. Stern eds., 1999).

MILLENNIUM DEVELOPMENT GOALS (MDGs)

and

SUSTAINABLE DEVELOPMENT GOALS (SDGs)

MDG	Type	SDG	Costs	Type
1 Eradicate extreme poverty and hunger	Individual Private Good/welfare	1: Ending Poverty and Hunger		Individual Private Good
2 Achieve universal primary education	Individual Private Good/welfare	2: End hunger, achieve food security, nutrition and sustainable agriculture	$44 bn. per year [EurActiv]*	Individual Private Good
3 Promote gender equality and empower women	Individual Private Good/welfare	3: Good health and well-being		Individual Private Good
4 Reduce child mortality	Individual Private Good/welfare	4: Quality education		Individual Private Good
5 Improve maternal health	Individual Private Good/welfare	5: Gender equality		Individual Private Good
6 Combat HIV / AIDS, malaria and other diseases	Individual Private Good	6: Clean water and sanitation	$27bn per year [EurActiv]*	Individual Private Good
7 Ensure environmental sustainability	Global Public Good	7: Affordable and clean energy	$50bn per year [EurActiv]*	Individual Private Good
8 Develop a global partnership for development	Global Public Good	8: Decent work and economic growth		Individual Private Good
		9: Industry, innovation, infrastructure		Global Public Good
		10: Reduced inequalities		Global Public Good
		11: Sustainable cities and communities		Global Public Good

MDG	Type	SDG	Costs	Type
		12: Responsible consumption, production		Global Public Good
		13: Climate action	$1,100 bn. per year [EurActiv]*	Global Public Good
		14: Life below water		Global Public Good
		15: Life on Land	$430 bn. per year [EurActiv]*	Global Public Good
		16: Peace, justice and strong institutions		Global Public Good
		17: Partnerships for the goals		Global Public Good
* EurActiv, *Infographic: Not All SDGs Were Created Equal,* http://www.euractiv.com/sections/development-policy/infographic-not-all-sdgs-were-created-equal-318558				

The commitment to GPGs raise a number of interconnected questions. First, will the SDGs diminish, depreciate, and devalue the individual human development goals of the MDGs? Second, who will pay the very high price tag of the SDGs? Third, will ODA be diverted from the human developmental goals of the MDGs to the GPGs of the SDGs? Fourth, what effect will the transfer of resources from the MDGs to GPGs have on the poorest of the poor, especially the least developed countries (LDCs) and the energy poor?

Some of these questions were anticipated by astute commentators while the SDGs were being developed. It was pointed out that the majority of the MDGs are goals of human development and refer to improvements in the well-being of individuals, such as education, health, and access to water and food, that can be measured at the micro-level. The SDG agenda, while adopting some of these individual human development goals, embrace a variety of GPGs that are not focused developmental objectives, as understood by development ethics, but are preconditions for sustainable development. They are conceptually and categorically different to the

MDGs and should not form part of the same program.[85] In pursuance of clarity and good public policy, it was suggested that the individual human development goals of the MDGs should be separated from the GPGs in the SDGs, and that the two sets of goals be located in two different documents.[86]

In an illuminating exchange of views,[87] Inge Kaul has accurately and perspicaciously pointed out that it was clearly agreed at the 1992 United Nations Conference on Environment and Development, (*supra* section D), that GPGs like biodiversity preservation, climate change mitigation, and related activities should be financed with new and additional funds, and not be takenout of ODA. Despite this decision, international organizations such as the Global Environment Facility (GEF), the World Bank, and the UN Development Programme (UNDP) use ODA money for climate change mitigation. Inge Kaul further demonstrated that 24 per cent to a third of ODA is primarily directed at climate change mitigation or adaptation. And many more ODA-funded activities promote climate change mitigation or adaptation as a secondary purpose. She regretted how ODA, contrary to its purpose was being siphoned off to deal with GPGs. A crucial question raised by Inga Kaul was how such policies were consistent with the need to address the rising number of LDCs, developing countries, and burdened peoples that rely on ODA to deal with their problems of poverty. She too advocated separating the case for aid under ODA from the new and different case for GPGs and the fresh additional funds they required. The case for GPGs should be independently made and funded, and should not be financed with ODA resources.

Furthermore, Inge Kaul compellingly pointed out that GPG financing is categorically different from development aid. ODA is a unilateral transfer of resources, not a contractual payment for services. Her argument is supported by numerous legal and political conclusions embodied in various treaties and political agreements cited above such as the UNFCCC (*supra* D), the CBD (*supra* D), the Rio Declaration (*supra* D) and the Johannesburg Declaration (supra F), that establish the right of developing countries to economic and social development and the eradication of poverty. International law and policy establish that foreign aid to developing countries is not

---

85 Markus Loewe, *Post 2015: How To Reconcile The Millennium Development Goals (MDGs) And The Sustainable Development Goals (SDGs)?*, GERMAN DEV. INST. (2012), available at http://edoc.vifapol.de/opus/volltexte/2013/4583/pdf/BP_18.2012.pdf (visited Dec. 5, 2015).

86 *Id.*

87 Inge Kaul, Robin Davies, Robert Glasser, Michael Gerber, & Luca Etter, *Financing The SDGs: Global Vs. Local Public Goods*, (2015), available at https://poldev.revues.org/2068 (visited Dec. 5, 2015). The three following paragraphs are based on this debate.

contractual and is not based on mutual advantage or reciprocity. Instead foreign aid consists of unidirectional disbursements whether premised on legal, political, or moral obligation. ODA is part of the distributive machinery of international governance that implements the legal and moral obligation of developed countries to support SD within poorer countries through individual economic and social development.

By contrast, when developing countries take actions to advance climate change mitigation, they are contributing to a GPG desired by developed countries, and are entitled to be reimbursed under the doctrine of CBDR. In the case of climate action the UNFCCC unequivocally states that developed countries are required to take the lead in meeting the GPG of stabilizing green-house gasses. Where developing countries take actions that should have been undertaken by developed countries, they should under CBDR, be reimbursed for their services through resource or monetary transfers. Kaul's conclusions resonate within a framework of global energy justice. ODA might be based on grounds of moral or legal obligation, or on those of charity or benevolence. Whatever its rationale, ODA is a redistributive method of using humanitarian aid advancing individual human welfare in developing countries. Developed countries do not receive any direct correlative utilitarian benefits by participating in ODA. By contrast, developed countries are the primary proponents of GPGs pertaining, for example, to climate change and biodiversity and these countries derive utilitarian, ecological and socio-biological benefit from them. Legally, the principle of CBDR embodied in the UNFCCC and CBD,—two almost universally accepted treaties dealing with climate change and biological diversity, require that developed countries should pay for these GPGs.

Goal 13 of the SDGs deals with the GPG of climate action and the need to take urgent action to combat climate change and its impacts. The explanation accompanying Goal 13 states that the ". . . UNFCCC or Framework Convention is a universal convention of principle, acknowledging the existence of anthropogenic (human-induced) climate change and giving industrialized countries the major part of responsibility for combating it."[88]

The responsibility placed on developed countries is indubitably correct. Article 3 (1) of the UNFCCC institutionalizing CBDR,required developed countries to pay for climate action. But

---

[88] *UNFCCC COP 21/ CMP 11*, DIV. FOR SUSTAINABLE DEV., UN-DESA, *21st Session of the Conference of the Parties and 11th Session of the Conference of the Parties Serving as the Meeting of the Parties to the Kyoto Protocol, (2015)*, https://sustainabledevelopment.un.org/index.php?page=view&type=13&nr=1359&menu=1634 (visited Dec. 29, 2015).

having acknowledged the legal obligation placed on developed countries by CBDR, the SDGs then renounces CBDR by placing the primary responsibility for climate change action on developing countries. In doing so, MDG 13 clearly violates the UNFCCC which draws a clear distinction between the GPG addressing climate change, and the humanitarian goals of economic advancement and eradication of poverty.

The Objective embodied in Art 2 of UNFCCC is

> " . . . to achieve in accordance with the relevant provisions of the Convention, the stabilization of greenhouse gas concentrations in the atmosphere at a level that could prevent dangerous anthropogenic interference with the climate system. Such a level should be achieved within a time-frame sufficient . . . to enable economic development to proceed in a sustainable manner."

It is to be observed that the stabilization of greenhouse concentrations is to be achieved in conjunction, first, with the other relevant provisions of the Convention, and second, in a manner that enables sustainable development. The other relevant provisions of the Convention make it abundantly clear that climate stabilization is not an unalloyed GPG to be sought at the expense of sustainable economic development and its corollary of humanitarian assistance.

The preamble to the UNFCCC asserts that the Parties should take into full account " . . . the legitimate priority needs of developing countries for the achievement of sustained economic growth and the eradication of poverty." The preamble then recognizes that in order to achieve sustainable social and economic development, the energy consumption of developing countries will need to grow. The body of the Convention continues to emphasize the extent to which economic and social development tempers the quest for climate stability.

Article 3(4) on Principles, states that "The Parties have a right to and should promote sustainable development. Policies and measures to protect the climate system against induced change should be appropriate for the specific conditions of each Party . . . taking into account that economic development is essential for adopting measures to address climate change." Article 4(7) is even more emphatic in asserting that economic and social development and poverty eradication are the overriding priorities of the developing country parties.

These legal provisions are found in a treaty whose objective is to stabilize climate change. The compelling extent to which even the most important treaty dealing with climate change is qualified and modified by the reiteration of the primary importance of economic and social development cannot be ignored.

The argument of Inge Kaul that the funding of GPGs should be separated from ODA addressing humanitarian assistance is based on the UNFCCC. Article 4(3) is unequivocal in asserting and stressing that developed countries shall provide *additional financial resources (emphasis added)* to meet the full costs of the developing countries in complying with their GPG obligations. The degree to which such new financial and technology transfers are crucial to the implementation of the Convention is further highlighted by Article 4(7). The language of Article 4(7) emphasizes that the extent to which developing countries implement their commitments under the Convention will depend on the effective implementation of developed country commitments. In sum, implementing the GPG of climate stabilization would need new, fresh, and additional financing. The financial and other resource needed to advance climate change should not be funneled or siphoned from ODA which is intended for individual human advances through economic and social development.

The cardinal importance of developed countries finding additional financing for promoting climate stabilization is further affirmed by Article 3(1), incorporating the Principle that Parties should protect the climate system ". . . on the basis of equity and in accordance with their common but differentiated responsibilities and respective capabilities. Accordingly, the developed country Parties should take the lead in combating climate change and the adverse effects thereof."

Furthermore, as we have noted, the UNFCCC confluenced with the other widely accepted treaty adopted at the United Nations Conference on Environment and Development, 1992, the CBD. Both treaties forcefully and unequivocally expressed the developmental priority of SD. Article 4(7) of the UNFCCC, and Article 20(4) of the CBD, reaffirm in unison that Parties "will take fully into account that economic and social development and poverty eradication are the first and overriding priorities of the developing country Parties."

C. The Attenuation of Economic and Social Development and the Growth of GPGs

The legal and political importance of economic and social development was expressed in the MDGs. But, as we have seen, the human-focused developmental goals of the MDGs, though incorporated in the SDGs, are clearly relegated to a diminished position when compared to the nine GPGs. These GPGs require enormous new amounts of additional funding, and the question of how they would be funded was discussed at the Third International

Conference on Financing for Development and the resulting Addis Ababa Action Agenda (AAAA) agreed to by that conference.[89]

Most importantly, the AAAA highlights the fact that each country (including the LDCs) will bear the main responsibility for its own sustainable development. Such a conclusion represented a disavowal of the earlier premise of international law, noted above, that developed countries shoulder this responsibility.

The AAAA also made three changes to the architecture of development assistance. First, it called for a new approach to taxes, in which countries commit to

> "enhancing revenue administration through modernized, progressive tax systems, improved tax policy and more efficient tax collection and to work[ing] to improve the fairness, transparency, efficiency and effectiveness of our tax systems, including by broadening the tax base and continuing efforts to integrate the informal sector into the formal economy in line with country circumstances."[90]

Strikingly, a key focus of ODA was identified as supporting developing countries in strengthening their capacities for effectively mobilizing and efficiently spending their domestic resources. This represented an about-face and an abrogation of established policy, in which ODA was used to finance individual human advancement, not revamp taxation.

Second, the AAAA called for a prominent role for private business and finance in implementing the SDGs. The main thrust of chapter 2 of the AAAA is incentivizing long-term private investment in areas that are key to sustainable development. The section on "Domestic and International Private Business and Finance" highlights the importance of aligning private sector incentives with public goals by incentivizing the private sector to adopt sustainable practices. This includes measures for increased transparency in investment decisions that will allow consumer pressure to push investments in sustainable sectors and businesses in the same way it has increased the supply of sustainable products over the past decade. There are references to blended finance in the AAAA and about the potential for well-designed public-private partnerships to help unlock necessary private finance in key areas, particularly infrastructure.[91]

---

[89] *Financing for Development*, Addis Ababa, 2015 http://www.un.org/esa/ffd/ffd3/index.html (visited Dec. 6, 2015).

[90] UNITED NATIONS DEP'T OF ECON. & SOC. AFFAIRS, FINANCING FOR DEVELOPMENT OFFICE, *Third International Conference: Financing for Development* (2015). http://www.un.org/esa/ffd/ffd3/index.html (visited Dec. 29, 2015).

[91] *Id.* at arts 35–37.

A third aspect of AAAA represents another significant weakening of humanitarian assistance. It suggested a reshaping of ODA, under the working title of "Total Official Support for Sustainable Development" (TOSSD).[92] Under the proposed measure, ODA may be applied to activities promoting and enabling sustainable development, including contributions to global public goods. Despite rhetoric to the contrary in the AAAA, doing so changes the character of ODA from a source only funding human developmental aid, to one that is now free to fund GPGs. As we have seen, ODA is already being used to fund climate change. The proposed new changes, open the door for ODA to fund climate change programs at the cost of developmental assistance. Not surprisingly, the OECD, the main funding source of ODA, is now on a path to doing precisely this.[93]

D. Global Energy Justice and the SDGs

Any assessment of how the SDGs impact global energy justice must begin with the fact that SDG 7, on affordable and clean energy, aims to ensure access to affordable, reliable, sustainable, and modern energy for all. As we have discussed in Chapter 1, the MDGs did not include access to energy as one of its goals. There is no doubt that institutionalizing access to clean energy is a major step forward in securing energy justice for the energy poor. However, there are a number of questions that arise when implementing SDG 7.

First, how much energy constitutes access to energy? According to Simon Trace, a recognized expert on this matter,[94] the diverse needs of the EP give rise to different types of access to energy. There are variances between the household (domestic), enterprise (livelihood or commercial), and community needs. Energy for households include lighting, cooking, water and space heating, cooling, and information. For billions among the EP the ability to earn a living depends on access to energy. Trace states, "(H)aving lighting after dark to keep a shop open longer, or fuel for an engine to mill grain, or a pump to irrigate land, can be the difference between earning a decent livelihood and remaining at or below the subsistence level and in poverty . . . "[95] Additionally, community services provided by hospitals, schools, and street lighting require energy. He demonstrates why the goals of Sustainable Energy for All

---

[92] *Id.* at art. 55.

[93] ORG. FOR ECON. CO-OPERATION & DEV., DCD/DAC, *Proposed Roadmap For Developing the Total Official Support for Sustainable Development Measurement Framework for 2015–2016* (Sept. 4, 2015), available at http://www.oecd.org/official documents/publicdisplaydocumentpdf/?cote=DCD/DAC(2015)26&docLanguage=En (visited Dec. 7, 2015).

[94] Simon Trace, *Measuring Access for Different Needs*, in *International Energy And Poverty: The emerging contours* 160 (Lakshman Guruswamy ed. 2015).

[95] *Id.*

(SE4All) require a better definition and understanding of what constitutes access for different purposes and services.

In moving forward, it is important that access to electricity remain the immediate, future, and final objective of access to energy for all. Nonetheless, it is important and that we better define what we mean by access to electricity. The US consumes about 13,400 kWh per year, per person of electricity, while the consumption in Bulgaria and South Africa, which are at the bottom of the energy consumption ladder, is about 4,500 kWh.[96] In calculating the energy required to provide access to energy for all, the International Energy Agency (IEA), defines an initial threshold for energy access to be 250 kWh per year for rural households and 500 kWh per year for urban households, assuming five people per household.[97] This equates to 50 to 100 kWh per year per person, or about 0.5 percent of that consumed by the average American and 1.7 percent of that of the average Bulgarian and South African. It is difficult to envisage how the domestic, livelihood, or community needs for energy, referred to above, can be met by such a meagre and inadequate supply of electricity.

Second, what are the costs of access to clean energy? Experts differ. According to EurActive (see Table) it would cost $50 billion per year, but it does not offer evidence supporting this figure. Others estimate about $1 trillion to achieve the total global access, rising to 750 kWh per capita for new connections by 2030, and 17 times more ($17 trillion), to achieve a level of worldwide access equivalent to that in Bulgaria.[98] The Global Tracking Framework of the IEA and World Bank has estimated the cost of achieving the three SE4All goals of electricity for all, doubling energy efficiency, and doubling the use of renewable energy by 2030. Doing so will cost at least $600 to $800 billion per year over and above existing levels, entailing a doubling or tripling of financial flows over current levels.[99]

Third, to what extent do the resources needed for the individual private good of access to energy (SDG 7) conflict with those required for numerous other GPGs? These GPGs include those combating climate change (SDG 13) Sustainable Infrastructure and Green Development (SDG 9), Sustainable Cities (SDG 11), Responsible

---

[96] Morgan Bazilian and Roger Pielke, *Making Energy Access Meaningful, 29(4)* ISSUES IN SCIENCE AND TECHNOLOGy 74–79 (2013).

[97] International Energy Agency, *World Energy Outlook 2012* (2012).

[98] Bazilian and Pielke, *supra* note 96.

[99] Nicolina Angelou, et al., *Global Tracking Framework: Executive Summary, Sustainable Energy For All* (May 28, 2013), available at http://www-wds.worldbank.org/external/default/WDSContentServer/WDSP/IB/2013/05/23/000442464_20130523110507/Rendered/PDF/778890WP0v10EN0y0Box377317B00OUO090.pdf. (visited Dec. 8, 2015).

Consumption and Production (SDG 12), and Peace, Justice and Strong Institutions (SDG 16). The costs of achieving these other SDGs become critical in answering this question.

According to UN estimates, an additional $3.3 trillion to $4.5 trillion would be needed in the developing world to deliver these SDGs. Current investment in these sectors is around $1.4 trillion, creating an annual investment gap of about $2.5 trillion.[100] But, action to combat climate change alone will cost between 1 to 3 percent of global gross domestic product.[101] According to the IPCC, cutting CO2 emissions to limit global temperature rises to 2 degrees Celsius would cost up to 4 percent of GDP in 2030, 6 percent of GDP in 2050, and 11 percent in 2100.[102] These estimates have been criticized as underestimating the true costs.[103]

Admittedly producing these estimates remains a challenge, particularly because of relatively well known, but limited integration of scientific knowledge across disciplines. The integrated assessment community, on the one hand, has extensively assessed the influence of technological and socio-economic uncertainties on low-carbon scenarios and associated costs. The climate modeling community, on the other hand, has spent years improving its understanding of the geophysical response of the Earth system to emissions of greenhouse gases.[104] The result is that knowledge about the impact of climate change on socio economics and earth systems is not integrated.

Notwithstanding differing estimates of the costs of climate action, the fact is that it will cost trillions of dollars. Together with the costs of the other GPGs, the previously noted predisposition of

---

[100] Sophie Yeo, *Sustainable Development Goals Face $2.5 Trillion Funding Shortfall*, CLIMATE HOME (Jan. 20, 2015), http://www.climatechangenews.com/2014/06/24/sustainable-development-goals-face–2–5–trillion-funding-shortfall/; Aaron Maasho, *U.N. Conference Agrees on Plan to Finance Development Goals*, REUTERS (July 16, 2015), http://www.reuters.com/article/us-africa-development-idUSKCN0PQ21D20150716 (visited Dec. 3, 2015).

[101] Juliette Jowit & Patrick Wintour, *Cost of Tackling Global Climate Change has Doubled, Warns Stern*, THE GUARDIAN (June 25, 2008), http://www.theguardian.com/environment/2008/jun/26/climatechange.scienceofclimatechange (visited Dec. 2, 2015).

[102] Christopher B. Field et al., *IPCC, 2014: Summary for Policymakers*, in *Climate Change 2014: Impacts, Adaptation, And Vulnerability, Part A: Global And Sectoral Aspects, Contribution Of Working Group I to The Fifth Assessment Report of The Intergovernmental Panel On Climate Change* 1–32 (Cambridge Univ. Press 2014), available at https://ipcc-wg2.gov/AR5/images/uploads/WG2AR5_SPM_FINAL.pdf (visited Dec. 3, 2015).

[103] *'Carbon cure cost more painful than the illness', says Bjorn Lomborg,* The Australian, April 15, 2014, http://www.theaustralian.com.au/national-affairs/climate/carbon-cure-cost-more-painful-than-the-illness-says-bjorn-lomborg/story-e6frg6xf–1226884300046 (visited Dec. 3, 2015).

[104] Joeri Rogelj, David L. McCollum, Andy Reisinger, Malte Meinshausen & Keywan Riahi, *Probabilistic Cost Estimates for Climate Change Mitigation* 493 NATURE 79–83 (visited Jan. 3, 2013).

aid-granting bodies to favor these GPGs, and the deficit in funding, it is difficult to resist the conclusion that funding for access to energy faces a mottled, even daunting future. In Chapter 4 we will discuss the extent to which energy justice converges or diverges with the emphasis on GPGs, and to what extent GPGs are favored over goals addressing poverty in general and energy poverty in particular.

Chapter 4

ENERGY JUSTICE AND SUSTAINABLE DEVELOPMENT

I. Introduction

Globally, around 2.8 billion people (the "Other Third" or "Energy-Poor") have little or no access to beneficial energy to meet their needs for cooking, heating, water, sanitation, illumination, transportation, or basic mechanical power.[1] The dearth of energy applies to their households; their chances of making a living through agriculture, industry, or crafts; and the hospitals and schools serving their communities.

More than 95 percent of the energy-poor (EP) live either in sub-Saharan Africa or developing Asia, predominantly (84 percent) in rural areas. They cook by burning polluting energy such as biomass, resulting in 3.5 to 4. 2 million deaths every year, primarily of women and children.[2] The lack of motive power or mechanical energy for pumping water for domestic and agricultural use, ploughing fields, transport, metal works, and agro-processing (such as grinding food), thwarts the possibility of any livelihood dependent on exogenous energy. Generating income through small businesses requires energy to transport and distribute goods and services to markets, and to enable telecommunications. Even the most rudimentary forms of rural agriculture need energy for water-pumping, irrigation, ploughing, harvesting, milling, grinding, and processing food. Water treatment plants that provide safe drinking water for communities and schools require energy. Polluted drinking water causes 3.5 million deaths per year, largely among children. The lack of energy impairs functioning of hospitals and schools. Hospitals need energy for refrigerating vital medications and vaccinations; education calls for energy for the lighting and heating of schools; and a lack of energy for illumination prevents women and children from studying at night and makes life dangerous after dark.

As we have seen in Chapter 3, (see text accompanying footnotes 35 to 59), access to efficient and affordable energy services is also a prerequisite for achieving the Millennium Development Goal (MDG)

---

[1] This chapter reproduces duly noted published and pending work of the author.

[2] *Global Burden of Disease, Injuries, and Risk Factors Study 2013*, 743, *THE LANCET*, June 18, 2015. Estimating 3.5 million deaths per year. WHO, *Household Air Pollution and Health, Fact Sheet N 292 Updated Feb. 2016, http://www.who.int/mediacentre/factsheets/fs292/en/ Estimating 4.2 million deaths per year.*

relating to poverty eradication. To recap very briefly, the MDGs formed a blueprint agreed to by all the world's countries and leading development institutions in the year 2000 to meet the needs of the world's poorest. Unfortunately, they, did not institutionalize a right to energy.[3]

Responding to the need for energy, the United Nations (UN) declared 2012 the "International Year of Sustainable Energy for All" and declared the entire decade the "Decade of Sustainable Energy for All."[4] Moreover, the UN announced a goal of universal, primarily electrical, energy access by 2030, and SDG 7 as we have seen in Chapter 3, calls for access to affordable, reliable, sustainable, and modern energy for all. Access to electricity and modern energy must remain the ultimate objective of energy justice. But, as noted in section D of Chapter 3 (Global Energy Justice and the SDGs) the daunting additional costs of electricity and the time it will take to do so—realistically, thirty years, will shunt the energy-poor into limbo unless interim measures like those suggested in this book, are also taken. Chapter 1 discusses how beneficial energy, based on appropriate/affordable sustainable energy technologies (ASETs), can provide such intermediate energy. ASETs bridge the gap between capital-intensive electricity and the traditional subsistence technologies of the EP. ASETs include: clean fuels; clean cookstoves; illumination by photovoltaic lights; decentralized mini grids based on solar, wind, and biomass-generated electricity; treadle pumps; improved harnesses and yokes to boost the performance of draft cattle; better axels for transport by cart; simple windmills for pumping water; grain-grinding appliances; and low-cost bicycles.

SDG 7 on Affordable and Clean energy discussed in Chapter 3 (H. The Sustainable Development Goals (SDGs) 2015), was also called for by the Global Conference on Rural Energy Access, hosted by the United Nations in early December 2013, agreed that the reformulation of international economic development goals should include a discrete goal to "make sustainable energy for all a reality, and through this, help to eradicate poverty."[5] The aide memoire of the Global Conference on Rural Energy Access reiterated: "There is a strong nexus between energy and other important development factors such as education, health, gender, environment, economic growth, food security, and water. Sustainable access to modern energy services is a critical input and catalyst for improving the

---

[3] MILLENNIUM PROJECT, *What They Are*, http://www.unmillenniumproject.org/goals/index.htm (visited Dec. 29, 2015).

[4] *See,* SUSTAINABLE ENERGY FOR ALL *About Us: Setting a Vision in Motion* 2012, available at http://www.se4all.org/about-us/ (visited June 28, 2015).

[5] GLOBAL CONFERENCE, ECONOMIC COMMISSION FOR AFRICA, *Rural Energy Access: A Nexus Approach to Sustainable Development and Poverty Eradication (2013),* Addis Ababa, Ethiopia, December 4–6, 2013.

productive capacities and welfare of rural isolated communities, leading to poverty eradication and sustainable development."[6]

Access to energy, within the framework of SD, calls to be secured on the foundations of energy justice. The needs of the energy-poor must be addressed within the ethical, political, and legal framework of sustainable development (SD). In order that the universally accepted principles of SD be applied in earnest, it is essential that the world accept an ethical and rational justification for SD. Chapter. 2 suggested that concepts of justice, applicable to global energy poverty, may be found within different global jurisprudential lineages, including Western, Islamic, Buddhist, and Confucian. Consequently, it is possible to discover general principles of law and justice within the world's jurisprudential heritage. SD is predicated on these unarticulated general principles of law and justice and they should continue to fashion the legal response to global energy poverty.

This chapter recapitulates and weaves together various themes explored in Chapters 1, 2 and 3 with a view to establishing the importance of energy justice in addressing energy poverty. The first part of this chapter draws on materials in Chapter 1 to demonstrate why energy is a primary determinant of human progress. The second part, expands on Chapter. 1 by explaining the factual and socio-political phenomenon of the energy-poor, who lack clean energy for cooking, illumination, sanitation, drinking water, and mechanical or motive power. The third part makes the case for using ASETs to supplement the quest for electricity and provide an intermediate source of energy during the transition to electricity. The fourth part restates the conceptual and theoretical grounds found in moral and political philosophy and jurisprudence, positing that the world ought to remedy the lack of access to energy.

A. The Importance of Energy[7]

Energy's presence and influence in the human and social world is essentially ubiquitous.[8] Humans are endlessly engaged in transforming or converting energy found in the environment into energy useful for human purposes.

By the late nineteenth century, energy demand in industrialized countries had grown considerably.[9] This demand was met by the development of electric energy, an incredibly versatile energy source

---

6 *Id.*

7 This section is based on Lakshman Guruswamy, *Global Energy Justice*, in *International Energy and Poverty: The emerging contours,* (Lakshman Guruswamy, ed. 2015).

8 *Supra* Chapter 1. Text accompanying notes 15 to 30.

9 *Id.*

that can be transmitted over vast distances and put to a wide variety of uses. The first electric power plants were hydroelectric facilities relying on flowing water as their energy source, converting mechanical energy to electrical energy. Subsequent power plants have employed fossil fuels, and more recently nuclear fission and geothermal, wind, and solar power, to produce electricity. The development of alternating current technology allowed the transmission of electricity over long distances, enabling the development of regional power transmission grids to distribute the electricity generated across a network of large-scale power plants.[10] By the early twentieth century, electricity had emerged as the favoured method for transmitting energy and researchers responded with a range of products that extended the ways in which humankind could apply this electricity.[11]

B. The Energy-Poor[12]

The energy predicament of the LDCs and the EP has been described in Chapter 1. A general lack of access to beneficial energy plays an enormous role in both creating and promulgating the condition of the LDCs, and because the phenomenon of energy poverty is overwhelmingly a problem of the LDCs, the primary focus of this chapter will be on them.

The current era of globalization is driven by modern innovation and advanced technologies that occur in industrialized countries. These technologies are not necessarily affordable, appropriate, or accessible for the EP. On the other hand, traditional uses of energy, and the technologies surrounding them, are frequently harmful, inefficient, and unproductive. Appropriate/Affordable Sustainable Energy Technologies (ASETs) seek to bridge the gap between the capital-intensive advanced technologies of the developed world, and the traditional subsistence technologies of the EP. The purpose of ASETs is to free the EP from the oppressive impacts of unhealthy and unreliable energy access, and to facilitate sustainable development in the LDCs.

1. *Cooking*

A disturbingly large swathe of humanity is caught in a time warp. They rely on biomass-generated fire as their principal source of energy. These fires are made by burning animal dung, waste, crop residues, rotted wood, other forms of harmful biomass, or raw coal.

---

[10] *Id.*

[11] *Environmental Decision Making, Science, and Technology, History of the Energy System*, http://environ.andrew.cmu.edu.

[12] This section is based on and reproduces parts of Lakshman Guruswamy, *Energy Poverty*, 36 ANNUAL REVIEW OF ENVIRONMENT AND RESOURCES 139 (2011).

Smoke from the fire used for cooking leads to the premature deaths by respiratory infection of 3.5 to 4.2 million people annually, primarily women and children.[13] Moreover, fire fails to supply the majority of other basic energy needs. In the LDCs, 715 million people rely on solid fuels for cooking, 703 million of these people rely on traditional biomass, and 615 million of those relying on biomass live in sub-Saharan Africa alone.[14] In the LDCs, the overwhelming majority of people forced to use solid fuels for cooking are rural, and more than 80 percent of rural dwellers rely on solid fuels for cooking, including wood, coal, charcoal, crop residues, and dung; 85 percent of those people rely on wood and its byproducts only.[15] This means that a mere 15 percent of the EP in the LDCs enjoy access to modern fuels for cooking.

The general lack of access to modern fuels and overwhelming reliance on biomass for cooking has a number of adverse consequences for human health and also for the global phenomenon of climate change. First, the EPs that rely on biomass for their fuel for cooking generally cook over an open fire or with some other form of a traditional stove. This process is exceedingly inefficient, as only about 18 per cent of the energy from the fire transfers to the pot.[16] Depending on the type of fuel and stove being used, indoor air pollution can contain a variety of dangerous pollutants, such as carbon monoxide, nitrous oxides, sulfur oxides, formaldehyde, carcinogens (such as benzene), and small particulate matter.[17]

Second, 3.5 to 4.2 million deaths per year are attributed to indoor pollution due to combustion of solid fuels worldwide,[18] with more than 99 percent of these deaths in developing countries.[19] Specifically, though the population of the LDCs makes up a mere 12 percent of the global citizenry, it accounts for 30 percent of all deaths caused by indoor pollution.[20] The seriousness of indoor air pollution among the EP may be put in perspective by comparing their air quality with the health standards of the US. The U.S. Environmental

---

[13] Note 2, *supra*. For earlier assessments of mortality, *see* World Health Organization, *Household Air Pollution and Health*, March 2014, www.who.int; Global Alliance for Clean Cookstoves, *Igniting Change: A Strategy for Universal Adoption of Clean Cookstoves and Fuels*, November 2011, www.cleancookstoves.org.

[14] G. Legros, I. Havet, N. Bruce, and S. Bonjour, *The Energy Access Situation in Developing Countries: A Review Focusing on Least Developed Countries and Sub Saharan Africa* (2009) http://content.undp.org/go/cms-service/stream/asset/?asset_id=2205620 (last visited Mar. 06, 2016).

[15] *Id.*

[16] H. Warwick and A. Doig, *Smoke—The Killer in the Kitchen* (2004).

[17] World Health Organization, *Fuel For Life: Household Energy and Health*, 10 (2006).

[18] Note 2, *supra.*

[19] Note 22, *infra.*

[20] *Id.*

Protection Agency (EPA) sets an air pollution limit of 150 micrograms per cubic meter for small particulates in the United States. By contrast WHO reports that a typical 24-hour mean level for homes burning biomass fuels is between 300 and 3,000 micrograms per cubic meter.[21] This results in pollution levels that are far more deadly in EP countries than the levels of atmospheric pollution allowed by the developed world. According to WHO, exposure to high concentrations of indoor air pollution presents one of the ten most important threats to public health worldwide, resulting in diseases such as pneumonia, chronic pulmonary disease, lung cancer, asthma, and acute respiratory infections.[22] Furthermore, three published studies suggest that the risk of active tuberculosis is 2.5 times greater for people in homes using wood for cooking than for those who do not and there is growing evidence suggesting that indoor air pollution causes cataracts.[23]

Third, women and children are disproportionately affected by the use of biomass for cooking. Women are traditionally responsible for cooking and childcare in the home, and they spend more time inhaling the polluted air that is trapped indoors. Thus, women and children have the highest exposure to indoor air pollution and suffer more than anyone from these negative health effects.[24] Specifically, the risk of child pneumonia increases by 2.3 times in homes that burn solid fuels for cooking, and women are about twice as likely to be afflicted with chronic pulmonary disease than men in homes using solid fuels.[25] Beyond suffering adverse health effects, women and children are also disproportionately affected by the time constraints needed for collecting fuel. Women are burdened with the majority of the work involved in collecting fuel, which can present other serious risks such as an increased risk of being raped, as occurred in the refugee camps of Darfur.[26]

Fourth, there are also severe environmental impacts of biomass dependence. The reliance on wood as a fuel source puts considerable pressure on local forests, particularly in areas where fuel is scarce and demand for wood outstrips natural regrowth.[27] Depletion of

---

[21] WHO, *supra* note 17, p. 10.

[22] WHO, *Indoor Air Pollution Takes Heavy Toll on Health,* April 30, 2007, http://www.who.int.

[23] Warwick and Doig, *supra* note 16.

[24] Global Alliance for Clean Cookstoves, *Clean Cookstoves can Save Lives and Empower Women,* https://cleancookstoves.org/binary-data/RESOURCE/file/000/000/278-1.pdf (visited Mar. 6 2016).

[25] Legros et al. *supra* note 14.

[26] Cookstove Projects, *Overview,* http://darfurstoves.lbl.gov. This is equally the case in other refugee camps such as the Horn of Africa. See L. Shannon, *The Rape of Somalia's Women is Being Ignored*, *The Guardian*, October 12, 2011.

[27] WHO, *Broader Impacts of Household Energy*, http://www.who.int/indoorair/impacts/en/ (visited Mar. 6, 2016).

woodland can lead to soil erosion and loss of a carbon sink.[28] Furthermore, it is well established that burning dung and agricultural residues emits carbon dioxide and methane.[29] Research has identified emissions from the burning of biomass as a significant cause of anthropogenic global warming. For example, according to an article in *Nature Geoscience*,[30] discussed in *Science*,[31] the black carbon emitted by burning biomass is the second largest contributor to current global warming after carbon dioxide emissions. The article concludes that black carbon warms the atmosphere more severely than other GHGs, such as methane, halocarbons, and tropospheric ozone, by absorbing both direct and reflected solar radiation.[32] Unlike GHGs, ambient black carbon dissipates in a very short period of time. Thus, helping to move one third of the global population away from biomass burning will have the effect of reducing global warming more immediately than merely reducing carbon dioxide emissions. Furthermore, removing black carbon would reduce the effects of black soot on impairing the albedo, or reflectivity, of polar ice.[33] The presence of overlying black carbon may result in ice retaining more heat, leading to increased melting and further global warming.

The dependence on biomass for cooking can be addressed, among others, by using two tested ASETs,. First, by using biogas digesters, agricultural waste or animal dung can be converted to other useable forms of energy to create better fuels. Citing to a number of case studies Jason Aamodt and Blake Feamster make a compelling case as to how biogas can meet the cooking and heating needs of the EP.[34]

The National Biodigester program, a well documented successful program, is a joint enterprise between the Cambodia Ministry of Agriculture, Forestry and Fisheries, and the Netherlands Development Organisation. Unfortunately, the cost of each biodigester runs into hundreds of dollars, which may place it outside

---

28 S. Cairncross, D. O'Neill, A. McCoy, and D. Sethi, *Health, Environment and the Burden of Disease, Guidance Note,* Department for International Development UK (DFID) (2003).

29 A. Sagar, *Alleviating Energy Poverty for the World's Poor,* 33 *ENERGY POLICY* 1367 (2005).

30 V. Ramanathan and G. Carmichael, *Global and Regional Climate Changes Due to Black Carbon* 1 *NATURE GEOSCIENCE* 221 at 221 (2008).

31 R. Service, *Study Fingers Soot as Major Player in Global Warming* 319 *SCIENCE* 1745 (2008).

32 Ramanathan and Carmichael, *supra* note 30 at 221.

33 J. Hansen and L. Nazarenko, *Soot Climate Forcing via Snow and Ice Albedos* 101 *PROCEEDINGS OF THE NATURAL ACADEMY OF SCIENCES* 423 at 428 (2004).

34 Jason Aamodt and Blake Feamster, *The role of appropriate sustainable energy technologies (ASETs) as a means for providing access to energy for all,* in *International Energy and Poverty: The emerging frontiers* (Lakshman Guruswamy Ed. 2015).

the reach of most of the EP.[35] But Aamodt and Feamster cite to other case studies, and countries like China in which biodigesters are produced at much lower costs.[36] Other forms of fuel pellets or converted fuels have not proven to be practicable and have not gained wide currency.

Another way of addressing indoor air pollution is to increase access to improved cookstoves. The Global Alliance for Clean Cookstoves is an initiative led by the UN Foundation, supporting large-scale adoption of clean and safe household cooking solutions as a way to save lives, improve livelihoods, empower women, and reduce climate change emissions.[37] The Alliance's founding partners have set a goal of enabling an additional 100 million homes to adopt clean and efficient stoves and fuels by 2020.

Improved cookstoves can utilize a number of different fuel types, but in general are designed to conduct more efficient combustion and reduce particulate indoor air pollution. For example, Envirofit (a nonprofit corporation) has created a stove that can reduce emissions by as much as 80 percent and uses up to 60 percent less fuel, while reducing cooking cycle time by up to 50 percent compared to traditional open fires.[38] The University of California at Berkeley designed a cookstove for refugee camps in Darfur that saves more than 1.5 metric tons of CO^2 per year. In term of CO^2 reductions, this is equivalent to removing two average U.S. vehicles from the road for an entire year.[39] Both of these examples use local solid fuels, such as firewood, in order to facilitate sustainable practices within the community. There are a number of other stoves that use ethanol, gas, or other forms of liquid fuels to increase combustion efficiency and reduce particulate indoor pollution. Clean cookstoves can cost anywhere from $15 to $150 depending on the model and region in which they are assembled, again demonstrating a relatively low cost-benefit ratio, and presenting a timely opportunity to address the needs of the EP.[40]

2. Lighting

The EP also lacks access to lighting. Lighting is essential to human progress and without it humans would be comparatively

---

[35] National Biodigester Programme Cambodia, www.nbp.org.kh.

[36] Aamodt and Feamster, *supra* note 34.

[37] UN Foundation, *What We Do Global Alliance for Clean Cookstoves*, http://www.unfoundation.org/what-we-do/campaigns-and-initiatives/cookstoves/ (visited Mar. 5, 2016).

[38] Envirofit, www.envirofit.org (visited Mar. 5, 2016).

[39] *Potential Energy*, www.potentialenergy.org.

[40] Global Alliance for Clean Cookstoves, *Market Development*, http://cleancookstoves.org/market-development/ (visited Mar.3, 2016).

inactive about one-half of their lifetime.[41] The scorching sun and withering temperatures in the LDCs prevent agricultural labor during the daytime and reduce productivity. The absence of artificial light severely impedes working at night. Without lighting it is not possible for students to do homework after nightfall. The absence of lighting creates physical insecurity—particularly for women and children—while venturing out in the darkness and almost entirely prevents commercial activity after dark.

Almost 500 million people rely on kerosene for illumination.[42] The hazards of kerosene, such as fires, explosions, and poisonings resulting from children ingesting it, are extensively documented,[43] and children and women are disproportionately affected.[44] There is evidence implicating kerosene in ailments including the impairment of lung function, asthma, cancer, and tuberculosis.[45] The use of kerosene and candles is also costly: households often spend 10 to 25 percent of their income on kerosene.[46] Over $36 billion is spent on kerosene annually, U$10 billion of which is spent in sub-Saharan Africa.[47]

3. *Drinking Water and Sanitation*

Lack of access to clean drinking water and sanitation are two interconnected, deadly issues facing the EP. Worldwide, approximately one in eight people—884 million in total—lack access to safe water supplies.[48] While the MDG on sustainable access to drinking water was successfully reached in 2010, with the threshold of 88 percent of the world's population having access to improved water sources reached, the sanitation MDG remains off track, with only 63 percent of people having access to improved sanitation (short of the aim of 75 percent by 2015).[49] In preventing diseases such as diarrhea, tuberculosis, cholera, and other waterborne diseases, basic

---

41 M. Luckiesh, *Artificial Light: Its Influence Upon Civilization*, (1920).

42 N. Lam, K. Smith, A. Gautier, and M. Bates, *Kerosene: A Review of Household Uses and their Hazards in Low and Middle Income Countries* 15 *JOURNAL OF TOXICOLOGY AND ENVIRONMENTAL HEALTH,* 396 (2012).

43 *Id.* at 423.

44 M. D. Peck, *Epidemiology of Burns throughout the World, Part 1: Distribution and Risk Factors,* Volume 37, Issue 7, SCIENCE DIRECT 1087 at 1096 (2011).

45 Lam et al., *supra* note 42 at 399–401, 412–423.

46 *Lighting the Way*, *The Economist,* September 1, 2012, p. 14.

47 *Id.* p. 14.

48 WHO and UNICEF, *Progress on Drinking Water and Sanitation: Special Focus on Sanitation* (Geneva: WHO Library, 2008).

49 UNDESA, *Water for Life Decade 2005–2015: Access to Sanitation* (2015) http://www.un.org/waterforlifedecade/sanitation.shtm.

sanitation is just as important as fresh drinking water.[50] 2.5 billion people lack access to improved sanitation, including 1.2 billion people who have no facilities at all.[51] As a result, 3.4 million people died from water-related disease each year.[52] This number has been increased to 1. 5 billion.[53] Other consequences of the lack of clean drinking water and basic sanitation include crop failure in irrigated fields, livestock death, and environmental damage.[54] Energy is necessary to alleviate these problems through collecting, transporting, and distributing clean water, powering water treatment facilities, facilitating in-home water treatment (through boiling, for example), and constructing and powering sanitation facilities.[55] However, ASETs such as small-scale sustainable power grids and water transport mechanisms could help to remediate these issues.

Most of the 2.5 billion people without access to adequate sanitation, including the 1.2 billion people without any facilities at all, live in LDCs in rural Africa and Asia.[56] Consequently, the sanitation issue currently affects the EP in rural areas more dramatically than those in urban areas. However, the issue is increasingly becoming urban.[57] Of the sixty million people added to the world's towns and cities every year, most occupy impoverished slums and shanty-towns with no sanitation facilities.[58]

As with many other issues faced by the EP, children are intensely affected by lack of access to clean drinking water and sanitation facilities. Nearly one in five child deaths—about 1.5 million each year—is due to diarrhea, which is often caused by unclean drinking water and inadequate sanitation facilities.[59] These deaths occur primarily in LDCs, and the many of the children there who suffer from diarrhea also suffer from acute malnutrition, a condition that is

---

[50] Office of the High Commissioner for Human Rights, *Special Rapporteur on the Human Right to Safe Drinking Water and Sanitation*, (2015) http://www.ohchr.org/EN/Issues/WaterAndSanitation/SRWater/Pages/SRWaterIndex.aspx.

[51] *Id.*

[52] A. Prüss-Üstün, R. Bos, F. Gore, and J. Bartram, *Safer Water, Better Health: Costs, Benefits, and Sustainability of Interventions to Protect and Promote Health, Table 1,* Geneva: WHO Library, (2004, updated 2008), Table 1.

[53] Water.org, *Water Borne Diseases and Their Effects Around the World*, (2015) http://water.org/water-crisis/disease-facts/

[54] *Id.*

[55] International Energy Agency, *Water for Energy* (2012) http://www.worldenergyoutlook.org/resources/water-energynexus/ (visited Mar. 6, 2016).

[56] Water Supply and Sanitation Collaborative Council (WSSCC), *A Guide to Investigating One of the Biggest Scandals of the Last 50 Years* (2008). http://esa.un.org/iys/docs/san_lib_docs/WASH_media_guide_en%5b1%5d.pdf.

[57] *Id.*

[58] *Id.*

[59] *Id.*

exacerbated by diarrhea.[60] Child diarrhea is a serious global issue, as it painfully kills more young children than AIDS, malaria, and measles combined.[61]

In order to provide sanitation, energy is necessary to power water treatment and sanitation facilities to provide safe drinking water supplies and adequate sanitation facilities. Within the home, too, clean energy can provide people with the ability to boil water. While extending large-scale electricity grids to rural communities is often impracticable at the outset, decentralized mini grids based on solar, wind, and biomass-generated electricity comprise ASETs that can provide power to the EP for water treatment, sanitation facilities, and in-home water boiling.[62] Another example of an ASET that has been used to combat these issues is the implementation of "dry composting latrines" in Chalchuapa, El Salvador, by "Trees, Water, & People."[63] These latrines are fairly simple, inexpensive mechanisms that utilize sawdust in combination with human waste to produce a rich fertilizer that can be used on crops after six to eight months.[64]

Though the MDG for access to clean drinking water has been reached, several factors indicate that the water crisis is going to worsen over time. Over the last century, water use grew more than twice as fast as the population, and this trend is predicted to continue.[65] Population growth and urbanization are two factors stressing the global water supply. Additionally, as the effects of climate change intensify, the water cycle will change and water will become increasingly hard to come by, especially as rainfall is already irregular and water sources are already scarce in many LDCs.[66] Accordingly, it is crucial that ASETs be implemented to supply the need for clean water and sanitation among the EP.

---

60 UNICEF and WHO, *Diarrhoea: Why Children are Still Dying and What can be Done* (2009).

61 *Id.*

62 E. Visagie and G. Prasad, *Renewable Energy Technologies for Poverty Alleviation South Africa: Biodiesel and Solar Water Heaters* (South Africa: Energy Research Centre, 2006).

63 Trees, Water and People, *Dry Composting Latrines*, http://www.treeswaterpeople.org/programs/dry_composting_latrines/dry_composting_latrines.html (2016).

64 *Id.*

65 Deborah Zabarenko, *Water Use Rising Faster than World Population*, Reuters, October 25, 2011.

66 Matthias Bruckner, *Climate Change Vulnerability and the Identification of Least Developed Countries* 1 (2012). http://www.un.org/en/development/desa/policy/cdp/cdp_background_papers/bp2012_15.pdf.

4. Mechanical Power

According to the United Nations Development Programme, 2.5 billion people without access to modern energy services still depend on unimproved versions of mechanical power equipment that inefficiently use human or animal power to meet their energy needs.[67] Mechanical power refers to the transmission of energy through a solid structure to impart motion, such as for pumping, pushing, and other similar needs.[68] In a practical sense, this means either using human and animal power or "modern" energy sources such as wind, solar, gas, or electrical power to complete daily tasks. The energy services that stem from access to mechanical power include agriculture (irrigation, farming, and processing), water-pumping, and small-scale industry.[69] Unfortunately, specific data quantifying exactly how many of the EP in the LDCs lack access to mechanical power is lacking.[70] It is clear, however, that access to mechanical power is a problem for the EP, and that it has begun to receive attention on the international energy agenda.[71]

For the EP, the inability to access modern forms of mechanical energy results in the use of inefficient human and animal power to satisfy their most basic needs. To provide water for drinking, the arduous task of walking to a source, collecting it for use in the household, and carrying home is undertaken primarily by women.[72] Depending on the season, in parts of Africa, this can require spending up to four hours per day collecting water. In Uganda, women spend an average of 660 hours per year (a period equating to about a month) collecting water.[73] Even a very simple ASET, such as a water pump, could drastically cut collection time. Less time spent collecting water will also aid development and gender equality by allowing women to spend the time saved on other productive activities—whether they be economic, educational, or domestic.

While water pumps are widely used in parts of the LDCs, they are most commonly operated through the use of human power (by either hand or foot), and in many cases by women and children. Manually operated water pumps are physically demanding and time-consuming, and do not totally remove the burden placed on women and children. In some locations, it may be appropriate to employ

---

[67] Liz Bates et al., *Expanding Energy Access in Developing Countries: The Role of Mechanical Power, 2* (2009).

[68] Legros et al., *supra* note 14.

[69] Liz Bates et al., *supra* note 67, p. 2.

[70] *Id.* As of 2009, only three of the LDCs had data to report on access to mechanical power. *Id.* p. 3.

[71] Liz Bates et al, *supra* note 67, at pp. 11–14.

[72] *Id.* at p. 2.

[73] *Id.*

windmills, water wheels, or photovoltaic solar technologies to ease the burden caused by manual pumping. Selecting an effective ASET-based pump for lifting potable water requires investigating the groundwater depth, water characteristics, capacity demand, preferred method of operation, and maintenance in the target region. Fortunately, there are numerous nonelectric or fossil-fuel-based pumps that are up to the task.[74]

Another example of how ASETS can be used to provide useful mechanical energy involves the method for processing grain. Before grain can be consumed or sold, the EP must dry it in the sun or with a handheld fan, and then grind it by hand or with a flail. Because post-harvest processing is arguably the main factor in helping farmers increase their income, simple technologies such as watermills could drastically cut the amount of physical labor needed, increase production, and improve both food security and profit margins for farmers.[75] Although improving access to some basic services achieved through mechanical power can be addressed through expanding access to electricity, this energy deficit can also be addressed through non-electric, non-fossil fuel ASETs, such as hand operated grinding and pounding equipment.

A particularly innovative application of ASETs to the EP is the Gravity Goods Ropeways project conducted by Practical Action, Nepal.[76] The project, initiated in 2002, was conducted as a way to reduce the transportation time taken for communities to walk their agricultural produce from the village farmyards in the highlands down to the main roads. The technology was adroitly adapted to fit unique local conditions. What emerged is basically a system of gravity-operated pulleys that can carry up to 130 kilograms of goods in a trolley carriage 1.3 kilometers from an elevated platform to a lower platform, and about 40 kilograms of goods from the lower platform to the higher one. The ropeways have reduced transportation costs for farmers by 85 percent, and transportation time from three to four hours a day to just five minutes. Each individual pulley is locally managed, and operational costs are funded by use charges. The communities contributed 40 percent of the initial investment and the rest was funded by external sources. In sum, the ropeway required only about $6,500 of initial external investment. Community based systems such as this demonstrate the feasibility of applying efficient, simple, and sustainable solutions to the problems of energy poverty.

---

[74] E. Stewart, *How to Select the Proper Human-Powered pump for Potable Water*, Masters thesis, Michigan Technological University (2003).

[75] K. Watkins, *Human Development Report*: *Beyond Scarcity: Power, Poverty, and the Global Water Crisis* (2006).

[76] Practical Action, *Gravity Goods Ropeway* (2010).

The table below offers examples of ASETs.

EXAMPLES OF AFFORDABLE SUSTAINABLE ENERGY TECHNOLOGIES (ASETs)

NEED	ASET
Cooking	Efficient cook-stoves, charcoal, biogas, passive solar
Water Filtration and Heating	Efficient cook-stoves, passive solar, desalination, fog-collection, rainwater harvesting, household filters
Agricultural Technology	Improved plows, hand operated grinding and pounding equipment, animal husbandry, sustainable farming practices, passive solar greenhouses
Irrigation	Drip irrigation systems, treadle-pumps, ram-pumps, rope-pumps, play pumps
Draft Animal Technology	Improved harnesses, feed systems
Lighting	Solar bulbs, multifunctional biodiesel platforms, hand-held solar-lamps, mini-electric, micro-hydro
Transportation	Improved axels and wheels for carts, bicycles, local biodiesel, gravity ropeways
Sanitation	Pit latrines, composting toilets, biogasifiers
Mechanical	Pedal powered washing, pedal grain crusher, hand operated nutsheller, hand powered grain mill, pedal-powered grain mill

II. Sustainable Development and the Energy-Poor[77]

A. Right to Sustainable Development and Access to Energy

International law is the law that governs, and is restricted to, relations between legally sovereign coequal states. Treaties are the primary way in which international law is created. Treaties are written agreements between two or more states, governed by international law, creating or restating legal rights and duties. They are also described as conventions, agreements, protocols, covenants, and pacts. The Vienna Convention on the Law of Treaties (Vienna Convention) deals comprehensively with a number of complex questions concerning treaties.[78] A few are of relevance to this chapter. The first concerns the entry into force of a treaty, or the date on which it officially binds the parties. Even though signed, a multilateral treaty typically does not enter into force until a stipulated minimum number of states have deposited their ratifications. Ratification is the process by which the respective national governments give legal force to the signatures entered by their representatives.

The problem of access to energy relegates the EP to a life of desperation that affronts international concepts of justice and sustainable development (SD), discussed in Chapter 3. As we have seen, (Chapter 3: C.1983 World Commission on Environment and Development (Brundtland Commission)), the concept of SD was gestated by the World Commission on Environment and Development, also known as the Brundtland Commission, as a distributional principle to address the needs of the world's poor while maintaining environmental integrity. SD mandates that global environmental protection must be pursued in tandem with economic and social development.

International law, as expressed particularly in the UN Framework Convention on Climate Change[79] (UNFCCC) unequivocally institutionalizes SD. As we have emphasized in Chapter 3, the UNFCCC is the most important energy convention to date. Having obtained 194 instruments of ratification, it is probably the most extensively adopted treaty in the world. Article 3(1) of the UNFCCC states that the parties have a right to and should promote sustainable development, and that economic development is

---

[77] This section is excerpted and adapted from Lakshman Guruswamy, *Energy Poverty* 36 ANNUAL REVIEW OF ENVIRONMENT AND RESOURCES 139 (2011).

[78] *Vienna Convention on the Law of Treaties*, Vienna, 23 May 1969, 8 ILM 679 (1980).

[79] *Supra* Chapter 3, note 9.

essential for adopting measures to address climate change, while Article 3(2) affirms that full consideration be given to the special circumstances of developing countries. Parties are required to protect the climate system on the basis of equity and in accordance with their common but differentiated responsibilities and respective capacities. The principle of common but differentiated responsibility (CBDR), which is found in Principle 7 of the Rio Declaration on Environment and Development[80] and conclusively embodied in Articles 3(1) and 4(1) of the UNFCCC, affirms the responsibility of the developed country parties to take the lead in combating climate change and the adverse effects thereof.

The UNFCCC coalesced with another widely accepted treaty, the Convention on Biological Diversity[81] (CBD), by forcefully and unequivocally expressing the developmental priority of SD. Article 4(7) of the UNFCCC and Article 20(4) of the CBD reaffirm in unison that parties "will take fully into account that economic and social development and poverty eradication are the first and overriding priorities of the developing country Parties." Specifically, therefore, energy poverty can only be addressed within a framework of distributive justice, as part of the overall right to economic and social development established by the foundational norm of SD.

B. Jurisprudential Lineages of Sustainable Development

Chapter 2 examined the jurisprudential lineages of justice in Western, Islamic, Buddhist, and Confucian traditions. We referred *inter-alia*, to the writings of Aquinas, Plato, Aristotle, Grotius, and John Rawls to conclude that foundational concept of international justice based on natural law and ethics provides a moral justification for SD.

We delineated Rawls' thinking particularly in his book *The Law of Peoples*, and found a conclusion most pertinent to SD and the EP. Rawls elucidates the duty of liberal democratic and decent hierarchical peoples to assist "burdened societies" to the point where burdened societies are enabled to join the "Society of Peoples." It is of particular pertinence that Rawls' duty of assistance does not absolve developing country governments of their obligation to take appropriate action.

The legal and political acceptance of SD by the community of nations may be seen as validating Rawls' hypothesis. We have seen in Chapter 3, how existing legal and political frameworks of SD expressed, for example, in the UNFCCC and CBD, incorporate

---

80 *Rio Declaration on Environment and Development, supra* Chapter 3, note 20.

81 *Supra* Chapter 3, note 10.

Rawlsian ideals. But, as discussed in Chapter 3, the SDGs have moved away from the duty of assistance to burdened peoples as found in the MDGs, to GPGs incorporated in the SDGs. Such a move calls attention to the ongoing relevance of ensuring that SD is implemented in a manner consistent with Rawlsian principles. As is more fully discussed in the next section, the principle of SD has been invoked and erroneously applied to the ADCs, at the expense of the EP and the LDCs.

C. Rawlsian Sustainable Development as It Applies to the EP

To recapitulate the argument delineated in Chapter 2, a starting point for analyzing the international phenomena of the EP must begin with the fact that the EP should be identified primarily as "burdened societies" in the Rawlsian sense.[82] Rawlsian principles will ensure that SD is applied to the EP. Furthermore, their special status as burdened societies must be highlighted rather than hidden. Additionally, it is important to draw attention to Rawls' suggestion as to how the duty of assistance should be discharged, bearing in mind his particular conclusion that merely dispensing funds will not suffice to rectify basic and political injustice.[83]

Rawls' warning that the mere distribution of funds will not rectify the targeted problems now becomes of special relevance. Many rulers, Rawls points out, have been callous about the well-being of their own peoples,[84] and transferring resources to national governments does not ensure that they will be applied to the problems of the EP. For this reason, Rawls advocates that assistance be tied to the advancement of human rights. Tying assistance to human rights will also embrace the status of women, who are often oppressed. It has, moreover, been shown that the removal of discrimination against women has resulted in major economic and social progress.[85]

Such measures almost certainly will be resisted by authoritarian regimes, which will argue this approach amounts to an intrusion into the national sovereignty of a country and violates international law. These rulers might fear that establishing human rights as a condition for helping the EP will expose their own corruption and lack of good governance. Such rulers have reason to fear the granting of human rights where they have not confronted

---

[82] John Rawls, *The Law of Peoples*, *supra* Chapter 2, text accompanying notes 57 to 92.

[83] *Id.*

[84] *Id.*

[85] M. Yunus, *A World Without Poverty: Social Business and the Future Capitalism* (New York: Public Affairs, 2007).

their problems or have demonstrated weak governance. As an example of this, Rawls cites the works of Amartya Sen and Partha Dasgupta, who have demonstrated that the main cause of famine in Bengal, Ethiopia, Sahel, and Bangladesh was government mismanagement rather than shortage of food.[86]

Corruption remains a major problem in many developing countries, where large numbers of complex, restrictive regulations are coupled with inadequate controls. The United Nations Convention on Corruption, which came into force in 2005, was negotiated after *The Law of Peoples* and offers ample contemporary evidence of Rawls' conclusion.[87] It recognized the seriousness of problems and threats posed by corruption to the stability and security of societies, undermining the institutions and values of democracy, ethical values and justice, and jeopardizing sustainable development and the rule of law.[88] In his Foreword to the Convention, Kofi Annan, the UN Secretary-General at the time, refers to corruption as an "insidious plague" that has a wide range of corrosive effects on societies.[89] He continues by asserting that:

> It undermines democracy and the rule of law, leads to violations of human rights, distorts markets, erodes the quality of life and allows organized crime, terrorism and other threats to human security to flourish. This evil phenomenon is found in all countries—big and small, rich and poor—but it is in the developing world that its effects are most destructive. Corruption hurts the poor disproportionately by diverting funds intended for development, undermining a government's ability to provide basic services, feeding inequality and injustice and discouraging foreign aid and investment. Corruption is a key element in economic underperformance and a major obstacle to poverty alleviation and development.[90]

In both ADCs and LDCs, corruption is a pervasive problem. Not only are official decisions—for instance, the award of government contracts or the amount of tax due—bought and sold, but very often

---

86 Amartya Sen, *Poverty And Famines: An Essay On Entitlement And Deprivation* (1981); Jean Dreze and Amartya. Sen, *Hunger and Public Action* (1989); Partha Dasgupta, *An Inquiry Into The Well-Being and Destitution* (1995).

87 United Nations *Convention Against Corruption*, Merida, 9 December 2003, 43 ILM 37 (2004) [hereinafter Convention Against Corruption]. As of December 1, 2015, 178 parties have signed and ratified or otherwise acceded to the Convention: United Nations Office on Drugs and Crime, *United Nations Convention Against Corruption: Signature and Ratification Status as of 1 December 2015*, http://www.unodc.org/unodc/en/treaties/CAC/signatories.html.

88 *Id.* Preamble.

89 *Id.* Foreword.

90 *Id.*

citizens must pay for access to a public service or the exercise of a right, such as obtaining civil documents. The process of allocating political and administrative posts—particularly those with powers of decision over the export of natural resources or import licenses—is influenced by the gains that can be made from them. As these exchanges of privileges are reciprocated by political support or loyalty, the political foundations are cemented.[91] Corruption in turn can have a dramatic effect on a country's economy. It has been estimated, for example, that moving from a relatively "clean" government like that of Singapore to one as corrupt as Mexico's would have the same effect on foreign direct investment as an increase in the marginal corporate tax rate of 50 percent.[92]

A realistic attempt to remedy energy poverty should be alive to the serious problems posed by sovereignty, and it should try to overcome them. While there are limited ways of bypassing states where they are impediments to energy justice, the irremovable fact is that sovereignty is the basis of international law. Aid, assistance, or empowerment of the energy-poor cannot ignore national sovereignty. Under our present system of international law and governance, SD requires that developed countries play a dominant part in alleviating the condition of the EP. It also invokes the need for action by national governments. Justice requires both that assistance be given and that such assistance be properly administered. The failure of foreign aid has been debated, and better ways of granting assistance must be found. Justice also requires that national governments take on the task of addressing the EP. It is not possible to lay the blame on avaricious rich countries alone.

III. Interim Conclusions

The most important conclusions may be summarized at this point. First, the inability to access energy both causes poverty and disables impoverished people from developing. The connection between energy and poverty is fundamental to the discourse on sustainable development. Second, the plight of the energy-poor cannot be remedied by relying solely on the states within which they reside. The energy-poor have been glossed over by their identification only as national problems falling within the sovereign jurisdiction of the developing countries within which they reside. They are treated as problems of developing countries and not perceived as burdened societies calling for international action, sometimes independent of the countries in which they reside. It would be a giant step forward

---

[91] Irene Hors, *Fighting Corruption in the Developing Countries,* OECD Observer, April 2000.

[92] Shang Jin Wei, *How Taxing is Corruption on International Investors?,* LXXXII, THE REVIEW OF ECONOMICS AND STATISTICS, 1 (2000).

if civil society organizations could shake themselves from their preoccupation with climate change, to focus at least some attention on the real problems of energy poverty.

Third, allowing the EP to languish in their current state violates fundamental concepts of international justice and SD. These concepts are best justified by John Rawls, who outlined the duty of developed peoples "to assist burdened societies."[93] Rawls' concepts of duty and distributive justice, though not explicitly articulated, are embodied more generally in the principles of SD and more specifically in the MDGs, which can only be achieved if the need for energy is satisfied. The predominance of GPGs in the SDGs mark a retreat from addressing energy poverty.

Fourth, access to energy through electricity remains the ultimate objective. Unfortunately, it is a cost-prohibitive and protracted remedy that will take decades to implement, and does not offer any interim solutions. During the long wait for electricity, large segments of the EP will remain energy-deprived for many decades unless they are offered intermediate solutions based on ASETs. Employing ASETs can begin the journey out of energy poverty.

Finally, there is no doubt that the UN's recent recognition of the need for universal access to energy is potentially a great step forward because it acknowledges the connection between energy and poverty and charts a new path for SD. UN recognition of the need for cookstoves indicates that it may be open to more immediately effective forms of development based on ASETs. Such a recognition will offer a new space for formulating appropriate sustainable energy solutions that address the needs of the energy-poor by providing timely, sustainable, and affordable ways to satisfy their energy needs.

---

[93] John Rawls, *The Law of Peoples*, *supra* Chapter 2, notes 59–72.

Chapter 5

NATIONAL LAWS ADDRESSING GLOBAL ENERGY POVERTY

MODEL LAWS ON COOKING[1]

I. Introduction

This chapter will canvass two premises of the concept of law. The first premise is that law, as a normative construct, can and should respond to social problems. Second, the law can respond to a problem only after it understands the nature of the problem and the challenges raised by it. The jurisprudential foundation will be first discussed, followed by the biophysical problem of indoor air pollution.

II. Jurisprudential Foundation

The jurisprudential thesis underlying the assertion that law should be used for societal problems solving is that law is an "instrument," "tool," "machine," or "engine" for serving or achieving social objectives. Law in this sense is being used to achieve practical aims.[2] Robert Summers, in discussing the use of the machinery of law to achieve socio-economic objectives, saw it as a particularly American form of legal theory spawned by theorists like Oliver Wendall Holmes, Roscoe Pound, John Dewey, John Chipman Gray, Karl Llewellyn, Walter Wheeler Cook, and Felix Cohen.[3] Summers coined the phrase "pragmatic instrumentalism" to describe how these theorists created a theory of adjudication focused on the role of judges in shaping and molding law to achieve social means or ends.[4] The pragmatic instrumentalists relied on courts as instruments or machinery for achieving their goals. Their attention was focused on what judges did when interpreting the written form of a legal text. They contended that judges engaged in interpreting a legal text to ascertain its true meaning cannot do so by a simple parsing of the plain words. Instead, judges should consider and construct their meaning in light of the context of the law as illustrated, for example, by the goals or objectives it was meant to achieve.

---

1 This chapter is based on and reproduces sections of Lakshaman Guruswamy, *Dissemination of Clean Cookstoves: Model Laws for Developing and Developed Countries*, 24 COLORADO NATURAL RESOURCES, ENERGY & ENVIRONMENTAL LAW REVIEW 319 (2013).

2 Robert S. Summers, *Instrumentalism and American Legal Theory* 20 (1982).

3 *Id.* at 11; *see generally id.* Chapters 2, 12.

4 Michael S. Moore, *Educating Oneself In Public: Critical Essays In Jurisprudence* 194 (2000).

In addition to the pragmatic instrumentalists who charted a new theory of adjudication, and "a distinctive type of legal theorizing"[5] In the United States, the use of law for social engineering could trace its jurisprudential lineage to the British philosopher, jurist, and social reformer Jeremy Bentham (1748–1832). Bentham, perhaps best known for his utilitarian philosophy, was also an English legal revolutionary who re-drew the contours of law. In doing so, he recreated a vastly expanded domain of law in a way that had not hitherto been done. He called for a complete, comprehensive, and integrated legislative re-envisioning of the existing system of law and government. Bentham expounded the necessity for a new "form" of law that laid the foundations of a reformed society, in which the "whole of the community's social system no less than the community's legal system was to be located analytically within the province of legislation."[6] Moreover, he explicated how to design, draft, implement, and generally use legislation to achieve the social objectives of the new kind of law he was calling for. The vast and theretofore shapeless socio-political expanse envisioned by him had to be legislatively mapped and populated, and become part of a great reformist enterprise based on a new concept of law.

One of the major problems he confronted was that such an expansive concept of law flew in the face of the reality of his day, as reflected in the existing corpus of law, received orthodoxy, and extant legal theory. Legal theory of his time envisioned a minimalist state. For example, William Blackstone, in his masterly Commentaries on the Laws of England, first published in 1766, provided a complete overview of English law.[7] Sections II and III of Blackstone's Introduction to the Commentaries on the Laws of England, "Of the Study, Nature and Extent of the Laws of England," offers an overview of the law in general. In this authoritative account of English law, Blackstone divides law into the unwritten common law and written or statutory law. According to Blackstone, "[s]tatutes are either declaratory of the common law or remedial of some defects therein."[8] What is evident is that Blackstone treats the common law as the primary source of law and confines legislation to either declaring the common law or remedying its defects. While the latter conclusion may be interpreted as resembling the expanded concept of legislation called for by Bentham, that is not the case. It is clear from Blackstone's account of written (or statutory) law that it

---

5 Summers, *supra* note 2, at 11.

6 David Lieberman, *The Province Of Legislation Determined: Legal Theory in Eighteenth Century Britain* 286 (1989).

7 William C. Sprague, *Blackstone's Commentaries Abridged* (9th ed. 1915), available at http://books.google.com/books?id=zDA0AQAAMAAJ&printsec=frontcover&source=gbs_ge_summary_r&cad=0#v=onepage&q&f=false.

8 *Id.* at 15.

occupied an adjectival or minor position below the foundational common or unwritten law. Common law was primarily, and nearly exclusively, concerned about the private rights of person and property.[9] By contrast, the statute book (statutory law), except in the area of criminal law, was almost bereft of public law such as administrative law, regulation, or governance which dominates the statutory law of the modern state. Blackstone did not favor the creation of a new and expanded realm of statutory law, and neither did Edmund Burke, who was pleased that "the laws reach but a very little," and vehemently disliked expanding its province.[10] Law, clearly, was not seen as an instrument of social engineering as understood in today's terminology.

In sharp contrast to Blackstonian orthodoxy, Bentham set his face to liberating existing law "from the trammels of authority and ancestor-wisdom on the field of law" and of modernizing the legal system through legislation.[11] Bentham expressed contempt for the common law and English judges, and scorned at the idea that the judiciary could transform law and society.[12] A distinguished English judge sums up Bentham's low opinion of judges and lawyers: "As he saw it, in order to enrich themselves, lawyers ensured that English civil justice was '. . . a system of exquisitely contrived chicanery which maximies delay and denial of justice.' "[13] In Bentham's view, the task of re-designing law was a task for the legislature, not the judges.

The following Model Laws are based on Bentham's jurisprudence. These Model Laws serve as blueprints for legislation that could be enacted by the legislatures of developed and developing countries. Legislatures enacting these Model Laws will be adopting problem-solving national legislative solutions that clearly fall within the compass of law envisioned by Bentham. For example, the Model Laws for developing countries are actually blueprints for the national dissemination of clean cookstoves. The Model Laws for developed

---

[9] *Id.* at 10.

[10] Edmund Burke, *Thoughts on the Cause of the Present Discontents*: *The Two Speeches on America*, *in Select Works Of Edmund Burke,* 69, 99 (E. J. Payne ed., Liberty Fund 1999) (1770) available at http://files.libertyfund.org/files/796/0005.01_Bk.pdf.

[11] *See generally* Jeremy Bentham, *A Comment On The Commentaries and A Fragment on Government* 424 n.1 (J. H. Burns & H. L. A. Hart eds., Athlone Press 1977) (1776).

[12] Jeremy Bentham, *An Introduction To The Principles Of Morals and Legislation* (J. H. Burns & H. L. A. Hart eds., Oxford Univ. Press 1996) (1789); Jeremy Bentham, *Of Laws In General* (H. L. A. Hart, ed., Athlone Press 1970).

[13] Lord Neuberger of Absbury, *Swindlers (Including the Master of the Rolls?) Not Wanted: Bentham and Justice,* Bentham Lecture 2011 (March 2, 2011) (emphasis in original), available at http://www.ucl.ac.uk/laws/alumni/presidents/docs/neuberger_11.pdf.

countries provide a blueprint to legislate support for combating these issues through the common but differentiated responsibility for sustainable development accepted by developed countries.

Nations adopting these Model Laws, or variations of them, will be using the machinery of law to achieve the compelling social objectives of combating indoor air pollution, global warming, and gender inequality. Indoor air pollution is a global problem that could be addressed within the broad global enterprise of law. While law encompasses public international, as well as national, laws, it is proposed that Model Laws can be adopted by municipal or national legislatures, as contrasted to treaties or other international law modalities. The main reasons for adopting such a course require explanation.

Public international law is the law that creates and governs inter-state (or country) relationships, primarily through contracts called treaties, conventions, and protocols. It is possible for the 192 countries in the world to come together as a lawmaking assembly with a goal of negotiating and drafting a global treaty to address issues associated with unsafe cooking. Under the international law approach, it is also possible for countries to enter into regional multilateral treaties restricted to regions identified by trade or geo-politics. It is also possible for one country to enter into a bilateral agreement with another country. Given the ubiquitous nature of indoor air pollution and the need for both developed and developing country responses, it may be reasonable to conclude that the facts could call for a multilateral global treaty.

However, it is becoming evident that large international treaties or conventions of this kind are exceptionally difficult to negotiate, and even more resistant to implementation and enforcement. Despite tremendous diplomatic- and media-backing, the faltering negotiation of a treaty to replace the Kyoto Protocol, culminating in the legally ambiguous Paris Agreement, of 2015,[14] is strong evidence of this retreat from large multilateral treaties. Additionally, the search for consensus between different legal traditions is not an easy enterprise. Some commentators struck by the ethnic, religious, and linguistic differences between countries, claim that international treaties and conventions are drafted and serve as multi-cultural compromises between different schemes of law. Consequently, they could be perceived as possessing less compliance pull than the

[14] Paris Agreement, http://unfccc.int/resource/docs/2015/cop21/eng/l09.pdf (visited Mar. 6, 2016). The US claimed during the negotiating process that the Paris Agreement should not be considered a treaty requiring Senate approval under US law.

individual legal systems found in each country.[15] Furthermore, if the United Nations Framework Convention on Climate Change (UNFCCC) is an example, it takes over a decade to advance from a framework agreement setting out the agenda to the negotiation of protocols requiring collective and specified action.[16]

Municipal or domestic legal systems, as distinct from international law, offer another way of providing legal answers to a global problem. The numerous developing countries actually afflicted by these issues could create legal remedies through domestic or municipal laws. Many of these countries have adopted analogous laws dealing with differing aspects of air and water pollution and hazardous wastes enacted by national legislatures. The present Model Laws seek to expand the ambit of national pollution and health legislation by providing blueprint legislation on indoor pollution that could be adapted and incorporated into domestic law.

A model law is a legislative text that is recommended to states for enactment as part of their national or state law, or tribal governance regimes. The United Nations Commission on International Trade Law describes Model Laws as "appropriate" vehicles for modernization and harmonization of national laws because they give States the opportunity, unlike an international treaty, to make adjustments to the text to accommodate local requirements. The Commission further states that this flexibility makes a model law "potentially easier to negotiate," though it emphasizes that once negotiated states are encouraged to change as little text as possible in adopting Model Laws.[17]

At a fundamental level, Model Laws use national legislation to generate private and public action to combat indoor air pollution. For example, the model law uses a needs assessment to find out what people want and need; encourage different civil society entities, from entrepreneurs and business entities to non-governmental organizations (NGOs), to invest and trade in the fabrication, sale, and servicing of cookstoves; ensure that standards are set and enforced; and solicit international aid and assistance, while establishing a systematic use of monitoring that will ensure that standards are actually being met.

---

[15] J.S. Hobhouse, *International Conventions and Commercial Law: The Pursuit of Uniformity*, 106 LAW Q. REV. 530, 533 (1990).

[16] Lakshman Guruswamy, *International Environmental Law* 215 (4th ed. 2012).

[17] U.N. Comm'n on Int'l Trade Law, *A Guide To UNICITRAl: Basic Facts About The United Nations Commission On International Trade Law* 14–15 (2013), available at http://www.uncitral.org/pdf/english/texts/general/12–57491–Guide-to-UNCITRAL-e.pdf.

III. The Problem of Indoor Air Pollution & the Legal Response

The model law responds to specific problems of indoor air pollution, and in order to do so successfully it needs to understand the nature of the problem it confronts. The problem we are examining, is the phenomenon of indoor air pollution caused by using biomass for cooking. The deadly impacts of indoor air pollution caused by biomass have been described in Chapter 4, and will not be repeated.

We need new laws because existing law and administration is either nonexistent or unable to address this challenge. In creating new laws, it behooves us to understand that law is an existing, established social mechanism grounded in reality, and that it must command the acquiescence of the peoples it governs. The new law is not an idealistic and aspirational code of conduct, removed from social reality and actual human behavior. It tries to change behavior, but should not engage in flights of idealistic fancy.

A good law must satisfy some basic criteria. To begin, the law should be based upon a correct identification and diagnosis of the problem or issue that it purports to address.[18] The Model Laws published herein present sets of Findings, which help in meeting the criteria of correct diagnosis.

Next, following the correct diagnosis, laws "should embody prescriptions aimed at the core of the problem, and deal with the sources of the malady."[19] They should accurately target the sources, and the substantial remedies they prescribe should include methods of implementation and compliance. Where behavioral changes are necessary, the law should be directed toward eliciting them. As Bentham has pointed out, prescriptions are only good if they are actually carried out. In order to secure the implementation of its prescriptions, legislation should set up concrete institutions, whether governmental or private, and contain details where necessary as to how the law should be administered. In the Model Laws published herein, we have tried to institute some of these social mechanisms.

Another criterion is that the remedies and methods employed by a law should have a demonstrably beneficial impact on the problem and help move the country or international community toward the practical attainment of its goals and objectives.[20] The extent of its beneficial impact will depend on the degree to which a

---

[18] This Subpart relies upon and re-produces parts of Lakshman Guruswamy, *Judging Treaties*, 101 AM. SOC'Y INT'L L. PROC. 175, 176 (2007).

[19] *Id.*

[20] *Id.* at 175–176.

law that may contain an accurate diagnosis and good prescriptions actually changes behavior and benefits people. Consequently, the impact of a law will depend on the nature of its goals or objectives, its methods, and the extent to which it succeeds in changing behavior That is why the Model Laws for developing countries require extensive and continuous monitoring, not just of cookstoves but also of human health and behavior.

The Model Laws are accompanied by commentaries or "guides to enactment" setting forth explanatory information to assist governments and legislators in using the text. These commentaries or guides include, for example, information that would assist states in considering what, if any, provisions of the model law might have to be changed to take into account particular national circumstances. The commentaries also include relevant discussions from the working and drafting groups and matters not addressed in the text of the model law that may nevertheless be relevant to the subject matter of the model law.

Adoption of the Model Laws by a significant number of countries will draw national and international attention to the problems caused by the burning of biomass for cooking ng and constitute an effective and much needed legal response to these problems.

IV. Model Law on Cookstoves for Developing Countries

A BILL to promote the development and deployment of clean cookstoves to save lives, improve livelihoods, empower women, and combat global warming by creating a thriving global market for clean, affordable, and efficient household cooking solutions, and for other purposes.

Be it enacted by the [legislative organ] of the [developed country] assembled.

Short Title

This Act may be cited as the ***Development and Dissemination of Clean Cookstoves*: Act of [year].**

Effective Date. This Act becomes effective on [date].

§ 1. Findings

a [Name of country] is a member of the community of nations that has accepted well-recognized principles of international law and policy establishing the right of developing countries to sustainable development.

b [Name of country] seeks to support sustainable development pertaining to energy poverty and access to safe and sustainable cooking technologies through this Act.

c According to the World Health Organization, approximately 3 billion people—nearly half of the world's population—cook their food over open fires or with inefficient, polluting, and unsafe cookstoves that use firewood, dung, or coal as fuel.

d Nearly 4.2 million people each year die prematurely from illnesses attributable to indoor air pollution resulting from inefficient, unsafe cookstoves. Indoor air pollution accounts for more deaths yearly than malaria, tuberculosis, or human immunodeficiency virus infection/acquired immunodeficiency syndrome (HIV/AIDS).

e [N, number of people] in [name of country] cook their food over open fires or with inefficient, polluting, and unsafe cookstoves that use firewood, dung, or coal as fuel.

f It is estimated that smoke from cooking accounts for nearly [N, number] deaths annually in [name of country], which is more than the deaths from malaria, tuberculosis, or human immunodeficiency virus infection/acquired immunodeficiency syndrome (HIV/AIDS). [N, number] are sickened by the toxic smoke and [N, number] suffer burns annually from open fires or unsafe cookstoves. Smoke from these traditional cookstoves and open fires is associated with a number of chronic and acute diseases, including respiratory illnesses, such as pneumonia, heart disease, and cancer. Women and young children are affected disproportionately.

g Women and children disproportionately shoulder the burden of collecting and managing biomass fuel for cooking. As nearby fuel supplies dwindle, women are forced to go farther to find fuel to cook their families' meals. In some regions, women and girls risk rape and other forms of gender-based violence during the up to 20 hours per week they spend away from their communities gathering firewood.

h Recent studies show that black carbon created by biomass cookstoves significantly contributes to global warming and climate change. Black carbon emissions from residential cookstoves in developing countries account for an estimated 21 percent of the total global carbon inventory and mitigation of black carbon is a cost-effective way of addressing global warming.

i Clean cookstoves positively impact the quality of life and the environment by:

i Freeing women and children to engage in educational and economic endeavors;

ii Promoting gender equality and women's empowerment;

iii Improving child and maternal health and safety;

iv Advancing environmental stability by reducing reliance on biomass; and

v Reducing contributions to global climate change.

§ 2. Policy

The [named Legislative Assembly] hereby declares it is the national policy of [name of country] to:

a Appropriate financial resources towards the research and development of the most appropriate and sustainable energy technologies for improved cookstoves that advance the objectives of this Act in [name of country];

b Encourage the growth of a domestic cookstove manufacturing industry by supporting entrepreneurs through tax incentives, loans, and micro- and other forms of financing that advance the objectives of this Act;

c Standardize, test, and certify all cookstoves based on ambient and durability standards;

d Distribute cookstoves in a manner that emphasizes accessibility while encouraging the recipient to contribute to the cost in currency, exchange, and/or sweat equity;

e Encourage community participation in financing, manufacturing, distributing, and promoting the objectives of this Act;

f Seek the assistance, expertise, guidance, and experience of non-governmental organizations (NGOs) and faith groups in all aspects of the implementation of the Act;

g Promote awareness and education about indoor air pollution;

h Promote the involvement of cookstove users, *inter alia*, in the research, design, development, manufacturing, distribution, monitoring, maintenance, evaluation, and marketing of cookstoves; and

i Conduct training on use and maintenance to cookstove users and community members.

§ 3. Definitions

For the purposes of this Act:

a “Administrator” means the Administrator of the Cookstoves for the Reduction of Energy Poverty Agency (CREPA).

b “Agency” means the CREPA.

c “Cookstove” refers to a cookstove that:

i Employs appropriate sustainable energy technologies; and

ii Has been prototypically demonstrated, tested, and certified as meeting the emission and durability standards set out in Section 4.

d “Certification” or “certified” refers to certification by an entity or organization authorized by the CREPA.

e “Court” means a court duly designated by the Adminstrator of CREPA.

f “Local conditions” means the holistic assessment of economic factors (ability to pay), cultural factors (willingness to change cooking patterns and behavior), and social factors (who the primary decision-maker in the household is, who is affected most by indoor air pollution, and who the primary social agents in the community are).

g “Organization” means an entity other than a governmental body, which was established or organized for any purpose relevant to this Act. This term refers to, inter alia, a corporation, company, guild, association, partnership, NGO, faith-based organization, trust, or trade union.

h “Endangerment” means the exposure, whether consented, voluntary, knowing, or without consent and involuntary, of individuals to conditions harmful to their physical health or the misrepresentation that certain harmful effects will in fact be reduced or removed by the actors’ conduct.

i “Micro-financing” refers to loans which are granted for design, production, marketing, distribution, sale, maintenance, and repair of cookstoves.

j “Sweat equity” refers to the labor, skill, goods, or community services offered by recipients, in part or in full, for cookstoves. Sweat equity shall be transferable among households. The following activities shall qualify as sweat equity under this Act:

i Labor provided in building or retrofitting cookstoves;

ii Transportation of materials for new or retrofitted cookstoves; and iii Participation in public education and community outreach.

§ 4. National Minimum Standards and Certifications

a Indoor Ambient Air Quality Standards

The term "indoor ambient air quality standards" means airborne pollution measurements that do not exceed the following:

i For particulate matter of 10 µm (PM_{10})—

(1) A 24-hour mean of 50 µg/m^3; or

(2) An annual mean of 20 µg/m^3.

ii For particulate matter of 2.5 µm ($PM_{2.5}$)—

(1) A 24-hour mean of 25 µg/m^3; or

(2) An annual mean of 10 µg/m^3.

iii For carbon monoxide (CO)—

(1) 100 mg/m^3 during any 15-minute period and not more than 1 time per day;

(2) 35 mg/m^3 during any 1-hour period and not more than 1 time per day;

(3) An 8-hour mean of 10 mg/m^3; or

(4) A 24-hour mean of 7 mg/m^3.

iv For nitrogen dioxide (NO_2)—

(1) A 1-hour mean of 200 µg/m^3; or

(2) An annual mean of 40 µg/ m^3.

b Interim Standards

The Administrator, acting upon reasonable grounds, may determine that the standards in Subsection (a) above cannot be achieved, and s/he may create interim standards that improve existing air quality, even if they are unable to meet the standards in Subsection (a). Such interim standards may be in force for 2 years, provided they are no longer in force 5 years after the coming into force of this Act.

c Durability Standards

The Administrator shall establish minimum durability standards based on needs and conditions of the country, taking into account standards stipulated by the Global Alliance for Clean Cookstoves when available.

d Testing and Certification

i All new cookstoves and/or component parts, including combustion chambers, chimneys, and cooking tops sold and/or marketed under this Act in [*name of country*] shall be tested and certified.

ii Testing and certification will be undertaken by approved private, public, or NGO owned and operated laboratories. Certification will attest that the products are capable of achieving the ambient air quality and durability standards referred to in this Section.

iii The Administrator will approve such laboratories based on relevant criteria to be determined after a public hearing, and shall publicly announce and publicize such standards.

§ 5. Administrative Discretion

The Administrator, acting on reasonable grounds, which shall be determined after public hearing, may postpone and/or phase in the implementation of this and other provisions of the Act for a period that shall not exceed 5 years.

§ 6. Establishment of Agency

The Cookstoves for Reduction of Energy Poverty Agency (CREPA) is hereby established to implement the provisions of this Act. The Administrator of the Agency shall administer this statute by, inter alia:

a Conducting Needs Assessments and Developing Specifications

Within 120 days of the adoption of this Act, the CREPA shall deploy [*N* (*the number of provinces or sub-national governments)*] provincial assessment officers (PAOs), one in each of the country's [N] provinces. PAOs shall, in collaboration with [*name of appropriate NGO*] and local health personnel, conduct needs assessments that will identify and investigate:

i Types of fuel and cookstoves being used in their respective region for cooking;

ii Local exposure to indoor air pollution from existing cookstoves;

iii The needs and receptivity of the population to new cookstoves;

iv Possible cultural or geographical barriers to the adoption of new cookstoves;

v Environmental degradation and challenges to community;

vi The infrastructure of the areas assessed;

vii The financial status of the communities;

viii The high density of children; and

ix Provincial targets for the combustion efficiency of cookstoves, based on the minimum standards in Section 4(a) and local conditions.

b Cookstove Selection

CREPA, in collaboration with the Minister of Energy and the PAOs, will select cookstoves that culturally and economically suits the [name of country] and the type of biomass fuel used.

c Targeted Installation of Cookstoves—Pilot Programs

The PAOs, under the direction of the Administrator of CREPA, shall carry out pilot programs in each province, which can be replicated in the rest of the country for the purpose of identifying the challenges of creating a stove selection process, and implementing a national cookstove program. The communities selected for the pilot programs by the Agency shall be ones in which:

i Biomass is the sole method for cooking;

ii Surveys and Needs Assessments, which are carried out by the PAOs, reveal that a large majority in the community want to participate in the Pilot Project;

iii There are between 100 and 500 homes;

iv Individuals are willing and able to provide sweat equity, currency, or exchange for the cookstoves; and

v The population is demographically representative of the [number of people in the country] people who rely on biomass for cooking and are representative of the varying types of biomass fuel used in the region.

d Completion and Review of the Pilot Projects

i At least two Pilot Projects shall be completed within targeted communities for each province or biomass fuel type region before the widespread installation of cookstoves among the rest of the province population. The data revealed by each Pilot Project and the lessons learned shall be analyzed and reviewed in a Pilot Project Report.

ii If there is different fuel use or cooking methods in the province, separate Pilot Projects will be constructed and implemented in the areas to accurately determine the best clean cookstove.

§ 7. Implementation and Administration

a Implementation

The Administrator shall use the information revealed by the Pilot Projects to inform and implement this Act by:

i Consulting and collaborating, with the Ministers of (1) Health and Human Wellness, (2) Energy, (3) Environment & Natural Resources, (4) Education, and (5) Industry & Commerce, and within reasonable time constraints, receive their inputs.

ii Encouraging public participation in the implementation of the provisions of this Act, by incorporating:

1 Notice and comment prior to the adoption of any major rules implementing the provisions of this Act, as governed by the [name of country's administrative procedure act];

2 Open meetings whenever the CREPA has a quorum present for a meeting in which the CREPA discusses any regular business of the agency concerning this Act; and

3 A community liaison in all aspects of implementation of the Act.

iii Where appropriate, seeking international aid and assistance in the form of technological assistance and expertise for monitoring and evaluation from, inter alia, intergovernmental organizations, other states, NGOs, faith-based organizations, corporations, private individuals, and charitable trusts.

iv Establishing a nationwide program to train the citizenry on the design, production, marketing, distribution, sale, maintenance, and repair of cookstoves.

v Using innovation, appropriate sustainable technologies, and/or techniques that provide greater economic benefits, all at a limited cost to the end-user.

vi Utilizing technologies and organizational methods, which have been successfully tried, tested, and demonstrated by other developing countries.

vii Using sweat equity or exchange as a method for paying for the cookstoves.

viii Using comprehensive, holistic, cross-sectorial planning to capture the complexity of the cookstove initiative.

ix Seeking to establish in-country networks for the design, manufacture, marketing, and technological assistance of the cookstoves.

b Strategic 5-Year National Cookstove Plan (5-Year Plan)

After a widespread, open, and public consultation process, the CREPA shall draw up renewable strategic 5-Year Plans with annual targets and objectives that shall be publicly announced and publicized. The first Plan shall be completed within one year of the coming into operation of this Act. Once a 5-Year Plan has been completed, the CREPA shall issue annual reports that are announced and publicized on the actions taken pursuant to the 5-Year Plan and the extent to which the targets or objectives have or have not been met. The annual reports will be reviewed annually by the [*legislative organ*] of [*name of country*].

c Stimulate the Cookstoves Industry and Markets

The CREPA shall stimulate and encourage the creation of a robust domestic cookstove industry, by engaging, *inter alia*, in the following:

i Improving access to capital by providing tax incentives and loans and removing restrictions on foreign investment in the cookstove industry;

ii Establishing certification and standardization protocols for cookstove parts and equipment; and

iii Collaborating with the Ministry of Energy to disburse grants for research and development to qualified universities in [*name of country*], which are able to undertake research and development.

d Monitoring and Inspection

Through collaboration with PAOs, the Administrator shall, with immediate effect, begin the following activities towards implementation of this Act:

i *Assessment.* Quantitative monitoring of the ambient air quality of representative samples of existing homes before the installation of improved cookstoves.

ii *Post-Installation Air Quality Monitoring.* Quantitative monitoring of the ambient air quality of the homes referred to in Section 6(c) above after improved cookstoves are installed within the following time-frames:

- Phase 1—within 1 year of installation;
- Phase 2—within 18 months of installation;
- Phase 3—within 3 years of installation; and

- Annual monitoring once every year, thereafter.

iii *Use Monitoring.* Inspecting installed cookstoves to ensure they are being used and are working properly. iv *Reporting.* Submitting to Parliament a report (Administrators Report) on the findings of the monitoring and inspection efforts under this Section, 2 years after this Section comes into force and annually thereafter.

§ 8. Authorization and Appropriations

[*Appropriated amount (USD or national currency)*] shall be authorized and appropriated every year, beginning in 20[___], continuing for the next 5 years, and allocated as follows:

a [*Appropriated amount (USD or national currency)*] to the Administrator for the administrative costs of implementing this Act.

b [*Appropriated amount (USD or national currency)*] to a grant and loan mixed funding mechanism, which is administered by the CREPA and encourages entrepreneurship and creates new markets by stimulating the large-scale manufacture and distribution of improved cookstoves.

c No grant shall be made under this Section unless 75 percent of the products, materials, and supplies have been mined or manufactured in [*name of country*]. This Section shall not apply where the Administrator, after reasonable consideration of relevant factors, including cost, efficiency, availability, and international agreements, determines that it is in the public interest to waive this requirement, either generally or with regard to specific materials.

d [*Appropriated amount (USD or national currency)*] for NGOs, such as, but not restricted to [Appropriate NGO], if they can provide matching funds on a 1:4 ratio (match 1 USD provided in this Section with 4 USD of their own) for carrying out education and awareness campaigns and monitoring of indoor air pollution.

e [*Appropriated amount (USD or national currency)*] to the Ministry of Energy to administer a program for the research and development of appropriate cookstoves. The appropriated amount shall remain available until expended.

f [*Appropriated amount (USD or national currency)*] to the Ministry of Health on an established needs basis.

§ 9. Research and Development

The Minister of Energy is authorized to conduct, promote, coordinate, and accelerate research, development, studies, surveys, experiments, demonstration projects, and training related to:

a The development and application of cooking technologies that provide effective and efficient alternatives to open-fire biomass, including alternative fuels and efficient cookstoves that meet and exceed the minimum standards set out in Section 4 and which maximize the use of local materials; and

b Health and safety in the application of such technologies, methods, and means. c The Minister of Energy will actively solicit foreign aid, assistance, and collaboration in carrying out research and development from other governments, intergovernmental organizations, multinational corporations, NGOs, scientific bodies, and any other entities that will support objective scientific research and development.

d **Prioritization.** In conducting the activities authorized by this Section, the Minister of Energy may enter into contracts with and make grants to, qualified institutions, agencies, organizations, and persons. Priority shall be given to:

i The [*appropriate scientific or academic institution in country*];

ii Other public or private institutions that are scientifically equipped to conduct the required research; and

iii Other organizations that are equipped to create appropriate educational campaigns and workshops to engage communities and individuals.

e **Availability of Information to the Public.** Subject to the patent provisions of the [*name of country's patent act or other intellectual property law*], all discoveries, inventions, innovations, information, and data resulting from any research studies, surveys, experiments, assessments, or demonstration projects conducted or financed under this Section shall belong to the public domain and be available to the public for their use without charge.

§ 10. Education and Information

a The Ministry of Health shall be responsible for educating the public on the dangers of indoor air pollution. The Ministry of Health shall utilize existing health education channels to inform the public, including, but not limited to:

(1) rural and urban hospitals and clinics;

(2) school health awareness programs;

(3) churches and other places of worship;

(4) community leaders, including chiefs, faith leaders, and mid-wives; and

(5) mass media forums, including radio, television, and cellular phone messaging.

b The Minister of Health shall have final authority over all private programs for the dissemination of information to the public and shall exercise discretion in determining the appropriateness of the message communicated under programs governed by this Act.

c The Minister of Health shall approve the health-science aspect of marketing materials to ensure that only verifiable findings of Parliament are used to convey the nature of the problem.

§ 11. Public Health

The Minister of Health shall encourage early treatment of signs and symptoms of respiratory problems. To this end,

a Healthcare workers will report specific cases of respiratory illnesses, by creating individual records of patients and monitoring their treatment;

b Data on respiratory illnesses will be shared with the Administrator in accordance with the mandate of this Act under Section 10; and

c The Minister of Health will enlist the help of NGOs.

§ 12. Enforcement

a Civil Remedies

Non-Compliance Order. On the basis of information available to him/her, if the Administrator finds violations of this Act, s/he may issue a non-compliance notice to the identified party. Non-compliance orders may be issued by the Administrator for violations of this Act in accordance with [*name of country's administrative procedure act*]. In addition, the Administrator must:

i Issue a notice of the alleged violation to the offending party within 15 days of discovery of a violation;

ii Allow the offending party 10 days to rebut the evidence against him/her and submit to agency-inspected corrective measures; and iii Institute immediate suspension of activities that have or are reasonably expected to impose a grave health risk to the population.

b Citizen Enforcement

i Any citizen or resident of [*name of country*] may seek judicial remedies under this Section for violations of any mandatory provision of this Act. These citizen suits may be lodged in any District Court against any government agency, department, or private party that violates or fails to carry out any mandatory provisions of this Act. Prior to bringing an action, a citizen shall:

1 Give notice to the defendant agency, department, or private party about the alleged violation(s) of this Act; and

2 Allow a period of 2 months after receipt of notice to enable the defendant to rectify the alleged violation(s) of this Act before filing a lawsuit.

ii If the Plaintiff is successful, the court may order the defendant to comply with the Act and award damages. A successful litigant is entitled to recover full costs and the court shall include and order such costs in its judgment.

iii In the event an action is dismissed, the court may, in its discretion, order the citizen plaintiff to pay the defendant such costs as it deems reasonable and necessary.

c Criminal Penalties

i *Violation of Non-Compliance Order*. Any person who fails to comply within 3 months of receipt of a non-compliance order issued pursuant to Subsection (a) shall, after due inquiry by a District Court, be punished by a fine of not less than 250 USD [*or other typical fine in national currency*] nor more than 2,500 USD [*or other typical fine in national currency*] per day per violation, or by imprisonment for not more than 1 year, or by both.

ii *Negligent Misrepresentation*. Any person who negligently represents that cookstoves meet the minimum national standards of Section 4 or regional standards established pursuant to Section 4(a)(viii) shall be punished by a fine of 1,000 USD [*or other typical fine in national currency*] per cookstove sold under negligent misrepresentation.

iii *Knowing Endangerment*. Any person who knowingly endangers another person or community of persons by manufacturing, marketing and/or distributing cookstoves, and/or other cookstove parts that do not conform to the provisions of Section 4 (or regional standards established pursuant to Section 4(a)(viii)) shall be subject to a fine of not more than 25,000 USD or imprisonment of not more than 15 years. An organization shall be subject to a fine of not more than 100,000 USD.

V. Commentary: Model Law on Cookstoves for Developing Countries

Section-by-Section Analysis

Section 1: Findings

The model legislation provides a series of findings and lays the foundation for establishing the programs described in the following sections. The findings are based on generally and internationally available evidence.

Section 2: Policy

The policy articulated here is based on the premise that a solution to the problem of inefficient cookstoves must be comprehensive. It also involves public expenditures, as appropriated under this Act.

Section 3: Definitions

Many of these definitions simply explain terms and concepts in the model law. The adopting country will only use the definitions if the terms defined form part of the law being enacted by the adopting country.

Section 4: National Minimum Standards and Certification

Actual ambient air quality minimum standards under Section 4 will be country specific, based on what the adopting country determines is achievable. The World Health Organization (WHO) ambient air quality standards should serve as a guide/goal. In this context, it is important to emphasize the crucial importance of these standards. The ambient emission standards relating to indoor air pollution require improvement in air quality by reducing the emissions from cookstoves.

Section 4 also deals with certification. Product certification, undertaken by independent entities, is the process of certifying that a certain product has passed performance and quality assurance tests or qualification requirements and standards.

Section 5: Administrative Discretion

This Section grants discretion to the Administrator, after due procss and public inquiry, to adapt the standards and regulations to the compelling conditions of the country.

Section 6: Creating an Agency

The choices of whether to establish a new agency for the reduction of cookstove pollution or create a new cadre of provincial assessment officials clearly fall within the administrative governance of each adopting country. However, some of the other substantive goals set out in Section 6 are to be institutionalized as law.

Needs assessments are necessary to avoid a cookie-cutter approach to the promotion of cookstoves. Local needs assessments help to discover the local needs and conditions, and craft an area specific, bottom-up, rather than a topdown, cookstove program that addresses particular community needs.

Pilot programs are mini or scaled-down versions of a full-scale program. Pilot programs help to identify logistical problems, which might occur using proposed methods; estimate variability in outcomes; collect preliminary data; determine what resources (finance, staff) are needed for the full program; and assess the proposed programmatic techniques to uncover potential.

Section 7: Administration and Implementation

This Section refers to implementation by the Administrator of the new cookstove agency under Sections 6 and 7. The administration and implementation by the Ministers of Energy and Health are referred to in Sections 9, 10, and 11. As noted earlier, the adopting country does not need to create a new cookstove agency and could implement and administer this Act through its existing legal and administrative structures.

The Strategic Plan envisioned in Section 7(b) institutionalizes the need for the responsible agency to define its strategy or direction and make decisions on allocating its resources to pursue this strategy. In doing so, the strategic planning process should keep in mind the pivotal objective of encouraging the creation of markets for cookstoves and ensure that planning is an instrument for generating cookstove markets.

Section 8: Authorization and Appropriations

This Section deals with authorization and appropriations for three administrative/ governmental units: the new cookstove agency and the Departments of Energy and Health. The adopting country could change this to suit its own administrative structures.

What is critical is that the legislature authorizes and appropriates funds for the purposes referred to in Section 8, enabling the policy and purposes of the Act to be achieved.

The incorporation of NGOs into the administration and implementation of the Act is based on compelling evidence that NGOs and other non-governmental entities are in many cases more effective and efficient distributors of goods and services than government agencies. They are, thus, a resource that should be utilized.

The dangers of indoor air pollution are often unknown and cookstove programs should be premised on awareness and information. As a result, the public health dangers of indoor air pollution must systematically and continuously be publicized, hence the appropriation.

Section 9: Research and Development

The design and manufacture of cookstoves has attracted very little scientific funding. The developing world would be in a much better position to attract scientific attention and funding by showing its own commitment and resolve to address this problem.

Section 9 places the prime responsibility for research and development on the Ministry of Energy and emphasizes the importance of soliciting and attracting foreign funds and assistance. As in every other administrative allocation of duties, the adopting country is free to make its own arrangements, provided that the substantive importance of research and development is in fact institutionalized.

Section 10: Education and Information

This model law places primary responsibility on the Health Ministry to educate the public about the dangers of indoor air pollution and the availability of remedies like cookstoves. The adopting country can make its own administrative arrangements, provided it commits to promoting awareness and education.

Section 11: Public Health

This Section requires public health officials to be aware of the health impacts of indoor air pollution and that such conditions need to be treated. In doing so, Section 11 attempts to integrate the largely ignored health hazards of indoor air pollution with other more recognizable ailments and conditions.

Section 12: Enforcement

Judicial and administrative enforcement is a necessary facet of the broader implementation of the Act. While civil and criminal enforcement by public officials is a familiar feature of the laws of many developed countries, the citizen suit provisions may need some explanation in the context of developing countries.

In essence, a citizen suit is a form of private enforcement whereby the private litigant calls for enforcement against the official enforcers or government agencies. For a variety of reasons, government agencies are often unable or unwilling to enforce regulatory laws. When armed with citizen suit authority, private citizens are enabled to take over the enforcement of such laws, free of some of the bureaucratic and political constraints that can hobble government enforcers.

Any government that enacts this statute, seeking to address the problems of indoor air pollution, should not try to cover up the poor conduct of their agencies. Bringing questionable conduct into the light of judicial scrutiny will help governments meet the challenges they seek to address through this Act.

VI. Model Law on Cookstoves for Developed Countries

A BILL To promote the development and deployment of clean cookstoves to save lives, improve livelihoods, empower women, and combat global warming by creating a thriving global market for clean, affordable, and efficient household cooking solutions, and for other purposes.

Be it enacted by the [legislative organ] of the [developed country] assembled,

§ 1. Short Title

This Act may be cited as the "Clean Cookstoves Support Act of [year]."

§ 2. Findings

[*Legislative organ*] finds that:

1 [*Name of country*] is a member of the community of nations that has accepted well-recognized principles of international law and policy establishing—

A the right of developing countries to sustainable development; and

B the CBDR of [*name of country*] and other developed nations to institutionally, financially, and technologically support sustainable development among developing countries by alleviating energy poverty and providing access to safe and sustainable cooking technologies.

2 [*Name of country*] seeks to support sustainable development and carry out its CBDR pertaining to energy poverty and access to safe and sustainable cooking technologies through this Act.

3 According to the World Health Organization, approximately 3 billion people—nearly half of the world's population—cook their food over open fires or with inefficient, polluting, and unsafe cookstoves that use firewood, dung, or coal as fuel.

4 An estimated 4.2 million people each year die prematurely from illnesses attributable to indoor air pollution resulting from inefficient, unsafe cookstoves. Indoor air pollution accounts for more deaths yearly than malaria, tuberculosis, or human immunodeficiency virus infection/ acquired immunodeficiency syndrome (HIV/AIDS).

5 Particulate matter, heavy smoke, and carcinogens created by inefficient cookstoves and open fires can cause chronic and acute illnesses, such as pneumonia, heart disease, and lung cancer. There also is evidence linking indoor air pollution to low birth weight, tuberculosis, and other types of cancer. Women and children are disproportionally affected because they are the main household members regularly breathing cooking smoke.

6 Open fires and unsafe cookstoves lead to hundreds of thousands of burn deaths each year, and burn survivors often sustain permanent injuries ranging from debilitating scarring to loss of movement.

7 Open fires are extremely inefficient at converting energy from biomass, so the amount of biomass required as fuel for cooking can reach up to 2 tons per family each year. Collecting this amount of fuel is time consuming and environmental problems may result where demand for biomass exceeds the natural regrowth of resources.

8 Women and girls disproportionately shoulder the burden of collecting and managing biomass fuel for cooking. As nearby fuel supplies dwindle, women and girls are forced to travel farther to obtain fuel, increasing their risk of injuries from carrying heavy loads long distances and of sexual harassment and assault. Furthermore, women and girls may spend 20 or more hours a week collecting fuel, leaving them with less time to attend school, fulfill domestic responsibilities, earn money, engage in public activities, learn to read, acquire other skills, or simply rest.

9 Inefficient cookstoves contribute to global warming and environmental decline through deforestation and the release of

black carbon, methane, nitrous oxide, and carbon dioxide into the atmosphere. Although biomass is primarily a renewable energy source, harvesting of unsustainable levels of biomass can lead to pressure on natural resources and eventually cause deforestation. Black carbon, methane, and nitrous oxide, produced through incomplete biomass fuel combustion, not only are dangerous when inhaled, but also are principal agents of global warming. Black carbon warms the atmosphere by decreasing the reflectivity of the earth's surface and has a significant impact in areas close to ice and snow accumulations. Additionally, black carbon contributes to extensive brown haze that can affect temperature and precipitation.

10 The development and deployment of clean cookstoves is essential for achieving the United Nations Millennium Development Goals to reduce child mortality, improve maternal health, eradicate poverty, promote gender equality, and create environmental sustainability.

11 Clean cookstoves positively impact the quality of life and the environment by—

A freeing women and children to engage in educational and economic endeavors;

B promoting gender equality and women's empowerment;

C improving child and maternal health and safety;

D advancing environmental stability by reducing reliance on biomass; and

E reducing contributions to global climate change.

§ 3. Policy

It is the policy of the [*name of country*] to create programs and policies to—

1 encourage manufacturing industries for clean cookstoves in developing countries by supporting international partnerships and local entrepreneurs with financial, institutional, and technological assistance;

2 encourage the promotion, distribution, and maintenance of clean cookstoves for individuals in developing countries;

3 provide funding for research, development, and deployment of clean cookstoves and the necessary air quality monitoring systems for developing countries; and

4 support and disseminate research and monitoring of the adverse human health and environmental effects associated with the

black carbon and other pollutants emitted by inefficient cookstoves.

§ 4. Definitions

In this Act:

1 CLEAN COOKSTOVE.—The term "clean cookstove" means a cookstove that—

A employs appropriate sustainable energy technologies;

B has been prototypically demonstrated, tested, and certified as meeting—

i indoor ambient air quality standards; or

ii if a developing country determines that indoor ambient air quality standards cannot be achieved, the reasonable interim air quality standards established by the developing country that improve existing indoor ambient air quality; and

C meets minimum durability standards based on the needs and conditions of such developing country and its peoples, taking into account the available standards established by the Global Alliance for Clean Cookstoves.

2 INDOOR AMBIENT AIR QUALITY STANDARDS.—The term "indoor ambient air quality standards" means airborne pollution measurements that do not exceed the following:

A For particulate matter of 10 µm (PM_{10})—

i a 24-hour mean of 50 µg/m^3; or

ii an annual mean of 20 µg/m^3.

B For particulate matter of 2.5 µm ($PM_{2.5}$)—

i a 24-hour mean of 25 µg/m^3; or

ii an annual mean of 10 µg/m^3.

C For carbon monoxide (CO)—

i 100 mg/m^3 during any 15-minute period and not more than 1 time per day;

ii 35 mg/m^3 during any 1-hour period and not more than 1 time per day;

iii an 8-hour mean of 10 mg/m^3; or

iv a 24-hour mean of 7 mg/m^3.

D For nitrogen dioxide (NO_2)—

i a 1-hour mean of 200 µg/m3; or

ii an annual mean of 40 µg/m3.

§ 5. Clean Cookstove Manufacturing, Promotion, and Distribution

a IN GENERAL.—There is established within the [*ministry or agency for international aid*] a Clean Cookstove Manufacturing and Distribution Program.

b PURPOSE.—The purpose of the program established by subsection (a) is to provide international partnerships and local entrepreneurs with financial, institutional, and technological assistance to develop, manufacture, promote, distribute, and maintain clean cookstoves in developing countries.

c FUNDING.—

1 IN GENERAL.—The program established by subsection (a) shall be funded in the amount of $15,000,000 each year for 10 years.

2 CRITERIA.—The administrator of the program established by subsection (a) shall establish criteria for the use of funds provided by paragraph (1) to carry out the purpose of the program.

3 CONSULTATION.—The criteria established under paragraph (2) shall be developed in consultation with—

A governmental and community leaders in developing countries;

B non-governmental organizations working to promote clean cookstoves;

C [*other relevant ministries or agencies within the developed country*]; and

D the interested public.

4 NOTICE AND COMMENT.—The administrator of the program established by subsection (a) shall provide public notice and an opportunity for any interested government, business, organization, or individual to comment on any proposal to establish criteria under paragraph (2) or amendments thereto.

5 AVAILABILITY OF FUNDS.—The funding provided by paragraph (1) shall be available to any offices or programs within the [*appropriate agency or agencies within the ministry for international aid*] in accordance with—

A the criteria established under paragraph (2); and

B such other rules as are established by the [*minister or agency head*].

6 GRANTS AND OTHER AID.—The program established by subsection (a) may, in accordance with the criteria established under paragraph (2) and without the need for any matching or base funds, use up to 20 percent of the funding provided by paragraph (1) to provide grants, loans, or other methods of financial support to businesses and other non-governmental organizations working to develop, manufacture, promote, distribute, or maintain clean cookstoves in developing countries.

d MONITORING; REPORTING.—The administrator of the program established by subsection (a) shall—

1 monitor the effectiveness of the program; and

2 report every 5 years after the date of enactment of this Act to the [*appropriate developed country officials and entities*] and the public on the effectiveness of the activities supported by and carried out under the program.

e ACCOUNTING.—The administrator of the program established by subsection (a) shall account for the funds it receives and distributes. The accounting shall comply with generally accepted accounting principles and shall be made available to the [*appropriate developed country officials and entities*] and the public within 90 days of the end of each fiscal year.

§ 6. Applied Research and Development

a IN GENERAL.—There is established within the [*ministry or agency for applied energy research and design*] a Clean Cookstove Research, Development, and Demonstration Program.

b PURPOSE.—The purpose of the program established by subsection (a) is to enable and facilitate the research, development, testing, and demonstration of—

1 effective and efficient appropriate sustainable energy technologies that provide alternatives to the use of damaging biomass cooking;

2 alternative fuels; and

3 efficient and effective clean cookstoves.

c FUNDING.—

1 IN GENERAL.—The program established by subsection (a) shall be funded in the amount of $15,000,000 each year for 10 years.

2 CRITERIA.—The administrator of the program established by subsection (a) shall establish criteria for the use of funds provided by paragraph (1) to carry out the purpose of the program.

3 CONSULTATION.—The criteria established under paragraph (2) shall be developed in consultation with—

A domestic and international businesses, academic institutions, and non-profit institutions that are developing or are interested in the research, development, testing, or demonstration of clean cookstoves;

B [*other relevant ministries or agencies within the developed country*]; and

C the interested public.

4 NOTICE AND COMMENT.—The administrator of the program established by subsection (a) shall provide public notice and an opportunity for any interested government, business, organization, or individual to comment on any proposal to establish criteria under paragraph (2) or amendments thereto.

5 AVAILABILITY OF FUNDS.—The funding provided by paragraph (1) shall be available to any offices or programs within the [*ministry or agency for applied energy research and design*] in accordance with—

A the criteria established under paragraph (2); and

B such other rules as are established by the [*minister or agency head*].

6 GRANTS AND OTHER AID.—The administrator of the program established by subsection (a) may, in accordance with the criteria established under paragraph (2) and without the need for any matching or base funds, use up to 80 percent of the funding provided by paragraph (1) to provide grants, loans, or other methods of financial support to academic, business, and other non-governmental entities for research, development, testing, or demonstration of clean cookstoves.

d MONITORING; REPORTING.—The administrator of the program established by subsection (a) shall—

1 monitor the effectiveness of the program; and

2 report every 5 years after the date of enactment of this Act to the [*appropriate developed country officials and entities*] and the public on the effectiveness of the activities supported by and carried out under the program.

e ACCOUNTING.—The administrator of the program established by subsection (a) shall account for the funds it receives and distributes. The accounting shall comply with generally accepted accounting principles and shall be made available to the [*appropriate developed country officials and entities*] and the public within 90 days of the end of each fiscal year.

§ 7. Health and Environmental Research

a IN GENERAL.—There is established within the [*ministry or agency for health or environmental research*] a Clean Cookstove Health and Environmental Research Program.

b PURPOSE.—The purpose of the program established by subsection (a) is to—

1 conduct and support research and monitoring on the household, local, and global production of black carbon and other pollutants emitted by inefficient cookstoves;

2 conduct and support research and monitoring on the adverse human health and environmental effects associated with the black carbon and other pollutants emitted by inefficient cookstoves;

3 research and develop best practices and programs to reduce the adverse human health and environmental effects associated with black carbon and other pollutants through the use of clean cookstoves; and

4 inform governments, researchers, and the public of the research, monitoring, best practices, and programs developed under paragraphs (1) through (3).

c FUNDING.—

1 IN GENERAL.—The program established by subsection (a) shall be funded in the amount of $15,000,000 each year for 10 years.

2 CRITERIA.—The administrator of the program established by subsection (a) shall establish criteria for the use of funds to conduct the research, monitoring, and other activities described in subsection (b).

3 CONSULTATION. The criteria established under paragraph (2) shall be developed in consultation with—

A domestic and international businesses, academic institutions, and non-profit institutions that are interested in reducing the adverse health and environmental effects of inefficient cookstoves;

B domestic and international businesses, academic institutions, and non-profit institutions that are developing or are interested in the development of clean cookstoves;

C the [*other relevant ministries or agencies within the developed country*]; and

D the interested public.

4 NOTICE AND COMMENT.—The administrator of the program established by subsection (a) shall provide public notice and an opportunity for any interested government, business, organization, or individual to comment on any proposal to establish criteria under paragraph (2) or amendments thereto.

5 AVAILABILITY OF FUNDS.—The funding provided by paragraph (1) shall be available to any offices or programs within the [*ministry or agency for applied energy research and design*] in accordance with—

A the criteria established under paragraph (2); and

B such other rules as are established by the [*minister or agency head*].

6 GRANTS AND OTHER AID.—The administrator of the program established by subsection (a) may, in accordance with the criteria established under paragraph (2) and without the need for any matching or base funds, use up to 80 percent of the funding provided by paragraph (1) to provide grants, loans, or other methods of financial support to academic and other non-governmental entities for the health and environmental research, monitoring, and other activities described in subsection (b).

d MONITORING; REPORTING.—The administrator of the program established by subsection (a) shall—

1 monitor the effectiveness of the program; and

2 report every 5 years after the date of enactment of this Act to the [*appropriate developed country officials and entities*]

and the public on the effectiveness of the activities supported by and carried out under the program.

e ACCOUNTING.—The administrator of the program established by subsection (a) shall account for the funds it receives and distributes. The accounting shall comply with generally accepted accounting principles and shall be made available to the [*appropriate developed country officials and entities*] and the public within 90 days of the end of each fiscal year.

VII. Commentary: Model Law on Cookstoves for Developed Countries

Section-by-Section Analysis

Section 1: Short Title

Section 1 provides the short title for the model legislation.

Section 2: Findings

The model legislation provides a series of factual findings and lays the foundation for establishing the programs described in Sections 4 through 6.

Section 3: Policy

Section 3 describes the basic policies generated by the model law.

Section 4: Definitions

Section 4 provides important definitions for a "clean cookstove" and "indoor ambient air quality standards." Paragraph (1) includes three important components of the definition of a "clean cookstove." Of note, the definition references "appropriate/affordable sustainable energy technologies" ("ASETs"). ASETs "seek to bridge the gap between the capital-intensive advanced technologies of the developed world and the traditional subsistence technologies of the [energy poor]."[21] (In the context of cookstoves, ASETs include relatively simple technologies that satisfy basic cooking needs through sustainable engineering tailored to the particular needs of the intended community.[22]

Second, the definition emphasizes the importance of testing, demonstrating, and certifying cookstoves as meeting or exceeding indoor ambient air quality standards to ensure that the cookstoves developed countries support will achieve the intended benefits in developing countries. In some cases, achieving the specified

---

[21] Lakshman Guruswamy, *Energy Poverty*, 36 ANN. REV. ENVT. & RESOURCES 139, 141 (2011).

[22] *Id.* at 146.

standards may not be immediately achievable, so the definition recognizes the need to tailor the standards to best serve the developing country and its communities.

Third, the definition provides for the establishment of minimum durability standards. Experience has demonstrated that cookstove durability is a critical component for the long-term success of any clean cookstove deployment program.

Paragraph (2) defines "indoor ambient air quality standards," based on standards recommended by the World Health Organization.[23]

Section 5: Clean Cookstove Manufacture, Promotion, and Distribution

Section 5 establishes a program to support the development, manufacturing, promotion, and distribution of clean cookstoves in developing countries.

The model legislation recommends $15,000,000 annually to carry out the Clean Cookstove Manufacturing and Distribution Program. The adopting country may consider more or less funding; this amount provides a realistic example of the amount of funding that is needed to address the challenge, assuming that it is multiplied both by numerous developed countries and through the multi-program approach envisioned by this model law. In establishing criteria for the use of the funds, the model law calls for opening the process to the participation of all interested persons and entities, regardless of nationality.

The model law also calls for significant and transparent monitoring, reporting, and accounting. Such practices are important for establishing and maintaining an effective and efficient international aid program.

Section 6: Applied Research and Development

Section 6 establishes a program to support applied research and development of effective, efficient, and affordable clean cookstove technologies. There is a critical need for significant advancements in appropriate and sustainable clean cookstove technologies.

Unlike the program established under section 5, the program established by section 6 contemplates that a large portion of the research and development funding will be used to support non-governmental efforts. This recommendation is based on the recognition that the most common structure for carrying out such

---

[23] See *Air Quality and Health Fact Sheet No. 313*, WORLD HEALTH ORGANIZATION (September 2011), www.who.int/mediacentre/factsheets/fs313/en/index.html.

research and development efforts is through public-private partnerships, which often provide the most efficient and effective approach to the kind of program that is contemplated here.

Section 7: Health and Environmental Research

Section 7 establishes a program to (1) conduct and support research and monitoring on the pollutants that are produced by inefficient cookstoves; (2) 314 conduct and support research and monitoring on the adverse human health and environmental effects associated with such pollution; (3) research and develop best practices and programs to reduce those adverse human health and environmental effects; and (4) inform governments, researchers, and the public of the research, monitoring, best practices, and programs developed through the program established by this section.

Chapter 6

NATIONAL LAWS ADDRESSING GLOBAL ENERGY POVERTY

MODEL LAWS ON LIGHTING

I. Introduction

This Introduction will outline four foundational premises on which the Model Laws on lighting are built. The first is factual and deals with the unmet global need for lighting. Second, the jurisprudential foundations of Model Laws are delineated. The third explains the use of national legislation, and not public international law. Finally, the importance of executing and implementing the Model Laws is emphasized. Some of the matters discussed in this chapter are based on materials already canvassed in previous chapters. These previously examined areas will not be regurgitated. Instead this chapter will reference and rely on those earlier chapters.

II. Access to Energy for Lighting

We confront a global problem of energy poverty that besets the poorest peoples of the world. In stark contrast to the high-energy world, which depends on hydrocarbons or fossil fuels, nearly one-third of the world's population still lacks access to appropriate forms of energy adequate to meet their basic needs. Globally, around 2.8 billion people (the "Other Third" or "Energy Poor" [EP]) have little or no access to beneficial energy for: (a) cooking and heating; (b) illumination; (c) clean water; (d) sanitation; and (e) basic mechanical power essential for performing a variety of domestic and commercial functions.[1]

We have examined the phenomena of the EP in Chapter 4, and this section will only summarize main findings. More than 95 percent of the EP live either in sub-Saharan Africa or developing Asia, predominantly (84 percent) in rural areas. The EP cannot be classified within simplistic sociopolitical divisions of the world, that is, into developing and developed countries. This because there is a subset of nations within the developing world, called the least developed countries (LDCs). In 2014, the LDCs consisted of 48 countries and 880 million people located primarily in Africa and Asia. The LDCs have been officially identified by the UN as "least developed" in light of their low income, (three-year-average gross national income [GNI] per capita of less than $992), weak human

[1] Lakshman Guruswamy, *Global Energy Justice,* pp. 55–60, in *Energy and Poverty; The emerging frontiers* (Lakshman Guruswamy, ed. 2015).

assets (low nutrition, high mortality, lack of school enrollment, and high illiteracy), high economic vulnerability, exposure to natural shocks and disasters, prevalence of trade shocks, economic smallness, and economic remoteness. While 28 percent of people in developing countries lack access to electricity, the number in the LDCs is 79 percent.

These LDCs may be contrasted to another subset of developing countries, sometimes called newly industrialized countries (NICs) or advanced developing countries,(ADCs that have made tremendous economic strides in recent decades. This category includes the BRIC countries of Brazil, Russia, India, and China, South Africa, and the "Asian Tigers" of Taiwan, Singapore, Hong Kong, and South Korea. It also includes Thailand, Indonesia, Malaysia, and the Philippines, which are following the trajectory of exceptional economic growth and rapid industrialization of the Asian Tigers and have consequently been dubbed "Tiger Cub Economies."

However, access to clean energy or electricity is not uniform within NICs. The EP are a significant population in NICs like India, and to a lesser extent China. The EP in these countries suffer from a dearth of energy in their households, are denied the chance of making a living whether by way of agriculture, industry, or crafts and lack energy for their hospitals and schools serving their communities. The lack of beneficial energy prevents and negates development.

The EP also lack access to lighting, and these Model Laws on Lighting for Developing and Developed countries address this phenomenon. Lighting, or illumination, is essential to human progress and without it humans would be comparatively inactive about one-half of their lifetime. The scorching sun and withering temperatures in the LDCs prevent agricultural labor during the daytime and reduce productivity, and the absence of artificial lights severely impedes working at night. Without lighting, it is not possible for students to do homework after nightfall. The absence of lighting creates physical insecurity, particularly for women and children, while venturing out in the darkness, and almost entirely prevents commercial activity after dark. Almost 500 million people rely on kerosene for illumination. The hazards of kerosene, such as fires, explosions, and poisonings resulting from children ingesting it, are extensively documented, and children and women are disproportionately affected. The use of kerosene and candles is costly. Households often spend 10–25 percent of their income on kerosene Over $36 billion is spent on kerosene annually, $10 billion of which is spent in sub-Saharan Africa.

III. Jurisprudential Foundation

The jurisprudential thesis underlying the assertion that law should be used for societal problem—has been analyzed in the Introduction to the Model Laws on Cooking in Chapter 5 and will not be repeated.

IV. Using National Legislation

This chapter advocates the use of model national laws, rather than international laws, to address the lack of access to lighting. We have not considered it necessary to reproduce the common jurisprudential foundations for using law to solve societal problems, which that have been delineated in Chapter 5. But, the relevant facts pertaining to access to lighting are different to those dealing with indoor air pollution. Consequently, the case for using national legislation to address access to lighting will be re-stated.

This may also be necessary because chapter 6 is being offered as a self-contained chapter that could be used by decision makers to enact laws dealing with lighting. In making the case for using national legislation, dealing with access to lighting, there will be some unavoidable overlap between Chapter 5 and the present Chapter.

As we have seen in Chapter 5, Model Laws use national legislation to address a global problem. A model law is a legislative text that is recommended to states for enactment as part of their national or state law, or tribal governance regimes. At a fundamental level, Model Laws use legislation to generate private and public action. In doing so national legislation may restate fundamental principles of public international law. For example, the model law uses a needs assessment to find out what people want and need; encourage different civil society entities, from entrepreneurs and business entities to non-governmental organizations (NGOs), to invest and trade in the fabrication, sale, and servicing of lighting ensuring that standards are set and enforced; and solicit international aid and assistance, while establishing a systematic use of monitoring that will ensure that standards are actually being met.

On the other hand, international law is the law governing relations between legally sovereign co-equal states, and treaties are the primary way in which international law is created. Treaties are written agreements between two or more states, governed by international law, creating or restating legal rights and duties. The *Vienna Convention on the Law of Treaties*[2] deals comprehensively

---

[2] Vienna Convention on the Law of Treaties, 23 May 1969, 115 U.N.T.S. 331.

with questions concerning treaties which are also described as conventions, agreements, protocols, covenants, and pacts.

We will examine how one of the most important principles of law could be expressed and better implemented through national rather than international law. The principle highlighted is the right to sustainable development (SD). It is specifically embodied in international law, in the *UN Framework Convention on Climate* Change.[3]

The UNFCCC is the most important and extensively adopted energy treaty, having obtained 194 instruments of ratification. Article 3(4) of the UNFCCC states that the Parties have a right to and should promote SD, and that economic development is essential for adopting measures to address climate change, while Article 3(2) affirms the principle of common but differentiated responsibility (CBDR).

As we have seen in Chapter 4, the UNFCCC coalesced with another widely accepted treaty, the *Convention on Biological Diversity* (CBD)[4] by forcefully and unequivocally expressing the developmental priority of SD. Article 4(7) of the UNFCCC and Article 20(4) of the CBD reaffirm in unison that parties "will take fully into account that economic and social development and poverty eradication are the first and overriding priorities of the developing country Parties." Specifically, therefore, energy poverty can only be addressed within a framework of distributive justice, as part of the overall right to economic and social development established by the foundational norm of SD, so that full consideration can be given to the special circumstances of developing countries. Parties are required to protect the climate system on the basis of equity and in accordance with their common but differentiated responsibilities and respective capacities. The principle of common but differentiated responsibility, which is found in Principle 7 of the *Rio Declaration on Environment and Development*[5] is conclusively embodied in Articles 3(1) and 4(1) of UNFCCC, and affirms the responsibility of the developed country parties to take the lead in combating climate change and the adverse effects thereof (UN General Assembly 1992).

SD and CBDR applies to access to energy for the EP, and the question arises whether these principles could be better implemented through international or national laws. At the level of international law, it is possible for the 192 countries in the world to come together

---

[3] United Nations Framework Convention on Climate Change, June 9, 1992, 31, I.L.M. 849 (1992). *Supra* Chapter 3 note 9.

[4] Convention on Biological Diversity, 5 June 1992, 31 I.L.M. 818 (1992).

[5] Rio Declaration on Environment and Development, 13 June 1992, 31 I.L.M. 874 (1992).

as a lawmaking assembly with a goal of negotiating and drafting a global treaty to address issues associated with lack of lighting. Under the international law approach, it is also possible for countries to enter into regional multilateral treaties restricted to regions identified by trade or geopolitics. It is also possible for one country to enter into a bilateral agreement with another country. Given the ubiquitous nature of the lack of lighting, and the need for both developed and developing country responses, it may be reasonable to conclude that the situation calls for a multilateral global treaty.

However, it is becoming evident that large international treaties or conventions of this kind are exceptionally difficult to negotiate and even more resistant to implementation and enforcement. Despite tremendous diplomatic- and media-backing, the faltering negotiation of a treaty to replace the Kyoto Protocol is strong evidence of this retreat from large multilateral treaties. In fact, the Paris Agreement under the United Nations Convention on Climate Change (2015), which emerged from this negotiation, is based on nationally determined contributions that will be implemented through domestic measures. It employs national legislation, rather than a treaty provision, to create legally binding obligations.[6]

Additionally, the search for consensus between different legal traditions is not an easy enterprise. Some commentators claim that international treaties and conventions are drafted as multicultural compromises between different schemes of law. Consequently, they could be perceived as possessing less merit than the individual legal systems from which they have been derived. Furthermore, UNFCCC is an example, that it takes over a decade to advance from a framework agreement setting out the agenda to the negotiation of protocols requiring collective and specified action.

Legal answers to a global problem could also be viewed through the lens of domestic or municipal legal systems. The numerous developing countries actually afflicted by lighting issues could respond through domestic or municipal laws. Many of these countries have other laws dealing with differing aspects of pollution and hazardous waste. These laws are enacted by national legislatures, and the present Model Laws seek to expand the ambit of national pollution and health legislation by providing blueprint legislation on lighting that could be adapted and incorporated into domestic law.

The Model Laws creating national legislation assumes that the lack of lighting is a global and not just a national challenge. Therefore, it is important that the task of providing access to lighting

---

[6] The Paris Agreement under the United Nations Framework Convention on Climate Change, 12th Dec. 2015. http://unfccc.int/resource/docs/2015/cop21/eng/l09.pdf.

be acknowledged and undertaken by the community of nations consisting of developed and developing nations in which the energy poor live. The Model Laws function within this global compass by creating different Model Laws for developed and developing countries. The two species of law constitute contrasting sides of the coin of access to energy, where one remains indivisible from the other. It is important that developing countries accept their common responsibility through their Model Laws. It is crucial, however, that developed countries undertake their common but differentiated responsibility by bearing their primary moral and legal responsibility for alleviating energy poverty.

Consequently, Model Laws, serve as the functional equivalent of a hypothetical treaty on energy poverty in which both developed and developing country parties agree to address the issue of lighting. Such a hypothetical treaty will contain provisions uniformly binding on all parties be they developing or developed countries. Admittedly, the Model Laws being enacted by developing and developed countries might not contain identical or uniform language, and to that extent, will not bind parties like the common uniform contractual provisions of a treaty. But the laws being enacted nationally must remain faithful to the core elements of the model law if they are to be treated and counted as part of the model law enterprise. By enacting national legislation adopting the core elements of the model law, the nations of the world will each be creating a stick that will form part of the collective bundle of laws expressing rights and duties addressing global energy poverty.

National laws are the primary laws of the land, and call to be implemented according to their terms. By contrast, treaties typically are not self-executing,[7] and treaty implementation requires another layer of action. The obligations contained in a treaty need to be incorporated into the national law and administration of a country, through implementing or enabling legislation or regulation. This process of implementation can cause problems and delays as it involves invoking and using a new machinery of implementation not contained in the treaty. National laws based on Model Laws are not confronted by this barrier. National laws are the law of the land that is binding and enforceable.

[7] A self-executing treaty is a treaty that becomes judicially enforceable upon ratification. As opposed to a non-self-executing treaty, which becomes judicially enforceable through the implementation of legislation. A treaty could be identified as either self-executing or non-self-executing by looking to various indicators, including the language of the treaty, and the extent to which it falls within the exclusive powers of the national legislature. *Self-Executing Treaty, Legal Information Institute, Cornell University.* [https://www.law.cornell.edu/wex/self_executing_treatyhttps://www.law.cornell.edu/wex/self_executing_treaty].

Nations adopting these Model Laws, or variations of them incorporating the core principles of the Model Laws, will be using the machinery of law to achieve the compelling social objectives of access to lighting, and also combating indoor air pollution, global warming, and gender inequality. The Model Laws can be adopted by municipal or national legislatures.

We need new laws because existing law and administration is either nonexistent or unable to address this challenge. In creating new laws, it behooves us to understand that law is an existing, established social mechanism grounded in reality, and that it must command the acquiescence of the peoples it governs. It is not an idealistic and aspirational code of conduct, removed from social reality and actual human behavior. It tries to change behavior, but should not engage in flights of idealistic fancy. A good law must satisfy some basic criteria. These criteria have been discussed in Chapter 5.

The Model Laws are accompanied by commentaries or "guides to enactment" setting forth explanatory information to assist governments and legislators in using the text. The guides include, for example, information that would assist states in considering what, if any, provisions of the model law might have to be changed to take into account particular national circumstances. The commentaries also include relevant discussions not addressed in the text of the model law that may nevertheless be relevant to the subject matter of the model law.

Adoption of the Model Laws by a significant number of countries will draw national and international attention to the problems caused by lack of access to lighting, the harms caused by use of kerosene for lighting, and constitute an effective and much needed legal response to these problems.

V. Implementation and Execution

Recognizing the problems of energy poverty and enacting Model Laws as a method of addressing this problem, would be incomplete without methods of implementing such laws. Bentham's conception of the domain of law explains why implementation is an integral part of the law. He argued that "law" does not refer to an enacted single law but is part of a complete body of law, that forms a circle round the whole extent of jurisprudence.[8] He concluded that " . . . A body of laws is a vast and complicated piece of mechanism of which no part

[8] Manuscript of Jeremy Bentham cited by Lieberman, *supra* note 6, Chapter 5.

can be fully explained without the rest."[9] It was necessary in his view for implementing methods to ensure that the goals and objectives of a remedial statute were realized.

Bentham goes on to explain why the enactment of the primary or principal legislation which embodies the will of the legislator is incomplete " . . . The will of the legislator concerning the matter in question has indeed been declared, and the punishment has been threatened . . . but of the means of carrying such threats into execution, nothing of this sort has hath yet been made to appear."[10] This required another "subsidiary" law addressed to those executing the law.[11]

The importance of execution anticipated by the development of the modern administrative state cannot be overemphasized. Bentham's Constitutional Code sketched the organization and managing of a centralized and hierarchical officialdom with a government of thirteen ministries including health, finance, trade, preventive service or police, and indigent relief.[12] In the view of one commentator, this detailed scheme looks forward to Weber's work on bureaucracy and led to the building piecemeal of an administrative machine of great complexity. It resulted in the formation of an effective police force for London (1829), the rigorous and systematic application of the poor law (1834), and the creation of authorities for the enforcement of laws to promote public health in the 1840s.[13]

The manner and methods of implementation and enforcement of the Model Laws on Lighting for Developing and Developed Countries is written into and forms part of the statute itself. It should be noted at the outset that statutes do not contain footnotes substantiating the conclusions they reach. Consequently, each model law contains commentaries that explain the rationale and provide substantiation and backing for the various sections of the statute. These commentaries may contain materials that might otherwise be found in footnotes.

A brief delineation of the anatomy or architecture of the two Model Laws gives us a window into how they address the need for

---

9 Jeremy Bentham, *An Introduction to the Principles of Morals and Legislation,* 299 fn. b2, (J.H. Burns, & H.L.A Hart eds., (1996) (1789).

10 *Id.* 137.

11 *Id.* 139–140.

12 *The Works of Jeremy Bentham, IX,* 62, 121, 204, 226, 229 and 428–53, John Bowring ed. (1838–1843).

13 C.P. Ilbert, *Legislative Methods and Forms,* pp.212 and 213 (1901). See also: D. Roberts, *Victorian Origins of the British Welfare State* (1960); H. Parris, *Constitutional Bureaucracy* (1960); F.M.G.Wilson, *Ministers and Boards: Some Aspects of Administrative Development since 1832,* 32 PUBLIC ADMINISTRATION 43 (1954).

lighting. The Model Law for Developing and Developed Countries contain different features but some are common. They both contain Sections on Findings that summarize the facts surrounding the absence of access to lighting. Another common set of Sections deal with Policy, stating the policies of the governments in dealing with this issue, and the third covers Definitions.

The other substantive sections of the Model Laws of developing and developed countries differ from one another. The Model Law on Developing Countries deals with the issues germane to developing countries, while the Model Law on Developed Countries deals with the matters relevant and applicable to developed countries.

The Developing country law has sections dealing with national minimum quality and performance standards along with testing and certification of lights. The law creates administrative agencies with discretion to change some of the specifics and extend deadlines after proper inquiry. The administrative agency is charged *inter alia* with conducting needs assessments and carrying out pilot programs as well as with implementation in general. This includes collaboration with other agencies and bottom up peoples' input, and solicitation of international assistance for technological and commercial assistance. The law provides for the creation of a strategic five-year lighting plan and the encouraging of entrepreneurship and private lighting product industry through tax incentives and loans. Other sections of the Developing Country Law deal with research and development, seeking foreign aid, education, and public health issues. The court-based, Enforcement sections provide for citizen enforcement as well as criminal penalties.

The Developed country law provides for the Developed countries to create international partnerships and to provide local entrepreneurs with financial, institutional, and technological assistance to develop, manufacture, promote, distribute, and maintain improved lighting products and centralized charging stations in developing countries. It further requires Developed countries to create a fund amounting to $15 million each year for 10 years and stipulates mechanisms for the disbursement of those funds to promote joint research, development and demonstration of appropriate and affordable lighting products, as well as to track environmental and public health problems created by the use of kerosene.

What is presented are two sets of laws that are actually blueprints for promoting affordable and sustainable lighting for the energy poor.

VI. Model Law on Lighting for Developing Countries

A BILL To promote the development and deployment of clean lighting to save lives, improve livelihoods, empower women, and combat global warming by creating a thriving global market for clean, affordable, and efficient household, commercial and community lighting, and for other purposes.

Be it enacted by the [legislative organ] of the [developed country] assembled,

Short Title

This Act may be cited as the ***Development and Dissemination of Clean Lighting*** **Act of [year].**

Effective Date. This Act becomes effective on [*date*].

§ 1. Findings

(a) [*Name of country*] is a member of the community of nations that has accepted well-recognized principles of international law and policy establishing the right of developing countries to sustainable development.

(b) [*Name of country*] seeks to support sustainable development pertaining to energy poverty and access to safe and sustainable lighting products through this Act.

(c) It is estimated that of the 1.3 billion people worldwide without access to electricity, most rely on kerosene for illumination.

(d) The use of kerosene for lighting generates indoor air pollution, contributing to the deaths of 1.8 million people per year. Kerosene fires kill more than 1 million people per year.

(e) [*Number of people*] in [*name of country*] currently use kerosene for lighting.

(f) Kerosene fires and indoor air pollution cause the deaths of [*number of people*] in [*name of country*] per year.

(g) Children are disproportionately vulnerable to the dangers of kerosene. Accidental ingestion of kerosene leads to fever, cough, abdominal discomfort, or death.

(h) Light generated by kerosene lamps is poor and inefficient, rendering it virtually impossible for people, especially women and children, to accomplish household and social tasks, or engage in economic activity after nightfall.

(i) Lighting costs for kerosene are 325–1625 times higher than those for electric light bulbs, and are borne by some of the world's poorest people.

(j) Kerosene is fossil fuel-based, thus a nonrenewable energy source. Kerosene lamps consume an estimated 77 billion liters of fuel per year. Each year, the burning of kerosene for lighting emits 240 million tons of carbon dioxide into the atmosphere, thus contributing to global climate change.

(k) Safe, sustainable lighting positively impacts the quality of life and environment by:

   (i) Allowing women, children, and men to engage in educational and economic endeavors after nightfall,

   (ii) Promoting gender equality and women's empowerment,

   (iii) Improving household health and safety,

   (iv) Alleviating the financial burden presented by kerosene,

   (v) Advancing environmental stability by reducing use of kerosene, and

   (vi) Reducing contributions to global climate change.

§ 2. Policy

The [legislative organ] hereby declares it is the national policy of [*name of country*] to:

(a) Appropriate financial resources towards the research and development of the most appropriate and sustainable energy technologies for improved indoor lighting products that advance the objectives of this Act in [*name of country*];

(b) Foster the growth of a domestic indoor lighting manufacturing industry by supporting entrepreneurs through tax incentives, loans, and micro- and other forms of financing that advance the objectives of this Act;

(c) Ensure that all indoor lighting products meet relevant standards for physical durability, product life-span, and light output;

(d) Install and distribute indoor lighting products in a matter that emphasizes accessibility while encouraging the recipient to contribute to the cost in currency, exchange, and/or sweat equity;

(e) Stimulate community participation in the financing, manufacturing, distribution, and promotion of the objectives of this Act;

(f) Seek the assistance, expertise, guidance, and experience of non-governmental organizations (NGOs) and community advocacy groups in all aspects of the implementation of the Act;

(g) Promote awareness and education about indoor air pollution caused by kerosene lamps and lanterns;

(h) Promote the involvement of current kerosene lamp and lantern users, *inter alia*, in the research, design, development, manufacturing, distribution, monitoring, maintenance, evaluation, and marketing of improved indoor lighting products; and

(i) Conduct training on use and maintenance to indoor lighting product users and community members.

§ 3. Definitions

For the purposes of this Act:

(a) "Administrator" means the administrator of the Lighting Agency.

(b) "Agency" means the Lighting Agency ("LA").

(c) "Certification" or "certified" refers to certification by an entity or organization in the country of origin, which is authorized by the LA.

(d) "Endangerment" means the exposure, voluntary, or involuntary, of individuals to conditions harmful to their physical health, and includes circumstances arising from willful or negligent misrepresentation.

(e) "Lighting" refers to artificial indoor or outdoor lighting.

(f) "Lighting products," refers to indoor or outdoor lighting suitable for off-grid applications.

(g) "Local conditions" means the socioeconomic conditions in the area, based on an overall assessment of economic factors including the ability to pay, cultural factors including a willingness to change patterns or behavior in use of lighting products, and social factors, including the identification of primary decision-makers in households, those who are affected most by lack of beneficial lighting, and the primary social agents in communities.

(h) "Micro-financing" refers to loans that are granted for design, production, marketing, distribution, sale, maintenance, and repair of lighting products.

(i) "Minister of Energy" includes other executive branch equivalent administrators found in a non-parliamentary system (*e.g.* Secretary).

(j) "Organization" means an entity other than a governmental body, which was established or organized for any purpose relevant to this Act. The term refers, *inter alia*, to a corporation, company, guild, association, partnership, NGO, local community advocacy organization, trust, or trade union.

(k) "PAO," a provincial assessment officer, is defined in Section 4(a) of the Act.

(*l*) "Sweat equity" includes the labor, skill, goods, or community services offered as consideration by recipients, in part or in full, for lighting products. Sweat equity is transferable among households. Sweat equity includes, but is not limited to, the following activities:

(i) Labor provided in producing, installing or publicizing solar based lighting products;

(ii) Transportation of materials for lighting products; and

(iii) Participation in public education and community outreach.

§ 4. Establishment of Agency

The Lighting Agency (LA) is hereby established to implement the provisions of this Act. The Administrator of the Agency shall administer this statute by, *inter alia*:

(a) Conducting Needs Assessments and Developing Specifications

Within 120 days of the adoption of this Act, the LA shall deploy [*N (the number of provinces or sub-national governments)*] provincial assessment officers (PAOs), one in each of the country's [*N*] provinces. PAOs shall, within 6 months of designation, in collaboration with [*name of appropriate NGO or NGOs*] and local health personnel, conduct needs assessments that will identify and investigate:

(i) Types of household lighting currently being used in the province;

(ii) Typical expenses associated with household lighting in the province;

(iii) The needs and receptivity of the populace with respect to modern lighting products, with an emphasis on the needs of women and children;

(iv) Local aesthetics and its relationship to the desirability of lighting products;

(v) Any potential barriers to adoption of such lighting products, including cultural and geographic barriers and physical and environmental conditions;

(vi) Exposure to indoor air pollution and other hazards from fuel-based lighting;

(vii) The financial status and market infrastructure of local communities; and

(viii) The feasibility of decentralized power generations that can supply electricity for each community.

(ix) The practicability of installing charging units for batteries

(b) Lighting Product Selection

The LA, in collaboration with the Minister of Energy and the PAOs, will assist in the marketing of lighting products that suit the needs of [*name of country*].

(c) Pilot Programs

The PAOs, under the direction of the Administrator and with the assistance of [an appropriate organization], shall carry out pilot programs in each province, which can be replicated in the rest of the country, for the purpose of identifying challenges and developing procedures in advance of full national implementation. The communities selected for the pilot programs by the Agency shall be the ones in which:

(i) Electricity is not widely available;

(ii) Surveys and Needs Assessments, carried out by the PAOs, reveal that a majority in the community want to participate in the Pilot Project;

(iii) There are not more than 500 households;

(iv) Individuals are willing and able to pay for lighting products through sweat equity, currency, or other forms of exchange;

(v) The population is demographically representative of the [*number of people in the country*] that do not have access to modern lighting.

(d) Completion and Review of the Pilot Projects

At least two Pilot Projects shall be completed within targeted communities for each province before attempting the widespread installation of lighting products in the rest of the province. The data revealed by each Pilot Project and the lessons learned shall be analyzed and reviewed in a Pilot Project Report generated by the LA which will, among other things, clarify the goals of the pilot projects, and whether these goals were met. This report, as well as the projects themselves, shall be open to scrutiny by the public, NGOs, and by other government officials.

§ 5. Administrative Discretion

After holding a public hearing, the Administrator may reasonably phase in implementation of the Act over a period of time in accordance with an area's Local Conditions, but this period may not exceed 3 years.

§ 6. Implementation and Administration

(a) Implementation

The Administrator shall use the information revealed by the Pilot Projects to implement this Act by:

(i) Consulting and collaborating, with the Ministers of

- (1) Health and Human Wellness,
- (2) Energy,
- (3) Environment & Natural Resources,
- (4) Education, and
- (5) Industry & Commerce, and within reasonable time constraints, receive their inputs.

(ii) Encourage public participation in the implementation of the provisions of this Act, by incorporating:

- (1) Notice and comment prior to the adoption of any major rules implementing the provisions of this Act, as governed by the [*name of country's administrative procedure act, if applicable*];
- (2) Open meetings whenever the LA has a quorum present for a meeting in which the LA discusses any regular business of the agency concerning this Act;
- (3) A community liaison, answerable to the PAO, in all aspects of implementation of the Act; and
- (4) Providing accessible means for the public to offer input and feedback regarding the implementation of this Act's provisions.

(iii) Where appropriate, seeking international aid assistance in the form of technological assistance and expertise for monitoring and evaluation from, *inter alia*, intergovernmental organizations, other states, NGOs, community advocacy groups, corporations, private individuals and charitable trusts.

(iv) Creating and implementing a system whereby end users can acquire lighting products by sweat equity or exchange;

(v) Creating and implementing a program for recycling used batteries, which may require lighting product distributors, retailers, and charging stations to collect used batteries;

(vi) Using innovation, affordable and appropriate sustainable energy technologies, and/or techniques that provide greater economic benefits, at a limited cost to the end-user;

(vii) Using technologies and organizational methods, which have been successfully tried, tested, and demonstrated by other developing countries.

(b) Strategic National Lighting Plan (3-Year Plan)

After a widespread, open, and public consultation process, the LA shall draw up renewable strategic 3-Year Plans with annual targets and objectives that shall be publicly announced and publicized. The first Plan shall be completed within one year of the coming into operation of this Act. Once a 3-Year Plan has been completed, the LA shall issue annual reports that are announced and publicized on the actions taken pursuant to the 3-Year Plan and the extent to which the targets or objectives have or have not been met. The annual reports will be examined annually by the [legislative organ] of [*name of country*] through hearings and used as necessary to pass or amend laws.

(c) Stimulate the Lighting Product Industry and Market

The LA shall stimulate and encourage the creation of a robust domestic lighting product industry, by engaging, *inter alia*, in the following:

(i) Improving access to capital for new businesses by providing tax incentives and loans, and by removing restrictions on foreign investment in the lighting product industry. To this extent, the LA shall encourage the growth of markets that benefit the rural energy poor;

(ii) Establishing certification and standardization protocols for lighting product parts and equipment as described in Section 8; and

(iii) As stated in Section 9, collaborating with the Ministry of Energy to disburse grants for research and development to qualified universities in [*name of country*], which are able to undertake research and development.

(d) Monitoring and Inspection

In order to ensure that lighting product distribution requirements have been properly met, through collaboration with PAOs, the Administrator shall, with immediate effect, begin the following activities towards implementation of this Act:

(i) *Assessment*. Ascertain the rate and severity of accidents associated with kerosene before the installation of lighting products, and determine the rate at which members of households, notably women and children, are able to engage in educational or other productive activity after dark.

(ii) *Post-Installation Monitoring*. Monitor accidents, and after-dark activities (as described in (i), above) of the homes referred to in Section 4(c), above, after lighting products are installed within the following time-frames:

(1) Phase 1—within 1 year of installation;

(2) Phase 2—within 18 months of installation;

(3) Phase 3—within 3 years of installation; and

(4) Annual monitoring once every year, thereafter.

(iii) *Charging Station and Use Monitoring*. If applicable, inspecting centralized charging facilities and end-user sites to ensure they are being used and are working properly.

(iv) *Economic Sustainability Monitoring*. Procedures to monitor the financial performance of the program to ensure its economic sustainability.

(v) *Protocol for Testing*. Negotiating and finalizing with laboratories on a protocol for testing based on the provisions of this law.

(vi) *Reporting*. Submitting to Parliament a report (Administrator's Report) on the findings of the monitoring and inspection efforts under this Section, 2 years after this Section comes into force and annually thereafter.

(vii) *Applicability in relation to Pilot Projects*. The monitoring and inspection requirements here are applicable to final projects subsequent to the pilot project.

(e) Statistics and Communication

(i) The Lighting Agency shall consult data obtained under Article 4 to aid in implementation, in addition to other sources.

(ii) The Lighting Agency shall accurately report its findings for implementing final projects to the public and other government agencies, and keep administrative records.

§ 7. Authorization and Appropriations

[*Appropriated amount (national currency or currency of choice)*] shall be authorized and appropriated every year, beginning in [*year*], continuing for the next 5 years (or until the Act is), and allocated as follows:

(a) [*Appropriated amount (national currency or currency of choice)*] to the Administrator for the administrative costs of implementing this Act.

(b) [*Appropriated amount (national currency or currency of choice)*] for needs assessments and pilot programs pursuant to this Act and implementation of the required programs. These funds may be provided in part to appropriate NGOs for implementation of the required programs. These NGOs may also provide funding of their own.

(c) [*Appropriated amount (national currency or currency of choice)*] to the Ministry of Energy to administer a program for he research and development of appropriate lighting technologies. This funding shall remain available until expended.

(d) Pursuant to the effort to maximize adoption of lighting products within a five-year period, the Administrator shall endeavor to acquire at least [*appropriate amount*] of annual funding from domestic and international sources to be invested directly in national and NGO-sponsored programs involving the provision of illumination.

(e) [*Appropriated amount (national currency or currency of choice)*] to the Ministry of Health to carry out its duties under Section 10.

§ 8. National Minimum Standards, Testing and Certification

(a) Establishing Quality and Performance Standards. The Agency shall establish mandatory minimum quality and performance standards for lighting products, informed by internationally agreed standards. All lighting products marketed or sold in [*name of country*] shall be certified as meeting the standards established by the Agency.

(b) Quality standards shall require:

(i) That the brightness and luminosity of lighting be adequate for the purposes for which they are intended, such as domestic, commercial or community uses;

(ii) Durability standards for batteries, bulbs, PVC panels, circuit boards, charge converters, inverters, the casing, other equipment or mechanical parts of lighting products;

(iii) That spare parts are adequate;

(iv) Accurate product labeling in accordance with certification standards in subsection (d);

(v) No cadmium or mercury to be present in the product; and

(vi) Truth in advertising.

(c) Performance standards shall add specificity to quality standards and shall be reviewed at regular intervals. Performance standards shall differentiate, *inter alia, between* lighting for household or domestic use, commercial use, agricultural use, and community use in hospitals, schools, buildings, and roads.

(i) Levels of brightness and luminosity for general household or domestic use must provide a minimum output of 50 lumens. The LA may after open public hearings, change this standard, to others based on the best practicable, affordable, and technologically feasible standards.

(ii) Levels of brightness or luminosity for commercial, agricultural and community purposes shall be established by the Agency, within one year of the enactment of this statute, after open public hearings, based on the best practicable, affordable, and technologically feasible standards.

(d) Testing and Certification

(i) All new lighting products and/or component parts sold and/or marketed under this Act in [*name of country*] shall be tested and certified by approved private, public, or NGO-owned and operated laboratories at the country of origin or manufacture.

(ii) Certification will attest that the products have been tested according to protocol, and comply with the relevant quality and/or performance standards referred to in this section.

(iii) Labeling. Every lighting product and or component sold or marketed shall contain consumer-facing labels stating for which social sector(s) (household, commercial etc.) the product has been certified. All of the following must be accurately specified on the label:

(1) Manufacturer;

(2) Model name and #;

(3) Light output;

(4) Lamp type;

(5) Run time;

(6) Charger rating; and

(7) If the light has phone or small electronics charging capabilities, the change in brightness and power usage as a result of charging while the light is otherwise normally operating.

(iv) The Administrator will communicate with and approve the above-specified laboratories in paragraph (d)(i) based on relevant criteria determined after a public hearing.

(v) The Administrator will agree with the laboratories on a protocol for testing based on the provisions of this law.

(vi) After reaching an agreement on appropriate protocols, the Administrator shall publicly announce and publicize the names of the approved laboratories.

§ 9. Research and Development

(a) Authority

The Minister of Energy is authorized to conduct, promote, coordinate, and accelerate research, development, studies, surveys, experiments, demonstration projects, and training related to the development of lighting products and their components. The Minister of Energy shall vouch that the expenditure of any funds appropriated under this Act shall be coordinated with and reflect the needs and priorities identified by the Agency.

(b) Foreign Aid and Assistance

The Minister of Energy shall actively solicit foreign aid, assistance, and collaboration in carrying out research and development from other countries, intergovernmental organizations, scientific bodies, philanthropic organizations, non-governmental organizations, and any other entities supporting access to lighting.

(c) Grants

In implementing this Section, the Minister of Energy may enter into contracts with and make grants to qualified institutions, agencies, organizations, and persons. Priority shall be given first to [*country*]'s research universities, then to other public or private institutions suitably equipped to carry out scientific, economic, or social research related to indoor illumination in [*country*].

(d) Reporting

(i) The Minister of Energy shall submit an annual report to the Administrator of the LA and the [legislative organ] about the research projects funded pursuant to this Section, outlining the funding provided for each project, how such funds were used, and the nature and general progress of the project.

(ii) The Administrator of the LA and Minister of Energy shall promote accurate reporting of research and scientific data by organizations engaged in lighting development, and shall approve regulations to ensure accurate administrative record-keeping by government officials.

(e) Availability of Information to the Public

Subject to the patent provisions of the [*name of country's patent act or other intellectual property law*], all discoveries, inventions, innovations, information, and data resulting from any research studies, surveys, experiments, assessments, or demonstration projects conducted or financed under this Section shall belong to the public domain and be available to the public for their use without charge.

§ 10. Public Health

The Ministry of Health shall encourage early treatment of kerosene-related burns. To this end:

(a) Healthcare workers will report back to the Ministry of Health specific cases of kerosene-related burns by creating records of patients and monitoring their treatment;

(b) The Minister of Health will enlist the help of NGOs in carrying out duties under this section.

§ 11. Education and Information

(a) The Administrator shall be responsible for educating the public on the benefits of modern indoor lighting technologies and the dangers of fuel-based lighting. The Administrator shall use existing information channels, and enlist the assistance of the private sector, in doing so.

(b) Private programs whether voluntary or enlisted by the Administrator to disseminate information to the public regarding indoor illumination shall comply with all provisions of this Act.

(c) The Minister of Commerce shall oversee marketing materials to ensure that only verifiable findings are used.

§ 12. Enforcement

(a) Civil Remedies

Non-Compliance Order. On the basis of information available to him/her, if the Administrator finds violations of this Act, s/he may issue a non-compliance notice to the identified party. Non-compliance orders may be issued by the Administrator for violations of this Act in accordance with [*name of country's administrative procedure act*]. In addition, the Administrator must:

(i) Issue a notice of the alleged violation to the offending party within 30 days of discovery of a violation;

(ii) Allow the offending party 45 days to rebut the evidence against him/her, or submit to agency-inspected corrective measures; and

(iii) Institute immediate suspension of activities that have or are reasonably expected to impose a grave health risk to the population.

(b) Citizen Enforcement

(i) Any citizen or resident of [*name of country*] may seek judicial remedies under this Section for violations of any mandatory provision of this Act. These citizen suits may be lodged in any District Court against any government agency, department, or private party that either violates a standard established by this Act, or fails to carry out a mandatory duty required by this Act. Prior to bringing an action, a citizen shall:

(1) Give notice to the defendant agency, department, or private party about the alleged violation(s) of this Act; and

(2) Allow a period of 60 days after receipt of notice to enable the defendant to rectify the alleged violation(s) of this Act before filing a lawsuit.

(ii) If the Plaintiff is successful, the court may order the defendant to comply with the Act and award damages. A successful litigant is entitled to recover full costs and the court shall include and order such costs in its judgment.

(iii) In the event an action is dismissed, the court may, in its discretion, order the citizen plaintiff to pay the defendant such costs as it deems reasonable and necessary.

(c) Criminal Penalties

(i) *Violation of Non-Compliance Order*. Any person who fails to comply within 3 months of receipt of a non-compliance order issued pursuant to Subsection (a) shall, after due inquiry by a District Court, be punished by a fine of not less than an amount equivalent to 250 USD [*or other typical fine in national currency*] nor more than an amount equivalent to 2,500 USD [*or other typical fine in national currency*] per day per violation, or by imprisonment for not more than 1 year, or by both.

(ii) *Negligent Misrepresentation*. Any person who negligently misrepresents that lighting products meet the minimum national standards of Section 4 or regional standards established pursuant to Section 4(a)(viii) shall be punished by a fine of an amount equivalent to 250 USD [*or other typical fine in national currency*] per lighting product sold under negligent misrepresentation.

(iii) *Knowing Endangerment*. Any party who knowingly endangers another person or community of persons by manufacturing, marketing and/or distributing lighting products, and/or parts thereof that do not conform to the provisions of Section 4 (or regional standards established pursuant to Section 4(a) (viii)) shall be subject to a fine of not more than 100,000 USD.

(iv) *Other Sanctions*. Nothing in this subsection shall limit or reduce any other punishment, including imprisonment, under any other applicable criminal laws.

VII. Commentary: Model Law on Lighting for Developing Countries

Section 1: Findings

The Model Law provides a series of findings and lays the foundation for establishing the programs to support the distribution and use of off-grid lighting products as described in Sections 4 to 12. The Findings are based on domestically and internationally available evidence, and attempt to incorporate the latest available data. Lighting is an extremely crucial area that needs to be addressed among developing countries. Worldwide, 1.3 billion people still do not have sufficient access to light.[14] The Model Law takes a significant step toward implementing Goal Number 7 and its affiliated targets,

---

[14] Jörg Peters & Maximiliane Sievert, *On-Grid and Off-Grid Rural Electrification—Impacts And Cost Considerations Revisited* 2 (2014).

of the Sustainable Development Goals (SDGs) of 2015.[15] The objective of Goal Number 7 of the SDGs is to "[E]nsure access to affordable, reliable, sustainable and modern energy for all."[16] The targets associated with Goal Number 7 call for this goal to be achieved by 2030, and for the enhancement of international cooperation to facilitate access to clean energy research and technology, including renewable energy, energy efficiency, and promote investment in energy infrastructure and clean energy technology.[17] The targets also call for expanding infrastructure and upgrading technology for supplying modern and sustainable energy services, in particular to least developed countries, small island developing States, and land-locked developing countries.[18] The Model Law also advances the older United Nations' Millennium Development Goals (MDGs) pertaining to sustainable social development and environmental protection,[19] which have now been incorporated into the SDGs.

The Model Law addresses the prevalence of kerosene lighting in the developing world, particularly unpressurized wick kerosene lamps. Kerosene, while cheaply priced and used in a variety of applications, such as lighting, cooking and heating, poses burns hazards to children from open flames. As will be detailed in the Commentary for Section 10, women and children are the most susceptible to kerosene burns.[20] Air pollution from kerosene lamps is also a significant problem, as kerosene emits over 240 million tons of carbon dioxide annually.[21] Kerosene lamps consume 77 billion liters of oil per year, or 1.3 million barrels of oil per day.[22] Over the long term, kerosene begins to become expensive, potentially costing many times more than some electric light bulbs. A 2003 study conducted in

---

15 *Sustainable Development Knowledge Platform.* https://sustainable development.un.org/topics.

16 *Id.*

17 *Id.*

18 *Id.*

19 *Supra* Chapter 3 (E).

20 *See* Chamania et al. *Pilot Project In Rural Western Madhya Pradesh, India, To Assess The Feasibility of Using LED And Solar-Powered Lanterns to Remove Kerosene Lamps and Related Hazards From Homes*, 41 BURNS 595, 596.; *see also* Ashkan Golshan et. al., *A Systematic Review of the Epidemiology of Unintentional Burn Injuries in South Asia*, 35 J. PUB. HEALTH 391 (2013) (highlighting how female mortality outnumbered male mortality in the literature on burns in South Asia); Katrine Lofberg & Christopher C. Stewart, *Pediatric Burn Injuries In The Developing World,* GLOBAL HEALTH EDUCATION CONSORTIUM 9 (2012) (noting that children aged 5 and under and the elderly suffer the highest mortality from burns globally).

21 Clean Air Task Force, *Black Carbon Emissions From Kerosene Lamps* 1 (2013), available at http://www.catf.us/resources/publications/files/201311–Black carbonandkerosenelamps_BRIEF.pdf.

22 Jean-Claude Bolay, Alexandre Schmid & Gabriela Tejada, *Technologies and Innovations for Development: Scientific Cooperation for a Sustainable Future,* 308 (2012).

Berkeley found that LEDs cost 5 cents per thousand lux hours, while non-pressurized kerosene lamps could cost as much as $3.80 per thousand lux hours.[23] While pressurized hurricane lamps do not pose burn hazards, they cost much more, and still pose the same problems as unpressurized lamps in terms of indoor air pollution.

Some of the developing countries, challenged by the absence or inadequacy of access to lighting, have vast populations, are of enormous geographic size, and possess extensive cultural and socio-economic diversity. For example, India is a federal republic composed of 29 states, each with its own state legislature and a substantial degree of control over its own affairs. Given the sheer size of India's population and the vast differences between each individual state (as well as the sheer size and complexity of India's national government), it would be impractical to adopt these Model Laws for the entire country. However, individual states within India, like Tamil Nadu or Madhya Pradesh, could adopt these Model Laws and tailor them for their own unique geographical and socio-economic situations. Thus, in some cases, it might be more appropriate for these Model Laws to be adopted not by the central government, but by the country's smaller state and/or provincial governments.

While the Model Law aims to encourage the distribution of off-grid lighting products, it does not specify the specific types of lighting products that should be used or what methods should be employed to ensure effective product distribution. Such decisions will be dependent on the specific requirements of each country, such as how available off-grid lighting is or what types of products are available in the country.

Section 2: Policy

The policy articulated here is expressed in generic terms and is meant to be adopted by any country, and may be adapted to suit the particular circumstances of that country.

It is open to an adopting country to change wording of the Model Laws to comport with its own policies. The need to do so might become evident where the meaning of some words may be lost in translation from English into their own language. However, the policies articulated are based on a number of common factors shared by countries seeking to offer access to lighting.

The reference to NGOs acknowledges the fact that several for profit and non-profit initiatives are working to address lighting distribution around the developing world. These initiatives range

---

[23] Evan Mills, *Technical and Economic Performance Analysis of Kerosene Lamps and Alternative Approaches to Illumination in Developing Countries* 3 (2003), available at http://evanmills.lbl.gov/pubs/pdf/offgrid-lighting.pdf.

from small non-profit organizations distributing plastic bottles with bleach solution, which serve as lights when the bleach is added to water in the bottle,[24] to large multinational organizations such as the United Nations and the World Bank's Lighting Global initiative.[25] Even some musical performance artists are contributing to direct lighting schemes by establishing their own distribution and infrastructure for lighting.[26] In addition to these initiatives, private corporations such as Nokero are manufacturing their own lighting equipment and selling them directly to distributors working in developing countries.[27]

Providing lighting to developing countries can be a costly endeavor, even if the long-term benefits are shown to outweigh the initial costs. Extending and maintaining the main electrical grid out to remote rural areas is an expensive national undertaking. Even in India, one of the largest growing economies in the world, over 400 million people live in communities lacking reliable electricity supplies for more than three hours per day.[28] Solar lighting would at first seem like a cheaper solution, as much of India is located in a climate zone that receives, on average, at least eight hours of sunlight per day.[29]

Off-grid solar LED lights have been shown to be a relatively effective medium-term solution for areas that cannot be connected to the electrical grid. Again, to use India as an example: a single solar LED light can be purchased for, on average, about 549 Indian Rupees (nine US dollars at the time of the study), and has a warranty of six months.[30] Assuming that a warranty of six months represents the *absolute minimum lifetime* of the product, this would mean that the maximum the household using this light could spend is about 1,098 Rupees (eighteen US dollars) in one year, all other factors being equal (although, in the final study, most of the lights actually exceeded the initial six month period, lasting the full year, and thus bringing the actual cost down to only 549 Rupees for most of the

---

[24] *See*, Myshelter Foundation, *Liter of Light—About Us* (2015), http://literoflight.org/about-us/. These plastic lights have also been reported on by international news agencies. *See, e.g.*, Kotoe Oshima, *Plastic Bottles Light up Lives*, CNN.com (Aug. 30, 2011), http://www.cnn.com/2011/WORLD/asiapcf/08/30/eco.philippines.bottle/.

[25] *See* Home page, Lighting Global (2015), http://www.lightingglobal.org/.

[26] From February 2014, the rapper Akon has been working with Samba Bathily and Thione Niang on the Akon Lighting Africa project, which provides solar lights and small scale village and town lighting infrastructure projects. *See* Overview—Akon Lighting Africa, *Akon Lighting Africa* (2015), http://akonlightingafrica.com/our-activities/overview/.

[27] *See* Home page, Nokero Solar (2015), www.nokero.com.

[28] Chamania et al, *supra* note 20, at 596.

[29] *Id.*

[30] *Id.*

participating households).[31] The study cited by Chamania found that the average rural Indian household in Madhya Pradesh spends 1,800 Rupees per year on kerosene for one lamp (and that excludes other factors such as the cost of the lamp itself, or the external costs to health resulting from burns and inhalation of smoke).[32] Thus, even at its "most expensive" (*i.e.* assuming that each light needs to be replaced every six months), the use off-grid solar lighting products was still proven to be more economical than kerosene lighting, saving each participating household at least 702 Rupees. In addition, each household would avoid the associated health risks of using kerosene lighting.

The solar lights in this study were all produced, tested, and certified within India, thereby cutting down on the costs associated with procurement and distribution. These Model Laws are drafted to allow and encourage the adopting countries to establish a similar lighting market. As discussed above, having a lighting market may address corruption and would also allow for easier distribution and replacement or repair of the lighting products.

Section 3: Definitions

Many of these definitions are self-explanatory and simply explain terms and concepts in the model law. However, the fact that an agency or concept is defined does not mean that it should become a part of the laws or institutions of the adopting country. For example, it is possible that the adopting country does not propose to set up a Lighting Agency, and instead tasks an equivalent agency with the same responsibilities. In this case, the definition of "Agency" may be altered to reflect this change.

Section 4: Establishment of Agency

As just mentioned, and also made clear in Chapter 5,[33] the adopting country may not wish to establish a new agency to address the issue of insufficient lighting.[34] Similarly, the adopting country may also not wish to create a new cadre of provincial assessment officials.[35] The exact administrative and logistical choices clearly fall within the individual administrative structure of each adopting country's government. However, the task of implementing, overseeing, and enforcing these laws must be institutionalized within the administration and law of each adopting country.

---

31 *Id.* at 599.

32 *Id.*

33 Chapter 5, *supra.*

34 *Id.*

35 *Id.*

The first major objective for the agency, addressed in Section 4(a), is to perform needs assessments and develop specifications for what products and programs will be implemented based on the findings of these assessments. Needs assessments are expensive and time-consuming, but they are also necessary to avoid a "cookie-cutter" or "one size fits all" approach to the promotion of lighting.[36] While it is generally accepted that everyone needs lighting, the geographical, economic, and social and culture situation of each country and community is unique. Thus, local needs assessments help to discover the specific local needs and conditions, which then allow for the creation of an area-specific lighting program ensuring that the country's limited resources are expended in the most productive, efficient and effective manner.[37]

In conducting a needs assessment, a country does not necessarily have to "reinvent the wheel." A country could model its needs assessment after those that have been conducted in other locations. For example, some needs assessments consist of a brief five-to-ten minute conversations with each household that provide sufficient information to the administrator.[38] Furthermore, most functioning governments should already have a civil service in place that is used to regularly perform surveys and censuses of the population.[39] However, this may not always be the case.

Sections 4(c) and (d) concern the implementation and review of pilot programs, which are mini or scaled-down versions of a full-scale program.[40] Pilot programs fulfill a range of important functions and can provide valuable insights for assessing the feasibility of a full-scale program. Pilot programs: (1) help identify logistical problems, which might occur using proposed methods; (2) estimate variability in outcomes; (3) collect preliminary data; (4) determine what resources (finances, staff, et cetera) are needed for the full program; (5) assess the proposed programmatic techniques to uncover hidden potential; and (6) also serve as an important "quality control" test run for the products that the administrator eventually intends to use.[41]

Pilot program results depend on their duration and scope. For example, with regards to quality control, if the program lasts only

---

[36] *Id.*

[37] *Id.*; Fernando I. Soriano, Conducting Needs Assessments: A Multidisciplinary Approach 4 (2nd ed. 2013).

[38] Johannes Urpelainen & Semee Yoon, *Solar Home Systems for Rural India: Survey Evidence on Awareness And Willingness to Pay From Uttar Pradesh*, 24 ENERGY FOR SUSTAINABLE DEVELOPMENT 70, 72 (2015).

[39] Soriano, *supra* note 37, at 79.

[40] As contrasted with 4(a).

[41] *Id.* Section 4(c) and (d).

one year, then the administrator will know only if the products involved in the program will last one year or not. Thus, the administrator might modify the pilot program to be two years in duration, in order to see if the lighting products last at least two years.

The optimal duration of a pilot program must strike a balance. It should be long enough to provide sufficient information, but not too long so as to delay implementation of the full-scale program. Generally, many pilot programs last for 365 days, with at least one mid-term evaluation at the six-month mark.[42] One pilot project in Nigeria distributing off-grid lighting to 36 rural hospitals even used a program lasting as little as three to four weeks, and claimed that the introduction of these lighting products had an almost immediate effect of increasing the working hours of hospital employees by 30%.[43]

Two challenges in establishing a pilot program are determining the appropriate sample size, and selecting a sample that most accurately reflects the average conditions of the adopting country's small rural communities. Some pilot programs use 1,000 households, as 1,000 was found to be sufficiently large enough number to represent the larger population, while also being within the manageable limits of the agency's resources.[44] These Model Laws propose conducting two pilot programs consisting of 500 households to provide sufficient data.

The final part of Section 4 mandates that the lighting agency shall review and analyze the data from the pilot projects. This report should be made available to both the legislature and citizens of the adopting country. However, during this stage special care must be taken by the adopting country's government to ensure that the information is accurately analyzed. One of the biggest challenges in conducting research in the developing world is the reliability of the information collected.[45] Various political interests may act to skew data in ways beneficial to their own interests during the process of gathering information. Many of the governments of Sub-Saharan Africa are notorious for manipulating objective data.[46] Thus, the needs assessment and pilot programs should be overseen by an NGO, a citizen advocacy group, or by a different governmental agency.

---

42 Chamania et al, *supra* note 20 at 596.

43 Louis Gyoh, *Feedback On The Performance Of Off-Grid Lighting Products Deployed In 36 Health Centers In Nigeria* 7–13 (2014).

44 Chamania et al, *supra* note 20. at 599.

45 Morten Jerven, *Poor Numbers: How We Are Misled By African Development Statistics And What To Do About It* 83 (2013).

46 *Id.* at 85.

Section 5: Administrative Discretion

This Section grants discretion to the Administrator, after due process and public inquiry, to adopt and adapt standards and regulations to comport with the specific conditions of the country. It is important to grant such discretion to the Administrator as the Model Laws may need some adjustment due to compelling circumstances. While the Administrator shall have broad discretion, revised standards should be implemented within three years.

Section 6: Implementation and Administration

This Section refers to implementation by the Administrator of the provisions of the Model Law. The first part relates to Pilot Projects. The second, to the Strategic Plan envisioned in Section 6(b). The strategic planning process should endeavor to encourage the creation of markets for lighting and ensure that the plans are instruments for generating lighting markets. One aspect of market advancement, lies in creating standards, certifications, and monitoring. Another relates to public participation and consultation. It is important to undertake bottom-up planning that incorporates the views of the people

Corruption remains a major problem in many developing countries where large numbers of complex, restrictive regulations are coupled with inadequate controls. The United Nations Convention on Corruption offers ample contemporary evidence of the problems caused by corruption.[47] It recognizes the "seriousness of problems and threats posed by corruption to the stability and security of societies, undermining the institutions and values of democracy, ethical values and justice and jeopardizing sustainable development and the rule of law."[48] In his Foreword to the Convention, Kofi Anan, the UN Secretary General at the time, refers to corruption as an "insidious plague" that has a wide range of corrosive effects on societies.[49] He continues by asserting that:

> It [corruption] undermines democracy and the rule of law, leads to violations of human rights, distorts markets, erodes the quality of life and allows organized crime, terrorism and other threats to human security to flourish. This evil phenomenon is found in all countries—big and

---

47 U.N. Office of Drugs and Crime, Merida Conference, Dec. 9–11, 2003, Convention Against Corruption, GA res. 58/4, UN Doc. A/58/422 (Dec. 9, 2003); 43 ILM 37 (2004) [hereinafter Convention Against Corruption]. As of April 1, 2015, 177 parties have signed and ratified or otherwise acceded to the Convention. United Nations Office on Drugs and Crime, United Nations Convention Against Corruption: Signature and Ratification Status as of 1 April 2015, https://www.unodc.org/unodc/en/treaties/CAC/signatories.html.

48 *Id.* Convention Against Corruption, *supra* at 2.

49 *Id.* Convention Against Corruption, at iii.

> small, rich and poor—but it is in the developing world that its effects are most destructive. Corruption hurts the poor disproportionately by diverting funds intended for development, undermining a Government's ability to provide basic services, feeding inequality and injustice and discouraging foreign aid and investment. Corruption is a key element in economic underperformance and a major obstacle to poverty alleviation and development.[50]

In both advanced developing countries (ADCs) and least developed countries (LDCs,) corruption is a pervasive problem. Not only are official decisions—for instance, the award of government contracts or the amount of tax due—bought and sold, but very often citizens must pay for access to a public service or the exercise of a right, such as obtaining civil documents. The process of allocating political and administrative posts—particularly those with powers of decision over the export of natural resources or import licenses—is influenced by the gains that can be made from them. As these exchanges of privileges are reciprocated by political support or loyalty, it cements the political foundations.[51] Corruption in turn can have a dramatic effect on a country's economy. It has been estimated, for example, that moving from a relatively "clean" government like that of Singapore to one as corrupt as Mexico's would have the same effect on foreign direct investment as an increase in the marginal corporate tax rate of 50 per cent.[52]

Thomas Pogge offers a radical and trenchant criticism of corruption as something ingrained in the international structure of power. According to him "many developing countries are run by corrupt and incompetent leaders, unwilling or unable to make serious poverty-eradication efforts."[53] Pogge continues that, bad leadership, civil wars, and widespread corruption in the developing countries are not wholly homegrown, but strongly encouraged by the existing international rules based on the sovereignty of states.[54] As ordinary citizens of the rich countries, we are deeply implicated in these harms. We authorize our firms to acquire natural resources from tyrants, and we protect their property rights in resources so acquired. We purchase what our firms produce out of such resources and thereby encourage them to act as authorized. In these ways, we

---

50 *Id.*

51 I. Hors, *Fighting Corruption in the Developing Countries'* OECD OBSERVER, April 2000.

52 S-J. Wei, *'How taxing is corruption on international investors?'* Williams David Institute Working Papers Series 63 (2007).

53 T. W. Pogge, *World Poverty and Human Rights: Cosmopolitan Responsibilities and Reforms*, 2nd ed. (Cambridge: Polity Press, 2008).

54 *Id.*

recognize the authority of tyrants to sell natural resources of the countries they rule. We also authorize and encourage other firms of ours to sell to the tyrants what they need to stay in power—from aircraft and arms to surveillance and torture equipment.[55]

Whatever its particular form, public hearings, and the open nature of rulemaking, required by this model law is aimed at combatting corruption. Especially in areas where limited competition and cozy relationships between favored corporations and government officials may be present, open markets, and a market based system, may best promote access to lighting. Moreover, stimulating lighting markets and fostering the growth of the private sector may decentralize large scale decision making, and allow private entrepreneurs to invest in and disseminate energy efficient lighting products and systems. Additionally, incentivizing local market development may also provide an opportunity for small communities to understand and take charge of their lighting products, and the joint enforcement environment created by all community members may help alleviate corruption, thereby allowing the lighting agency to focus on more pressing areas of the Model Law.

Markets, however, may not always lead to a decrease in corruption. For example, if the market is left to its own devices, one large retailer may force many small competitors out of the market, and this may lead to monopolies. Monopolies are characterized by a lack of economic competition to produce the good or service, a lack of viable substitute goods, and the possibility of a high monopoly price well above the firm's marginal cost that leads to a high monopoly profit.[56] Monopoly power can be controlled by the government by anti-monopoly and anti-trust laws and restrictive trade practices legislation. These aim at removing unfair competition, preventing unfair price discrimination and fixing prices equal to competitive prices.[57]

Section 6(c), in particular, envisions a number of ways that local dissemination of lighting may occur through the market. In the "fee for service" system, households purchase or rent, at a nominal fee, a light that can be recharged after the end of its life.[58] The proceeds go towards maintaining the system and giving the lighting distributors

---

[55] *Id.*, p. 148.

[56] Alan S Blinder, William J Baumol, Colton L Gale, *Microeconomics: Principles and Policy* 212 (2001).

[57] Edward Hirsch Levi, *The Antitrust Laws and Monopoly*, 14 University of Chicago Law Review 153 (1947). The author contends, however, that the antitrust laws (of the U.S.).have not been successful in the monopolization field.

[58] Doug Vilsack, *Lessons Learned from Six Years of Selling Solar in Africa*, 253, in *Int'l Energy And Poverty: The emerging frontiers* (Lakshman Guruswamy, ed. 2015).

a small income,[59] Having multiple local vendors allows consumers to obtain lights at affordable prices, even where a supplier's business integrity may be compromised. This is compared to having a central authority supply lights to various towns and cities in a province, where a public official's corruption may severely affect how consumers are able to obtain adequate lighting equipment. A similar system is a rent-to-own system, where households purchase lights and make rental payments with the eventual goal of paying off the lights.[60] However, where rental payments are missed, agents have to seize the lights, and when cultural barriers prevent them from seizing lights, they must often make a collection visit.[61] Households may also pay for their lights through a "pay-as-you-go" system, whereby villagers must make payments at regular intervals to keep their lights operating, and may visit an agent or use a cloud-based app to make a payment when their light turns off.[62]

Research projects such as those described above, may help to understand the nature of incentives required to reach hard to reach areas, and illuminate how research projects help in the evaluation of lighting distribution projects. Lighting a Billion Lives found that girls studied for longer periods of time when there was adequate lighting, and villagers were able to provide more services to their villages, such as tutoring and local eco-tourism.[63] Houri and Khoury found that residents liked the CFL bulbs they implemented, but were disappointed with the amount of electricity they received, due to the blackouts.[64]

Section 7: Authorization and Appropriations

This Section deals with authorization and appropriations for three administrative / governmental units: the new Lighting Agency, the Department of Energy, and the Department of Health. The adopting country can change these provisions to suit its own administrative structures.

It is critical for the legislature to authorize and appropriate funds for the purposes referred to in Section 8 to enable the policy and purposes of the Act to be achieved. Section 8 discusses funds, including loans and other fiscal devices, to encourage lighting

---

[59] *Id.*

[60] *Id.* Doug Vilsack 254–55.

[61] *Id.*

[62] *Id.*

[63] Debajit Palit & Jarnail Singh, *Lighting a Billion Lives—Empowering the Rural Poor*, 59 BOILING POINT 42, 45 (2011).

[64] Ahmad Houri & Pierre Al Khoury, *Financial and Energy Impacts of Compact Fluorescent Light Bulbs in a Rural Setting*, 42 ENERGY AND BUILDINGS 658, 665 (2010).

markets and underlines the importance of promoting private investment and markets for lighting.

The incorporation of NGOs into the administration and implementation of the Act is based on compelling evidence that NGOs and other non-governmental entities are in many cases more effective and efficient distributors of goods and services than government agencies.[65] NGOs may also be able to raise funding independently of the government, whether through private donations or foreign aid, and thus, spare the adopting government some of the financial burdens discussed above. It is clear that a number of NGOs are committed to addressing the problems of access to lighting, and are a resource that should be utilized. However, it is important to note that NGOs are not intended to subsume the role of government. These Model Laws focus on a collaboration between the adopting country's government and the NGOs.

Section 8: National Minimum Standards and Certifications

National Minimum Standards and standardization, are crucial in lighting product funding, manufacture, fabrication, marketing and distribution. Establishing minimum standards helps to ensure that the lighting products are safe and reliable. The standards hold manufacturers accountable for producing suitable products. Certification allows the lighting agency to be certain that lighting products conform to its standards. Standardization brings important benefits to businesses, including a solid foundation upon which to develop new technologies and an opportunity to share and enhance existing practices. Standardization also promotes more business activities in the developing country and advances policy initiatives.

To conform with the SDGs, any lighting solution, while benefitting citizens in developing countries, cannot cause more pollution or environmental harm than the method of lighting it is replacing. Many modern lighting projects and products are solar or wind powered, and require little to no electrical components and do not generate excessive carbon emissions. Many lighting schemes are focusing on using LED lights in developing countries, given that LED bulbs last up to 25 times longer than incandescent bulbs.[66] Solar lights are becoming an increasingly common fixture in 2015 sub-Saharan Africa, as more vendors now sell a wide variety of solar

---

[65] Miklos Marschall, *Transparency Int'l, Legitimacy and Effectiveness: Civil Society Organizations' Role in Good Governance* 1 (Oct. 29, 2002) (transcript available at the World Bank Library.

[66] Lighting Made Easy—Just Look for the Energy Star, EnergyStar.gov 1, https://www.energystar.gov/ia/partners/manuf_res/ES_Lighting_ConsumerFactsheet.pdf?0b551475.

lights to on and off-grid customers, a phenomenon that was much less common in 2009.[67]

Actual minimum brightness standards under Section 8 will be country specific, based on what the adopting country determines is achievable. Metrics for measuring brightness and luminosity are often based on lumens. A lumen measures one square foot of light that is produced by a candle one foot away from a wall.[68] Although lux and watts may also be acceptable measurement standards in some instances, this Model Law will use lumens.[69]

There are five existing global electrification standards a lighting agency may adopt, if it does not already have an electrification standard applicable throughout its borders: US, French, Australia/New Zealand, SABS (South Africa), or IEC/ISO system, developed by the International Electrotechnical Commission (IEC).[70] These electrification standards, *inter alia*, specify what the voltage output at a power outlet would be, what plug type should be used for plug in appliances and equipment, and certification criteria used to test electrical equipment. In 2012, the IEC,[71] a Switzerland-based organization, promulgated the latest version of Recommendations for Small Renewable Energy and Hybrid Systems for Rural Electrification (IEC 62257–9–5) after conducting a survey across 30 countries.[72] The Recommendations were developed to assist

---

[67] Meg Harper, Peter Alstone & Arne Jacobson, *A Growing and Evolving Market for Off-grid Lighting*, LIGHTING GLOBAL 12–13 (2013).

[68] K. Soman, *International System of Units: A Handbook on SI Units for Scientists and Engineers* 16 (2009); *see also LED Flashlights Fact Sheet*, Starline Inc, available at https://us.starline.com/content/image/Forms/distributor_resources/Fact Sheets/Starline_FactSheet_LED.pdf.

[69] Wattage is a measure of power, and lux, a measure of the spread of light in an area, defined as one lumen per square meter. Power does not necessarily translate into luminance. While a lightbulb may use a certain wattage, if it is especially inefficient it will emit a low light output. Lumens are appropriate to use here because they measure the total light output from a source, and are useful as a base or foundation measure from which to work out a lux measurement, for example, if a light bulb is fitted in a home. Further, not all lights are likely to be used indoors and lighting equipment often draw more attention to a lumens measurement than a lux measurement. For example, the United States Dept. of Energy's EnergyStar program now measures bulb brightness in lumens. *See* "Lighting Made Easy—Just Look for the Energy Star" EnergyStar.gov 1, *supra* note 66.

[70] Leon Drotsche, *IEC TS 62257 Series*, Presentation in Oslo (2012).

[71] The IEC develops and promulgates internationally accepted technical specifications for electro-magnetic equipment. Member countries participate in the IEC through National Committees (NC), which represent all public and private electro-technical advocacy organizations in the country. *National Committees*, International Electrotechnical Commission ¶ 2, http://www.iec.ch/about/profile/members.htm. IEC currently has 83 members. *Id.* IEC has collaborated with the International Organization for Standardization (ISO) to develop over 200 technical specifications for developing country and affiliate members. *Adoption of IEC International Standards*, IEC para. 8–9 (2015), www.iec.ch/affiliates/adoptions.

[72] Leon Drotsche *supra* note 70, at 14 (2012).

electricity producers in rural areas of developing countries develop off-grid lighting methods using solar and wind-generated power.[73] The Joint Working Group for the IEC standards was meant to integrate further comments on renewable energy types it had received from those surveyed.[74]

Lighting Global, an initiative of the World Bank that focuses on spreading sufficient electrical lighting around the world, particularly in Asia and Africa, also revised its Global Quality Standards for lighting products as of March 2015; these standards are based on IEC 62257–9–5.[75] As part of Lighting Global's support for the growing global off-grid lighting product market, the Global Quality Standards are intended to create a baseline level for lighting quality, durability and truth-in-advertising, so that consumers are informed and have access to internationally-approved and certified lighting products.[76] Because the electrification standards discussed above may vary as to exact requirements for lighting equipment, at a minimum, the Model Law incorporates the truthful advertising and prohibition on mercury and cadmium requirements of the Lighting Global Standards.

Section 8 also deals with certification. Product certification, undertaken by independent entities, ensures that a certain product is authentic, has passed performance and quality assurance tests or standards, and is designed for its intended purpose. Understanding the light output and power that a product is expected to use will assist the lighting agency in approving lighting products that accord with the country's energy generation and distribution circumstances. Certification also helps consumers select the correct products for their needs, and helps the manufacturer gauge whether certain products should be promoted over others. The Model Law proposes that product certification should take place at the country of origin because it is likely better equipped to develop and enforce certification standards. In addition, it is not practical for manufacturers to ship lighting products to a developing country that, upon receipt, finds that the products are inadequate and uncertified. Over time, however, the developing country may take over such certification responsibilities once its lighting industry is further developed, and delegating certification to countries of manufacture

---

[73] Morand Fachot, *Supporting Rural Electrification*, IEC E-TECH (June 2014), http://iecetech.org/issue/2014–06/Supporting-rural-electrification.

[74] *Id.*

[75] *Lighting Global Quality Standards, version 5,* LIGHTING GLOBAL 2 (2015), available at https://www.lightingglobal.org/wp-content/uploads/2013/12/MQ Standards_Jan2015_V5.pdf.

[76] Quality Standards, LIGHTING GLOBAL (2015), https://www.lightingglobal.org/qa/standards/.

will help developing countries develop and adopt their own certification standards in the meantime.[77]

Section 9: Research and Development

Section 9 places the prime responsibility for research and development on the Ministry of Energy and emphasizes the importance of soliciting and attracting foreign funds and assistance. As in every other administrative allocation of duties, the adopting country is free to make its own arrangements, provided that the substantive importance of research and development is in fact institutionalized.

The design and manufacture of affordable lighting for the energy poor has not attracted large amounts of scientific funding. Affordable sustainable energy technologies (ASETs), such as solar bulbs advanced by the Model Law, rely on cutting edge modern lighting technology relating to photovoltaic cells (PVCs), batteries, LED lights, charge controllers, and casing materials that were developed for and marketed within developed countries. What has been lacking is funding on how to use and adapt such modern technologies to create the ASETs required by the energy poor. The absence of applied engineering research required to adapt modern technologies to the modest and prosaic needs of the energy poor may partly arise from the weak returns on investment. The Model Law seeks to overcome this funding shortfall by calling for scientific research and development (R&D) that can focus on the importance of designing and manufacturing effective, cheap, and durable lighting for the energy poor. This should be a joint collaborative enterprise involving scientists and engineers from both developed and developing countries. The R&D envisioned by the model law has been anticipated, for example, by the research undertaken by a group of Social Entrepreneurship Seminar students from Stanford University, who together with the NGO Light Up the World, developed three prototypes of a solar-powered LED lamp for Indian, Mexican and Chinese consumers.[78] They also created associated business plans to market the prototypes.[79]

In addition to natural science and technological research, socioeconomic research should also be encouraged as these studies help researchers ascertain consumers' reactions to lighting products, so that more consumer friendly ASETs may be implemented. For

[77] This proposal is based on comments solicited at the Access to Energy for All Conference, Sept. 11, 2015.

[78] A.S.U. University Design Consortium, *Affordable, Solar-Powered, Led Lights For Developing World,* A.S.U. UNIVERSITY DESIGN CONSORTIUM ¶ 5–10, https://universitydesign.asu.edu/db/affordable-solar-powered-led-lights-for-developing-world.

[79] *Id.*

example, in the Houri and Khoury study, researchers interviewed consumers for their thoughts on how the lighting products affected their daily activities and financial status.[80]

The Lighting a Billion Lives campaign and the "fee for service" system were developed by The Energy and Resources Institute (TERI), a small research university in New Delhi, as a response to the shortcomings of individual solar lantern distribution. These shortcomings included a lack of after sales service in rural areas and a lack of awareness among consumers as to how to operate and maintain individual solar lanterns.[81]

Section 10: Public Health

This Section acknowledges the importance of treating the health problems caused by kerosene use. To aid the adoption of lighting products by people who use kerosene lamps, it is important to educate them regarding the health risks associated with doing so. Therefore, Section 10 requires the government to support the treatment of kerosene-associated injuries, and also requires public health officials to document injuries caused by kerosene.

A 2014 estimate places the annual number of deaths resulting from all kinds of burns (not just kerosene) at about 300,000 globally (possibly even higher due to the number of deaths that go unreported).[82] Of this figure, over 90% of deaths are estimated to occur in low- to middle-income countries, and the prevalence of kerosene for both cooking and lighting is a major contributing factor to this trend.[83]

A localized study done in Indore, India, found that women aged 21 to 40 were disproportionately more likely to suffer burns than any other demographic, and that the main cause of this were kerosene-burning lamps.[84] A number of reasons were given for this: women aged 21 to 40 are more likely to be economically active in the home and during nighttime hours than men of the same age group, and traditional women's clothing in India compared to men's is more vulnerable to catching fire.[85] Another compounding factor was that most of the kerosene lamps used in this part of India were of bad quality or design, usually purchased second- or third-hand, or else homemade and improvised using materials like tins.[86] Thus, these

---

[80] Ahmad Houri & Pierre Al Khoury, *supra* note 64, at 659–60.

[81] Palit and Singh, *supra* note 63.

[82] Chamania et al, *supra* note 20, at 595.

[83] *Id.*

[84] *Id.*

[85] *Id.*

[86] *Id.*

statistics show that the issue of energy poverty can indeed be a matter of gender equality and women's health too.

"The challenge of burns lies not in the successful treatment of a 100% burn, but in the 100% prevention of all burn injuries."[87] The replacement of these dangerous open-flame lamps with safer LED lamps seems an obvious fix to the problem. However, the general public must first be educated and informed as to the dangers of kerosene lamps and the long-term benefits of electric lighting.

Section 11: Education and Information

The dangers of indoor air pollution and burn injuries resulting from kerosene are often unknown to those using kerosene, and lighting programs should be premised on providing awareness and information regarding kerosene's health risks.[88] If people are aware of the risks of using kerosene lamps, they may be willing to use off-grid lighting products instead. These Model Laws place the primary responsibility for educating the public on the Ministry Of Health. These Model Laws grant the adopting country the flexibility to make its own administrative arrangements, provided it accepts the importance of and commits to promoting awareness and education.

The most efficient channel for the dissemination of information to the general public may be through existing channels, such as public schools, or other educational programs for rural communities that the adopting country may already have in existence. The adopting country should first examine its existing programs on educating the public on other health matters to determine whether these same channels can be used to educate the public about the dangers of kerosene use. For example, many developing countries like India and Kenya already have extensive programs in place to provide for education on the issue of HIV/AIDS.[89] These programs may use the school system, or other channels such as television/advertisements or public bulletins that are private, NGO, or government-run.[90]

However, these existing programs may not be effective. For example, a recent study in India showed that while the vast majority of a sample of school-going children in India are aware that HIV and AIDS exist, most of these students still harbor great misconceptions, misunderstandings, and resultant prejudices over the exact nature

---

[87] Michael D. Peck, *Epidemiology of Burns throughout the World. Part I: Distribution and Risk Factors*, 37 BURNS 1087, 1100 (2011).

[88] *Supra* Chapters 5 & 6.

[89] Boler et al, *The Sound of Silence: Difficulties in Communicating HIV/AIDS in Schools; Lessons from India and Kenya*, ACTIONAID 53 (2003).

[90] Mitchell et al, *Community-based HIV/AIDS Education in Rural Uganda: Which Channel Is Most Effective?*, 16 HEALTH EDU. RES. 411, 420–422 (2001).

of AIDS.[91] For example, less than one third of the students sampled knew the difference between HIV and AIDS, and less than one half knew that condoms could be used to help prevent the spread of HIV.[92] Therefore, it is important to conduct follow-up surveys following a public education campaign to ensure that the information is being accurately conveyed and understood.

Finally, any education program must consider traditional, spiritual, and cultural norms and differences.[93] There can be severe cultural and traditional impediments to effective public health education. For example, a number of Western-based AIDS education and prevention programs in Africa failed because they failed to take into account "traditional African perceptions of causes of illness . . . , perceptions of sexuality, and cultural beliefs inhibiting the usage of condoms."[94]

Section 12: Enforcement

Judicial and administrative enforcement is a necessary facet of the broader implementation of the Model Laws. While civil and criminal enforcement by public officials is a familiar feature of the laws of many developed countries, the citizen suit provisions may need some explanation in the context of developing countries. In essence, a citizen suit is a form of private enforcement. With private enforcement, the private litigant steps into the public domain by calling for enforcement against the official enforcers or government agencies (for failing to enforce or uphold the laws that have been adopted), or against private actors (for violating the standards of performance, warranty, and safety required by this law).

For a variety of reasons, government agencies are often unable or unwilling to enforce regulatory laws, for a number of reasons, four of which merit special mention:

(1) Their efforts may be impeded by inadequate staff, funding, and information, a persistent problem even in developed nations.

---

[91] Sharma et al, *Mounting Aids Awareness through Educational Intervention: How Effective Can It Be?*, NAT'L J. MEDICAL RESEARCH, Apr.–Jun. 2013. at 155.

[92] *Id.*

[93] Matinga et al, *Behavioral Challenges and the Adoption of Appropriate Sustainable Energy Technologies*, in *Int'l Energy and Poverty: The emerging contours* 146 (Lakshman Guruswamy, ed. 2015).

[94] Alta C. Van Dyk, *Traditional African Beliefs and Customs: Implications for AIDS Education and Prevention in Africa*, S. AFR. J. PSYCHOLOGY, Jun. 2001, at 60, 66.

(2) Agencies may be slow off the mark and playing catch up with changing circumstances—often due to the backlog resulting from reason (1).

(3) Agencies may be "captured" by the very groups and special interests that they are supposed to regulate. Corruption, bribery, and cronyism at all levels of government can be huge problems in many of the developing nations these laws are meant for (and even in some developed nations as well).

(4) They could be ensnared in the procedural red tape that is a common facet in many developing countries' bureaucracies.[95]

When armed with citizen suit authority and given the standing necessary to pursue a case, private citizens are empowered to take over the enforcement of such laws, free of some of the bureaucratic and political constraints that can hobble government enforcers. Other advantages of allowing citizen enforcement is that the citizens in question often have a closer and more intimate connection with their environment, as well as providing a greater variety of non-institutional perspectives and information.[96]

It is possible for some governments and their bureaucracies to consider citizen suits as potential instruments for attacking government institutions who are doing their best in difficult circumstances. They may also consider such suits a device for drawing national and even international attention to their country. From a more objective perspective, any government that enacts this statute is seeking to address the problems of access to lighting and should not try to cover up the poor conduct of their agencies. A citizen suit allows the citizens of a country to draw attention to agency inaction and enables an independent judiciary to call for the implementation of mandatory and non-discretionary provisions of the Act. Bringing questionable conduct into the sunshine of judicial scrutiny will help governments meet the challenges they seek to address through this Act.

In the United States, many federal environmental statutes allow citizen suits.[97] These laws include the Clean Water Act, the Clean Air Act, the Resource Conservation and Recovery Act, and the

---

[95] Benjamin Van Rooij, *The People's Regulation: Citizens and Regulation of Law in China*, 25 COLUM. J. ASIAN L. 116, 177 (2012).

[96] Irene Villanueva Nemesio, *Strengthening Environmental Rule of Law: Enforcement, Combatting Corruption, and Encouraging Citizen Suits*, 27 GEO. INT'L ENVTL. L. REV. 321, 330.

[97] Altman et al, *Citizen Enforcement In Environmental Law*, D. DAVID ALTMAN CO., LPA, http://www.environlaw.com/pdf/citizen_suits.pdf.

Endangered Species Act.[98] For example, the Clean Air Act permits "any person" to "commence a civil action" against any other entity, including the government, "who is alleged to have violated [. . .] or to be in violation of an emission standard or limitation," as well against the Administrator "where there is alleged a failure of the Administrator to perform any act or duty under this chapter which is not discretionary with the Administrator."[99]

Following the example set by the United States, a number of both developed and developing states have recognized that public authorities are not always the best suited at enforcing compliance with environmental laws and have begun to allow private enforcement of environmental laws.[100] The first major international agreement was Article 18 of the 1993 Lugano Convention of the Counsel Of Europe, which states that "any association or foundation which according to its statutes aims at the protection of the environment" would be granted standing to litigate against any violators of each European state's respective environmental regulations.[101]

In many developing countries that have introduced environmental regulations, lack of citizen enforcement provisions ensure that citizens do not have standing to pursue their claims in the courts.[102] In addition, the costs and efforts involved in the process of litigation can be formidable.[103] For example, in China, a recent study found that one of the primary reasons that enforcement of environmental regulations remains lax and insufficient is due to the lack of public participation.[104] The study also suggested a number of measures that could be made to increase the active participation of the citizens in both the legislative process and in the enforcement of the laws once they are formally adopted.[105]

VIII. Model Law on Lighting for Developed Countries

A BILL To promote the development and deployment of lighting products to save lives, improve livelihoods, protect children, empower

---

[98] 33 U.S.C. § 1365 (2006); 42 U.S.C. § 7604 (2006); 42 U.S.C. § 6972 (2006); 16 U.S.C. § 1540 (2006).

[99] Section 7604(a).

[100] Werkman et al, *Improving Compliance with International Environmental Law* 53 (2014).

[101] Convention on Civil Liability for Damage Resulting from Activities Dangerous to the Environment, art. 18, Jun. 21, 1993, CETS 150.

[102] Nemesio, *supra* note 96 at 333.

[103] *Id.* at 334.

[104] Wang Canfa, *Chinese Environmental Law Enforcement: Current Deficiencies and Suggested Reforms*, 8 VT. J. ENVTL. L. 160, 191 (2007).

[105] *Id.*

women, and combat climate change by creating a thriving global market for clean, affordable, and efficient indoor lighting solutions, and for other purposes.

Be it enacted by the [legislative organ] of the [developed country] assembled,

§ 1. Short Title

This Act may be cited as the "Clean Lighting Support Act of [*year*]."

§ 2. Findings

[*Legislative organ*] finds that:

(1) [*Name of country*] is a member of the community of nations that has accepted well-recognized principles of international law and policy establishing—

(A) the right of developing countries to sustainable development;

(B) the common but differentiated legal and moral rights of [*name of country*] and other developed nations to institutionally, financially, and technologically support sustainable development among developing countries by alleviating energy poverty and providing access to safe and sustainable lighting products; and

(C) that there is an urgent and pressing need to promote the use of renewable energy resources and technologies to supply energy needs, including lighting.

(2) [*Name of country*] seeks to support sustainable and renewable development and carry out its common but differentiated legal and moral responsibility **(CBDR)** pertaining to energy poverty and access to safe and sustainable lighting products through this Act.

(3) It is estimated that of the 1.5 billion people worldwide without access to electricity, most rely on kerosene for illumination.

(4) The use of kerosene for lighting generates indoor air pollution, contributing to the deaths of 1.8 million people per year. Kerosene fires kill more than 1 million people per year, and children suffer health problems and die from the accidental ingestion of kerosene.

(5) Lighting fuels, such as kerosene, are nonrenewable sources of energy. The National Institute of Environmental Health Sciences estimates that worldwide 77 billion liters of liquid fuel, mostly kerosene, are used annually to light houses without electricity.

(6) The burning of kerosene for lighting in developing countries is estimated to cause the emission of 223 tons of carbon dioxide into the atmosphere per year, contributing to global climate change. Kerosene lamps are also major emitters of black carbon, which is both dangerous when inhaled and a significant agent of climate change.

(7) Without adequate indoor lighting, women and children cannot engage in educational or economic activities after dark. Lack of adequate lighting also contributes to insecurity and danger at night.

(8) Explosions and fires from kerosene-related accidents lead to hundreds of thousands of burn deaths each year, and burn survivors often sustain permanent injuries ranging from debilitating scarring to loss of movement.

(9) The development and deployment of improved indoor lighting products is essential for achieving the United Nations Sustainable Development Goal#7: Ensure access to affordable, reliable, sustainable and modern energy for all.

(10) Improved indoor lighting products positively impact the quality of life and the environment by—

(A) Enabling women and children to engage in educational and economic endeavors after dark;

(B) Promoting gender equality and women's empowerment;

(C) Improving health and safety;

(D) Advancing environmental stability by reducing reliance on fossil fuels;

(E) Reducing contributions to global climate change; and

(F) Ensuring and facilitating access and delivery of medical care, particularly after dark.

§ 3. Policy

It is the policy of [*name of country*] to—

(1) Promote universal access to lighting;

(2) Support energy supply from renewable and sustainable resources;

(3) Sponsor national and international efforts to promote, distribute, enable, and maintain universal access to lighting;

(4) Stimulate national and international research, development, and deployment of lighting products;

(5) Aid research, development, and deployment of lighting products which are safe and utilize renewable energy generation sources;

(6) Require the establishment of National Minimum Quality and Performance Standards such as United Laboratories or IEEE standards;

(7) Assist technology transfer of renewable and sustainable energy development and universal access to lightning.

§ 4. Definitions

In this Act:

(1) "Lighting Product" means one that:

(A) Employs appropriate durable, affordable, renewable, harmless and accessible sustainable energy technologies;

(B) Has been prototypically demonstrated, tested, and certified as meeting—

(i) Brightness Standards; and

(ii) Indoor ambient air quality standards; or

(iii) Where a developing country determines that indoor ambient air quality standards cannot be achieved, the reasonable interim air quality standards established by the developing country improves existing indoor ambient air quality; and

(C) Meets minimum durability standards based on the needs and conditions of such developing country and its peoples.

(2) "Brightness Standards" means that lighting products for general household use must provide an output of 20 lumens or illuminate an area equal to 2 sheets of paper at 25 lux.

§ 5. Lighting Product Manufacturing, Promotion, and Distribution

(a) In General.

There is established within the [*Ministry or Agency for International Aid*] a Lighting Product Manufacturing and Distribution Program.

(b) Purpose.

The purpose of the program established by subsection (a) is to provide international partnerships and local entrepreneurs with financial, institutional, and technological assistance to develop, manufacture, promote, distribute, and maintain certified safe, improved lighting products and charging stations in developing countries.

(c) Funding.

(1) The program established by subsection (a) shall be funded in the amount of $15,000,000 each year for 10 years.

(2) Criteria—The administrator of the program established by subsection (a) shall establish criteria for the use of funds provided by paragraph (1) to carry out the purpose of the program.

(3) Consultation—The criteria established under paragraph (2) shall be developed in consultation with:

(A) Governmental and community leaders in developing countries;

(B) Indigenous and affected populations and other stakeholders;

(C) Non-governmental organizations working to promote safe and sustainable indoor lighting;

(D) [*Other relevant ministries or agencies within the developed country*]; and

(E) The interested public.

(4) Notice and Comment—The administrator of the program established by subsection (a) shall provide public notice and an opportunity for any interested party to comment on any proposal to this section or amendments thereto; and the agency for receiving comments shall respond in a timely manner.

(5) Availability of Funds—The funding provided by paragraph (1) shall be available to offices or programs within the [*appropriate agency or agencies within the Ministry for International Aid*] in accordance with—

(A) the criteria established under paragraph (2); and

(B) such other rules as are established by the [*agency head*].

(6) Grants and Other Aid—The program established by subsection (a) may, in accordance with the criteria established under paragraph (2) and without the need for any matching or base funds, use up to 20 percent of the funding provided by paragraph (1) to provide grants, loans, or other methods of financial support to businesses and other non-governmental organizations working to develop, manufacture, promote, distribute, or maintain improved lighting products in developing countries.

(d) Monitoring; Reporting.

The administrator of the program established by subsection (a) shall—

(1) Monitor and evaluate the effectiveness of the program; and

(2) Report every 2 years after the date of enactment of this Act to the [*appropriate developed country officials and entities*] and the public on the effectiveness of the activities supported by and carried out under the program.

(e) Accounting.

(1) The administrator of the program established by subsection (a) shall account for the funds it receives and distributes. The accounting shall comply with generally accepted accounting principles and shall be made available to the [*appropriate developed country officials and entities*] and the public within 90 days of the end of each fiscal year.

(2) The program shall be audited by independent auditors, selected by the Agency for International Aid, at the end of every other fiscal year.

§ 6. Grant Program

(a) In General.

There is a grant program established within the [*Ministry or Agency for Applied Energy Research and Design*] to facilitate a Lighting Product Research, Development, and Demonstration in partnership with stakeholders in developing countries.

(b) Purpose.

The purpose of the grant program established by subsection (a) is to enable and facilitate the research, development, testing, and demonstration of—

(1) Effective and efficient appropriate/affordable sustainable energy technologies (ASETs) that provide alternatives to the use of fossil fuel-based lighting;

(2) Alternative lighting products and components thereof;

(3) Accessible and user-friendly centralized charging mechanisms and stations;

(4) Conduct and support research and monitoring on the household, local, and global production of black carbon and other pollutants emitted by fossil fuel-based lighting;

(5) Conduct and support research and monitoring on the adverse human health and environmental effects

associated with the black carbon and other pollutants emitted by bio-mass based lighting;

(6) Research and develop best practices and programs to reduce the adverse human health and environmental effects associated with black carbon and other pollutants through the use of bio-mass based andfuel-based lighting; and

(7) Inform governments, researchers, and the public of the research, monitoring, best practices, and programs developed under paragraphs (4) through (6).

(8) Leverage existing research and development in the sustainable energy sphere including wind turbines, hydro-electric, solar, biofuel, and lighting in general to create affordable sustainable lighting.

(c) Funding.

(1) In General—The program established by subsection (a) shall be funded in the amount of $15,000,000 each year for 10 years.

(2) Criteria—The administrator of the program established by subsection (a) shall establish criteria for the use of funds provided by paragraph (1) to carry out the purpose of the program.

(3) Consultation—The criteria established under paragraph (2) shall be developed in consultation with—

(A) Domestic and international businesses, academic institutions, and non-profit institutions that are developing or are interested in the research, development, testing, or demonstration of safe and sustainable lighting products;

(B) [*Other relevant ministries or agencies within the developed country*]; and

(C) Indigenous and affected populations/community leaders in developing countries, and other stakeholders; and

(D) The interested public.

(4) Notice and Comment—The administrator of the program established by subsection (a) shall provide public notice and an opportunity for any interested party to comment on any proposal under paragraph (2) or amendments thereto.

(5) Availability of Funds—The funding provided by paragraph (1) shall be available to offices or programs within the

[*Ministry or Agency for Applied Energy Research and Design*] in accordance with—

(A) The criteria established under paragraph (2); and

(B) Such other rules as are established by the [*agency head*].

(6) Grants and Other Aid—The administrator of the program established by subsection (a) shall, in accordance with the criteria established under paragraph (2) and without the need for any matching or base funds, use up to 80 percent of the funding provided by paragraph (1) to provide grants, loans, or other methods of financial support to academic, business, and other non-governmental entities for research, development, testing, or demonstration of safe and sustainable lighting products.

(d) Monitoring; Reporting.

The administrator of the program established by subsection (a) shall—

(1) Monitor the effectiveness of the program; and

(2) Report every 5 years after the date of enactment of this Act to the [*appropriate developed country officials and entities*] and the public on the effectiveness of the activities supported by and carried out under the program.

(e) Accounting.

The administrator of the program established by subsection (a) shall account for the funds it receives and distributes. The accounting shall comply with generally accepted accounting principles and shall be made available to the [*appropriate developed country officials and entities*] and the public within 90 days of the end of each fiscal year. (b) The program shall be audited by independent auditors, selected by the executive committee of the Agency, at the end of every other fiscal year.

§ 7. Health and Environmental Research

(a) In general.

There is established within the [*Ministry or Agency for Health or Environmental Research*] a Lighting Product Health and Environmental Research Program (PRM).

(b) Purpose.

The purpose of the program established by subsection (a) is to—

(1) Conduct and support research and monitoring on the household, local, and global production of black carbon and

other pollutants emitted by bio-mass, and/or fossil fuel-based lighting;

(2) Support research and monitoring on the adverse human health and environmental effects associated with the black carbon and other pollutants emitted by biomass and other fossil fuel-based lighting;

(3) Research and develop best practices and programs to reduce the adverse human health and environmental effects associated with black carbon and other pollutants resulting from the use of biomass and other fossil fuel-based lighting;

(4) Inform governments, researchers, and the public of the research, monitoring, best practices, and programs developed under paragraphs (1) through (3);

(5) Collaborate and integrate with existing research programs and standards to ensure relevance and interoperability globally.

(c) Funding.

(1) In General—The prm established by subsection (a) shall be funded in the amount of $15,000,000 each year for 10 years.

(2) Criteria—The administrator of the program established by subsection (a) shall establish criteria for the use of funds to conduct the research, monitoring, and other activities described in subsection (b).

(3) Consultation—The criteria established under paragraph (2) shall be developed in consultation with—

(A) Domestic and international businesses, academic institutions, and non-profit institutions that are interested in reducing the adverse health and environmental effects of fuel-based lighting;

(B) Domestic and international businesses, academic institutions, and non-profit institutions that are developing or are interested in the development of fuel-based lighting;

(C) The [*other relevant agencies within the developed country*];

(D) Indigenous and affected populations/community leaders in developing countries, and other stakeholders;

(E) The interested public.

(4) Notice and Comment—The administrator of the program established by subsection (a) shall provide public notice and an opportunity for any interested party to comment on any proposal to establish criteria under paragraph (2) or amendments thereto.

(5) Availability of Funds—The funding provided by paragraph (1) shall be available to any offices or programs within the [*agency for applied energy research and design*] in accordance with—

(A) The criteria established under paragraph (2); and

(B) Such other rules as are established by the [*agency head*].

(6) Grants and Other Aid—The administrator of the program established by subsection (a) may, in accordance with the criteria established under paragraph (2) and without the need for any matching or base funds, use up to 80 percent of the funding provided by paragraph (1) to provide grants, loans, or other methods of financial support to academic and other non-governmental entities for the health and environmental research, monitoring, and other activities described in subsection (b).

(d) Monitoring; Reporting—The administrator of the program established by subsection (a) shall—

(1) Monitor the effectiveness of the program; and

(2) Report every 5 years after the date of enactment of this Act to the [*appropriate developed country officials and entities*] and the public on the effectiveness of the activities supported by and carried out under the program.

(e) Accounting—The administrator of the program established by subsection (a) shall account for the funds it receives and distributes. The accounting shall comply with generally accepted accounting principles and shall be made available to the [*appropriate developed country officials and entities*] and the public within 90 days of the end of each fiscal year.

IX. Commentary: Model Law on Lighting for Developed Countries

Section 2: Findings

The first finding accepts and reinforces the principle of common but differentiated responsibility (CBDR) which requires developed countries to take the lead in advancing sustainable development.[106] Chapters 3 and 4 discuss the importance of CBDR. [107]

Findings 2 to 10 in this law and the rationale for them, are similar to those in the Model Law for Developing Countries, and do not require repetition in this commentary.

Section 3: Policy

Section 3 sets out seven proposed policies that support this legislation. These policies are stated in a manner allowing for their more complete expression by each adopting country. Most of the proposed policies relate directly to discrete sections within the proposed Model Law. Two of them do not: Policy No. 2, which promotes renewable energy technologies, and Policy 6 which suggests minimum performance standards.

Policy 2 considers the source of power in the promotion of sustainable lighting technology. This is an important problem that requires significant consideration because perceived low kerosene costs may impede the adoption of sustainable lighting technologies and frustrate the goal of this statute. A solar bulb or a microgrid tied to a wind generator will have significant up-front costs. [108] However, over the long term, kerosene becomes expensive, potentially costing many times more than some solar light bulbs. A 2003 study found that LEDs, at that time, cost 5 cents per thousand lux hours, while non-pressurized kerosene lamps could cost as much as $3.80 per thousand lux hours.[109] Accordingly, how to overcome the financial barriers obstructing renewable resources, must be considered at each level of implementation, under this model law.

Policy 6 deals with minimum quality and performance standards. Those products that are being endorsed or funded by national aid should be subject to testing and standards to ensure quality and performance. Standards seek to avoid and outcome where the goods or services provided at substantial costs, are ineffective or defective.

---

[106] The principle of common but differentiated responsibility (CBDR) is set out in Art. 3 (1) of the United Nations Framework Convention on Climate Change 1992, reprinted in 31 I.L.M. 849. Also see, Gwenaelle Legros et al., *The Energy Access Situation in Developing Countries: A Review Focusing on the Least Developed Countries and Sub-Saharan Africa* 10, United Nations Development Programme (2009). http://content.undp.org/go/cms-service/stream/asset/?asset_id=2205620.

[107] Chapter 3 *supra.*

[108] K. Kaygusuz, *Energy Services and Energy Poverty for Sustainable Rural Development*, 15 RENEWABLE AND SUSTAINABLE ENERGY REVIEWS 936, 940 (2011); Evan Mills, *The Specter of Fuel-Based Lighting*, 308 SCIENCE 1263, 1263 (2005).

[109] Evan Mills, *Technical and Economic Performance Analysis of Kerosene Lamps and Alternative Approaches to Illumination in Developing Countries* 3 (2003), available at http://evanmills.lbl.gov/pubs/pdf/offgrid-lighting.pdf.

Section 4: Definitions

Section 4 provides important definitions for the development and dissemination of clean lighting. First, paragraph (1) requires that lighting products are "appropriate durable, affordable, renewable, harmless, and accessible." There is no prioritization, all of them are equally important.

Second, lighting product are required to satisfy testing and certifications requirements.[110] These standards relate to brightness, ambient air quality and durability. Standards may be too burdensome or even practically unattainable for a particular developing country. If so less demanding interim standards may be applied.

Durability standards are based on the needs, conditions, and abilities of that particular developing country and its people. The requirement stems from the fact that durability of lighting products is essential for the long-term development of the lighting sector.

The "Brightness Standard," contains the requirement that lighting products for general household use must provide an output of 20 lumens[111] or illuminate an area equal to 2 sheets of paper at 25 lux. Metrics for measuring brightness and luminosity are often based on lumens. A lumen measures one square foot of light that is produced by a candle one foot away from a wall.[112] Although lux and watts may also be acceptable measurement standards, this Model Law will use lumens.[113]

---

110 The method of demonstration, testing, and certification has not been provided in the body of the model law, as it has to cater to the specific needs and conditions of a developing country that is implementing this model law. Therefore all actors and stakeholders involved in the establishment of lighting in that particular country should be engaged in structuring the method of demonstration, testing, and certification of "Lighting Products."

111 An output of 20 lumens is equated to an A 4 watt night bulb, which is the minimum of brightness in lumens. *See Lumens & LED Brightness*, http://www.power-sure.com/lumens.htm#Led0.

112 K. Soman, *International System of Units: A Handbook on SI Units for Scientists and Engineers* 16 (2009); *see also LED Flashlights Fact Sheet, Starline Inc.*, available at https://us.starline.com/content/image/Forms/distributor_resources/Fact Sheets/Starline_FactSheet_LED.pdf.

113 Wattage is a measure of power, and lux, a measure of the spread of light in an area, is defined as one lumen per square meter. Power does not necessarily translate into luminance; while a lightbulb may use a certain wattage, if it is especially inefficient it will emit a low light output. Lumens are appropriate to use here because they measure the total light output from a source, and are useful as a base or foundation measure from which to work out a lux measurement, for example, if a light bulb is fitted in a home. Further, not all lights are likely to be used indoors and lighting equipment often draw more attention to a lumens measurement than a lux measurement. For example, the United States Dept. of Energy's EnergyStar program now measures bulb brightness in lumens. *See "Lighting Made Easy—Just Look for the Energy Star* EnergyStar.gov 1, https://www.energystar.gov/ia/partners/manuf_res/ES_Lighting_ConsumerFactsheet.pdf?0b551475.

Section 5: Lighting Product Manufacturing, Promotion, and Distribution: Commentary

Section 5 establishes a program to support the manufacturing, promotion, and distribution of lighting products in developing countries. An adopting country may find that an existing office, agency, or program has the appropriate capacities to carry out the program,[114] in other cases, a new program or office may best serve the goals of the model legislation.[115] The preferred course is to avoid duplication and leverage existing administrative infrastructure to support the implementation of lighting product development, manufacturing, promotion, and distribution projects in developing countries. The designated agency should consider how to create and foster international partnerships, and partnerships with local entrepreneurs.[116]

Governments and civil society should contribute to the efforts of providing lighting for all.[117] For example, the United States Power Africa program has leveraged $43 billion in commitments from over 120 public and private sector partners. Power Africa plans to add

---

[114] An example of a developed country's agency that has the appropriate capacities to carry out the goals of this model legislation is the Office of International Affairs (IA) within the United States Department of Energy. The IA is primarily responsible for "international energy cooperation in energy, science, and technology . . . [by] lead[ing] and develop[ing] the Department's bilateral and multilateral R&D [research and development] cooperation, including investment and trade activities." U.S. DEPT. OF ENERGY, Office of International Affairs, http://www.energy.gov/ia/office-international-affairs (visited Nov. 4, 2015).

[115] An adopting country has a number of internal options in creating a new entity. One option is to create a quasi-governmental agency with a private organization or companies that have expertise in lighting products. *See generally* Kevin R. Kosar, *The Quasi Government: Hybrid Organizations With Both Government And Private Sector Legal Characteristics* (Congressional Research Service ed., 2011). Some examples of private companies working towards providing access to energy with lighting that an adopting country could partner with are Elephant Energy and Nokero, both of which are working towards creating and providing sustainable energy technologies. *See* NOKERO SOLAR, http://www.nokero.com/ (last visited Nov. 6, 2015); ELEPHANT ENERGY, http://www.elephantenergy.org/ (last visited Nov. 6, 2015).

[116] For example, the United States Environmental Protection Agency works with Brazil's Sao Paulo Sanitation Technology Company (CETESB), a Sao Paulo State environmental agency, by sharing information on environmental management and risk reduction. U.S. ENV'T. PROTECTION AGENCY, *EPA Collaboration with Brazil*, http://www2.epa.gov/international-cooperation/epa-collaboration-brazil#activities (last visited Nov. 4, 2015).

[117] For example, the Global Off-Grid Lighting Association (GOGLA), available at http://global-off-grid-lighting-association.org/; The World Bank Group & International Funding Corporation with their initiative: Lighting Global, available at http://www.lightingglobal.org/, Elephant Energy, available at http://www.elephant energy.org; and the U.S. Energy Department. According to the International Energy Agency, sub-Saharan Africa will require more than $300 billion in investment to achieve universal electricity access by 2030. Fact Sheet: Power Africa, Office of the Press Sec. June 30, 2013, https://www.whitehouse.gov/the-pressoffice/2013/06/30/fact-sheet-power-africa.

30,000 MW.[118] The overarching emphasis of such global efforts point to a bottom-up approach in providing access to lighting.[119] The Model Law on Lighting provides for bottom-up solutions.

Despite global attention and understanding of the urgent need to create access to lighting for everyone, current efforts fall short. On the one hand financial, institutional, technological, and research has significantly succeeded in creating advanced lighting for developed countries. On the other hand, Support for access to lighting for the EP has been weak, and these efforts have lacked the scale, and collective engagement essential for adequate progress. There is no established international funding mechanism or institutional body with the capacity to engage in research and development or the ability to raise the resources needed to combat the lack of lighting among the energy poor. The adoption and implementation of this Model Law, is not a silver bullet, but will open doors to more international collaboration.

The participation of the developed countries in programs under this Model Law is intended to complement and unify the global efforts of delivering sustainable electricity to every household. Developing rather than developed counties should be responsible for calculating and quantifying the lighting needed to implement this Model Law within its territory.[120] It not proposed that a developed country should not have an input in finalizing or amending the funding. The estimated funding should be a product of collaborative effort and dialogue between developed and developing countries (and/or their representatives), as the input from both countries is essential in arriving at the correct estimates.[121]

---

[118] US AID, *Power Africa,* https://www.usaid.gov/powerafrica. The funding incorporated technical assistance, grants, risk mitigation in private sector energy transactions, assistance in structuring governmental policies to attract investment of private sector, investment in energy infrastructure, regulatory reforms and institutional capacity building. Consequently, only with greater private sector investment can the promise of Power Africa be realized.

[119] *Power to the People*, THE ECONOMIST, Sep. 2, 2010, http://www.economist.com/node/16909923.

[120] When assessing the needed funding, barriers faced by the developing country need to be evaluated. Four such barriers have been identified.: 1) economic; 2) technical; 3) political/institutional; 4) cultural/social/environmental. Mark Safty, *Assessing Challenges to Development* 134–5, in *International Energy and Poverty: The emerging contours* (Lakshman Guruswamy, ed. 2015).

[121] The primary obstacle to foreign funding and investment is the inherent risk of investment in developing countries. Developing States could allay such fears by by the act of adopting this Model Law, and also incorporateing specific indemnities for the investors. Mark Safty, *Assessing Challenges to Development* 136. Elephant Energy, available at http://www.elephantenergy.org/african-ventures.

The Model Law also calls for significant and transparent[122] monitoring, reporting, and accounting. Such practices are important for establishing and maintaining an effective and efficient international aid program of the kind that is called for here.[123]

Section 6: Grant Program

Section 6 deals with grants, and provides a ministry or agency with options that may be utilized to develop sustainable lighting solutions for the energy poor.[124] Under Section 6, the agency will enable and facilitate: 1) the research and development of appropriate sustainable energy lighting technologies, and 2) evaluate the success of such research.

Kerosene is significantly cheaper than alternative lighting solutions, but as demonstrated in the commentary to Section 3, the risks greatly outweigh the benefits. One in three people use kerosene or other fuels as a light source but only receive 1% of the energy services due to mechanical inefficiencies. Funding for research will enable research on other sources of lighting estimated at saving $75–

---

[122] Transparency, a growing international concept, calls for governments to be more open, accountable, and responsive to citizens, with a view to creating trust. OPEN GOVERNMENT PARTNERSHIP, http://www.opengovpartnership.org/ (last visited Nov. 11, 2015).

[123] The adopting country must determine what method of monitoring will work best for the implementation of this model legislation. There are a number of methods an adopting country can choose from. One example is Social Impact Assessment ("SIA"), which is the process of "analyzing, monitoring and managing the intended and unintended social consequences, both positive and negative, of planned interventions and any social change processes invoked by those interventions." Frank Vanclay, *International Principles for Social Impact Assessment*, 21 IMPACT ASSESSMENT AND PROJECT APPRAISAL 5 (2003), http://www.tandfonline.com/doi/pdf/10.3152/147154603781766491. Another example is the Logical Framework Approach ("LFA") that is somewhat different from SIA. Gilroy Coleman, *Logical Framework Approach to the Monitoring and Evaluation of Agricultural and Rural Development Projects*, 2 PROJECT APPRAISAL 251, 252 (1987), and is directed at the initial planning and preparation of a project, rather than a monitoring mechanism. A third example, and perhaps the most efficient method of monitoring and reporting, is Integrated Assessment ("IA"). IA brings together natural, social, and economic information from scientists, policy makers, citizens, NGO, and industry representatives to evaluate and make decisions. Keely Dinse et. al., *Benefits of Integrated Assessment: Information for Decision Makers, Project Leaders and Scientists*, 2 (Michigan Sea Grant et. al. 2010), http://www.miseagrant.umich.edu/downloads/ia/10–200–Benefits-of-Integrated–Assessment.pdf. By bringing numerous groups and individuals together, IA can generate reports from diverse perspectives, and allows for a smoother transition where the program needs to be changed. *Id.* at 4–6.

[124] Vijay Modi et al., *Energy Services for the Millennium Development Goals*, THE INTERNATIONAL BANK FOR RECONSTRUCTION AND DEVELOPMENT, THE WORLD BANK, AND THE UNITED NATIONS DEVELOPMENT PROGRAMME, 61 2005; Evan Mills, *Why We're Here: The $230-Billion Global Lighting Energy Bill, Conference on Energy Efficient Lighting,* 376 CNICE, FRANCE (2002), available at http://citeseerx.ist.psu.edu/viewdoc/download?doi=10.1.1.202.5663&rep=rep1&type=pdf; Kristen Radecsky et al., *Solid-State Lighting on a Shoestring Budget: The Economics of Off-Grid Lighting for Small Businesses in Kenya*, THE LUMINA PROJECT, Technical Report #3, 2 (2009), available at http://escholarship.org/uc/item/2714q6kz.

115 billion a year.[125] Researching the health and environmental benefits will provide more motivation for developed countries to support developing countries to ensure access to illumination.[126]

The principle of CBDR, applies to research focused on creating technologies to combat the health and environmental impacts of kerosene. Developed countries with more sophisticated research institutions can lead research at a global level. Even more importantly, they should support, fund, and collaborate with research being conducted in developing countries on these issues. The collaboration could occur between government research institutes as well as private research initiatives, but the principle of CBDR must ensure that the primary responsibility for research is being shouldered by developed countries.

There is not a one size fits all solution to ensuring access to illumination for all. For example sub Saharan Africa is different to Arctic tundra environments. Funding and grants, should best support access to lighting around the world, in widely different environments. Therefore program goals should be determined through consultations with the parties outlined in paragraph c of Section 6. Consultations are not to be used as events to simply inform parties of the work being done. In order to ensure bottom up participation, all parties should be represented, invited, and empowered to engage in collective decision making. It will be wise for this ministry or agency to employ locals where research is being done to ensure proper representation.

The established agency head will administer and manage the distribution of funds, in accordance with international accounting principles. Robust financial controls must be implemented to ensure funds are used effectively, and not lost to the unfortunate realities of corruption in many nations. To ensure the proper usage of funding, like any sound business or agreed upon international standards, an accountant will be used to monitor fund spending and distribution.

---

125 Kristen Radecsky et al., *supra* note 124; Evan Mills, *supra* note 124.

126 William D. McNally, *Kerosene Poisoning in Children: A Study of 204 Cases,* 48 THE JOURNAL OF PEDIATRICS 296 (1956); P. Gupta et al., *Kerosene Oil Poisoning: A Childhood Menace,* Dep't of Pediatrics and Radiology, University College of Medical Sciences and G.T.B. Hospital, Shahdara, Delhi (1992); A Human Dimension to the Energy Debate, 26 NO. 4 J. ENERGY & NAT. RESOURCES L. at 532.

Section 7: Health and Environmental Research

This Section establishes a research program focused on the impacts that sustainable lighting can have both on health and environmental issues. While kerosene is being targeted, it is possible that biomass fires could be used as source of lighting. It is for this reason that both biomass and fossil fuel based lighting is included in Section 7. As the purpose section mentions, the most obvious health and environmental impacts are caused by black carbon.

Black carbon is known to contribute to global warming. According to some estimates, black carbon is the No. 2 contributor to climate change after carbon dioxide.[127] The impacts of carbon dioxide on the atmosphere last for decades, but black carbon's effects are short lived.[128] Unlike carbon dioxide, which remains in the atmosphere for centuries and even millennia,[129] black carbon attenuates in the atmosphere quickly when the source is removed.[130] As a result, reducing black carbon *production* would have a substantial impact on climate change—and it could have that impact

---

[127] Nicholas L., Lam, *et al.*, *Characterizing Kerosene Demand for Light in India and Evaluating the Impact of Measures Affecting Access and Dependence* in *Innovating Energy Access for Remote Areas: Discovering Untapped Resources: PROCEEDINGS OF THE INTERNATIONAL CONFERENCE*; April 10th to 12th, 2014, University of Berkeley. Universitätsverlag der TU Berlin, 2015 http://www.tu-berlin.de/fileadmin/FG/LBP/UCB-Symposium_MES-BREG_FINAL1.pdf; Nicholas L. Lam, *et al.*, *Household Light Makes Global Heat: High Black Carbon Emissions From Kerosene Wick Lamps*, 46 ENVIRON. SCI. TECHNOL., 13531 (Nov. 19, 2012); *Global Warming: The New Black*, THE ECONOMIST (Jan. 19, 2013), http://www.economist.com/news/science-and-technology/21569686–soot-even-worse-climate-was-previously-thought-new-black; Bryan Walsh, *Black Carbon: An Overlooked Climate Factor*, TIME (Nov. 19, 2009), http://content.time.com/time/health/article/0,8599,1938379,00.html http://www.time.com/time/health/article/0,8599,1938379,00.html. While it is clear that emissions from diesel locomotion, as well as black carbon from industrial facilities are major contributors to the problem, it would appear that controlling kerosene burning can result in a significant reduction of black carbon. *See* Bond, et al., *Bounding the role of black carbon in the climate system: A scientific assessment*, ___ JOURNAL OF GEOPHYSICAL RESEARCH: ATOMOSPHERES at ___ (2013) (accepted but not yet published). However, the impact of kerosene burning on black carbon emissions or the impact of black carbon emissions on climate change are not universally accepted. *C.f., Soot is Warming the World Even More Than Thought*, SCIENCE at 382 (Jan. 25, 2012) (discounting the impact of biomass burning on global warming).

[128] *Bond, Id.*; Drew Shindell, et al., *Simultaneously Mitigating Near-Term Climate Change and Improving Human Health and Food Security*, SCIENCE 183 (Jan. 13, 2012); Robert F. Service, *Study Fingers Soot as a Major Player in Global Warming*, SCIENCE 1745 (Mar. 28, 2008).

[129] David Archer, *et al.*, *Atmospheric Lifetime of Fossil Fuel Carbon Dioxide*, 37 ANNUAL REVIEW OF EARTH AND PLANETARY SCIENCES 117 (2009) Archer points out that the 2007 IPCC report more accurately states that "[a]bout half of a CO2 pulse to the atmosphere is removed over a timescale of 30 years; a further 30% is removed within a few centuries; and the remaining 20% will typically stay in the atmosphere for many thousands of years."

[130] Gregory R. Carmichael, *Short-Lived Climate Forcing Agents and Their Roles in Climate Change*, 77 PROCEDIA—SOCIAL AND BEHAVIORAL SCIENCES 227, 228 (2013).

quickly.[131] Indeed, as stated in recent testimony to the US Senate Committee on the Environment and Public Works, "Multiple, peer—reviewed scientific studies have shown that aggressive reductions of those air pollutants that cause warming, in particular methane and black carbon, can reduce the rate of warming over the next several decades by approximately half."[132]

Moreover, using kerosene lamps exposes those using the lamps directly to the smoke guttering from the flame. "As much as 7–9% of kerosene consumed in kerosene lamps is converted to carbonaceous particulate matter that is almost entirely black carbon."[133] The International Energy Agency (the IEA) predicts that the numbers of people expected to die from exposure to smoke from using ancient lighting like kerosene lamps and three stone fires is *likely increase* over the next 20–25.[134] In real world terms, the IEA's predictions mean that the number of deaths from smoke will in 2030 likely be essentially the same as the number of deaths caused by malaria, tuberculosis, and AIDS—combined—in that same year. As the IEA points out, such policies do not meet the goal of energy access for all.[135]

The remaining portions of Section 7 outline a funding, monitoring and accounting program that is identical to the other programs set out in Sections 5 and 6. Accordingly, reference is made to the commentary of those sections concerning the financial aspects of Section 7.

---

[131] *Id. See also*, Nicholas Lam, note 127, *supra*.

[132] Drew Shindell,. *Societal Benefits from Reductions in Emissions of Methane and Black Carbon* (2014), available at http://sites.nicholas.duke.edu/drewshindell/files/2015/01/Senate_EPW_testimony_Dec2014_Shindell_v3.pdf.

[133] Nicholas L. Lam, et al., *supra* note 127.

[134] International Energy Agency, *World Energy Outlook* 2011 at 489, fig. 13.10 (2011).

[135] *Id.* at 469.

Chapter 7

CONCLUSIONS

This chapter will attempt to braid the interim conclusions offered in previous chapters of this book, with a view to offering a clearer picture of the existence and application of laws and policies relating to global energy justice. What is evident, when arriving at any conclusions, is that the concept of global energy justice, and its application in law and policy, present complex, sociopolitical and legal challenges that interface and resonate with human rights, international development, the environment, healthcare, climate change, the global economy, and numerous other planetary issues. These issues must be confronted in achieving Sustainable Energy for All (SE4All), and Affordable and Clean Energy under SDG 7, Furthermore, laws, policies, and decisions implementing energy justice need to span energy poverty at all levels, beginning with individuals and traversing local, national, and international communities. These decisions, from local to international levels, should include Affordable Sustainable Energy Technologies (ASETs).

I. The Phenomenon of the Energy Poor

Three conclusions about the Energy Poor are worthy of recapitulation. First, Chapters 1, 3 and 4 establish and illustrate a foundational predicate of the book: The pivotal importance of energy for human progress and development.

Second, the fact of energy poverty is indisputable. Every chapter of this book confirms, in differing ways, that between 1.7 to 3 billion peoples, sometimes described as the Other Third or the Energy Poor (EP), are subject to one or more forms of energy deprivation. This energy deprivation arises from lack of access to clean energy for cooking, lighting, sanitation, drinking water, and motive or mechanical power. Chapter 4 demonstrates the importance of energy justice in addressing energy poverty.

Third, an important finding emerging from our examination of energy poverty is that the burdens of energy deprivation and lack of access to energy are carried preponderantly and disproportionately by women. The harm and hardship inflicted on women and children may amount to silent violence that contravenes their human and natural rights, and negates their right to sustainable development.

Furthermore, the plight of the energy-poor cannot be remedied by relying solely on the states within which they reside. The energy-poor have been glossed over by their identification only as national problems falling within the sovereign jurisdiction of the developing countries they populate. It has been inimical to the energy poor that they are treated as problems of developing countries and not perceived as burdened societies calling for international action, independent of the countries in which they reside.

Fourth, the almost total global fixation on climate change, often promoted by NGOs, has detrimentally impacted the energy poor. In this context, it would be a giant step forward if civil society organizations could shift their gaze from climate change, to focus at least some attention on the more immediate and real problems of energy poverty.

II. Justice and Law in Addressing Energy Poverty

Chapters 2, 4, and the Introduction to Chapters 5 and 6, explains why justice requires that law, as a normative construct, can and should respond to social problems. This book examines how law could be used as an instrument for achieving energy justice.

Chapter 2 delineates the jurisprudential lineages of energy justice, and underlines the unbridged and anomalous chasm between two disciplines: philosophical ethics, and the contemporary jurisprudence of international law. Political and moral philosophers, who have systematically probed issues of global justice, have inexplicably avoided the implications of their theorizing on international law. This omission is baffling, given the reality, relevance, and acceptance of international law by the sovereign states that constitute the international community of nations.

It is just as mystifying and unfortunate that modern international lawyers have been equally oblivious to the importance of structuring international law on the moral and ethical foundations of justice rooted in political and moral philosophy. To all intent and purposes, international lawyers on the one hand and political and moral philosophers on the other populate two different silos that ignore each other. This disconnect must be remedied and chasm between law and moral philosophy must be bridged. Chapter 2 points to how this might be done: International law should, be built upon foundations of justice.

The foundations for creating a principled basis for law, originated in the idea of the law of nations—the *ius gentium*—first articulated In the *Institutes* of the Roman jurist Gaius (130–180). The *ius gentium* is closely associated with the *ius naturale*.[1] Thomas Aquinas (1225–1274), examined the *ius gentium* and placed it within the framework of his theory of natural law. He concluded that the *jus gentium* was that aspect of positive law that was immediately

---

1 Samuel Gregg, *Natural Law and the Law of Nations*, THE WITHERSPOON INSTITUTE, http://www.nlnrac.org/earlymodern/law-of-nations (visited Dec. 5, 2015).

derived by deduction from the natural law and was universally applicable across jurisdictional boundaries[2] In the early modern world, Hugo Grotius (1583–1645), often known as the father of international law, developed his theory of natural law and natural rights from the Roman Law found in the Digest, and he concluded that this law was binding internationally.[3]

Chapter 2 then examines the work of the great moral philosopher John Rawls in order to demonstrate his relevance to contemporary international law. As we have noted, in *The Law of Peoples*,[4] Rawls addresses justice in the international context. In doing so, he extends his theories from liberal democratic states to "decent" peoples living in nondemocratic international societies. Rawls conceives that such "well-ordered hierarchical societies" will include "non-liberal societies" whose basic institutions meet specified conditions of political right and justice. Such conditions include the right of citizens to play a substantial role, such as participating in associations and groups making political decisions, and lead their citizens to honor a reasonably just law for the Society of Peoples.[5] Rawls demonstrated how the law of peoples may be developed out of liberal ideas of justice similar to, but more general than, the idea of "justice as fairness" presented in *A Theory of Justice*.[6]

The result most pertinent to our discussion of justice is that Rawls elucidates the duty of liberal democratic and decent hierarchical peoples to assist "burdened societies" to the point where burdened societies are enabled to join the "Society of Peoples." It is of particular pertinence that Rawls's duty of assistance does not absolve developing country governments of their obligation to take appropriate action.

Within legal theory and international law natural law remains orphaned despite its rich jurisprudential pedigree, and the fact that natural law is invoked and embodied in the Statue of the International Court of Justice. According to the Statute, the International Court of Justice (ICJ) shall apply "the general principles of law recognized by civilized nations" as a primary source of law.[7]

---

2 Fulvio Di Blasi, *Natural Law and Ius Gentium in Thomas Aquinas,* Thomas International Project (2005). http://www.thomasinternational.org/projects/step/conferences/20050712budapest/fdiblasi1.htm.

3 Benjamin Straumann, *Roman Law In The State Of Nature: The Classical Foundations Of Hugo Grotius' Natural Law* 4–5 (2015).

4 John Rawls, *The Law Of Peoples* (1997).

5 *Id.* at 106.

6 *Id.*

7 1945 I.C.J. 59 Stat. 1031 at art. 38(1)(c).

Our brief summary of chapter 2 suggests that concepts of justice, applicable to global energy poverty, may be found within different global jurisprudential lineages, including Western, Islamic, Buddhist, and Confucian traditions. Consequently, it is possible to discover general principles of law and justice within Thomian and non-Thomian natural law, which forms part of the world's jurisprudential heritage. These general principles of law and justice cannot be ignored when shaping the legal response to global energy poverty.

Chapter 4 describes how law, based on principles of energy justice, might respond to the global challenge of energy poverty. Allowing the EP to languish in their current state violates fundamental concepts of international justice and SD. The application of concepts of energy justice and SD, are best justified by John Rawls, who outlined the duty of developed peoples "to assist burdened societies."[8] Rawls' concepts of duty and distributive justice, are the unarticulated major premises of the principles of SD, and more specifically in the MDGs. As noted in chapter 4, the predominance of GPGs in the SDGs mark a retreat, but not a defeat, in addressing the energy poverty of the burdened peoples of the world.

III. Assessing Access to Energy

The SDGs create obstacles, but do not negate the objectives of providing clean energy for the EP. Admittedly, SDG 7 on affordable and clean energy is attenuated by the numerous GPGs particularly those dealing with climate change. But the existence of SDG 7, the incorporation of the MDGs, and the rhetoric on the importance of alleviating poverty in the SDGs, offer opportunities for crafting functional strategies for achieving the UN objective of SE4All.

In moving forward, it is important that access to electricity remain the immediate, future, and final objective of SE4All. But, Chapter 3 cites Simon Trace who points out the need to better define what we mean by access to energy. According to Bazillian and Pielke, also cited in Chapter 3, the US consumes about 13,400 kWh per year per person of electricity, while the consumption in Bulgaria and South Africa, who are at the bottom of the energy consumption ladder, is about 4,500 kWh. In calculating the energy required to provide access to energy for all, the International Energy Agency defines an initial threshold for energy access to be 250 kWh per year for rural households and 500 kWh per year for urban households, assuming five people per household. This equates to 50 to 100 kWh per year per person, or about 0.5 percent of that consumed by the

---

[8] Rawls, *supra* note 4, p. 106.

average American and 1.7 percent of that of the average Bulgarian and South African.

According to Bazilian and Pielke cited in Chapter 3, it would cost about $1 trillion to achieve the total global access rising to 750 kWh per capita for new connections by 2030—and 17 times more ($17 trillion), to achieve a level of worldwide access equivalent to that in Bulgaria.

The Global Tracking Framework of the IEA and World Bank has estimated the cost of achieving the three SE4All goals of electricity for all, doubling energy efficiency, and doubling the use of renewable energy by 2030. Doing so will cost at least $600 to $800 billion per year over and above existing levels, entailing a doubling or tripling of financial flows over current levels. The daunting additional costs, and the time it will take to do so—realistically 2045 to 2050—will shunt the EP into limbo unless intermediate energy sources are offered to them. Therefore, a number of experts suggest, it is also important to create a parallel track based on Affordable Sustainable Energy Technologies (ASETs).[9]

IV. Affordable Sustainable Energy Technologies (ASETs)

Chapter 4 discussed how beneficial energy, based on ASETs, can provide intermediate energy pending the arrival of electricity. ASETs alone cannot extract a country from poverty, but they can play a critical role in boosting economic development and improving the livelihoods of hundreds of millions of the Energy Poor. Some ASETs—such as improved cookstoves, portable water filtration systems, solar-charged illumination, and better mechanical and agricultural technologies—are already being distributed by a variety of projects around the world

ASETs bridge the gap between capital-intensive electricity and the traditional subsistence technologies of the EP. ASETs include: clean fuels, clean cookstoves, illumination by photovoltaic lights, decentralized mini grids based on solar, wind, and biomass-generated electricity, treadle pumps, improved harnesses and yokes which boost the performance of draft cattle, better axles for transport by cart, simple windmills for pumping water, grain grinding appliances, and low-cost bicycles.

---

[9] Jason Aamodt and Blake Feamster, *The role of appropriate sustainable energy technologies (ASETs) as a means for promoting access to energy for all;* Simon Trace, *Measuring access for different needs;* Margaret Matinga et al, *Behavioral challenges and the adoption of appropriate sustainable energy technologies, in International Energy and Poverty: The emerging contours* (Lakshman Guruswamy, ed. 2015).

Several companies and NGOs design, manufacture, and distribute ASETs to the Energy Poor and illustrate how they might be globalized.[10] It is not enough or sufficient for ASETs to be disseminated among just a segment of the EP. The challenge is enormous and calls for the dissemination of hundreds of millions of ASETs. The Global Alliance for Clean Cookstoves is an important international alliance or partnership addressing indoor air pollution and the need for cookstoves. The Global Alliance for Clean Cookstoves has set a target of 100 million households by 2020. But among the ASET needs of the EP for cooking, lighting, sanitation, clean water, and mechanical power, only cooking has received international recognition. Lamentably, the other needs of the EP have not received global recognition or institutional support. The challenge lies in globalizing ASETs that reach out to the unmet and relatively unacknowledged needs of the EP for lighting, sanitation, water, and motive or mechanical power.

The respondents to this challenge can benefit from a few clear lessons. First, it is crucial that NGOs and companies manufacturing and marketing ASETs, understand their markets and communities and act with the awareness that the EP are not a homogenous group.

Second, as noted above, there is a clear need to recognize gender equality as a critical element in achieving sustainable development, and the SDG 5 seeks to achieve gender equality and empower women and girls.[11] To achieve this goal it is necessary to emphasize the importance of recognizing that the lack of access to energy most seriously impacts women and children. In promoting ASETs, it behooves us to design gender- and child-specific policies that are aware of the greater risks confronting women and children.

Third, what constitutes access to energy will depend on whether energy is required for domestic, commercial or livelihood, and/or community purposes. Access to energy cannot be restricted to domestic needs. It is imperative that energy be available for commercial or livelihood purposes so that the EP can earn a living. It is equally important to offer access to energy for school and hospitals that serve the community. It is encouraging that the Global Tracking System[12] has begun taking a more comprehensive approach to energy access.

---

[10] *International Energy and Poverty: The emerging contours*, Chapters 4, 11, 12, 14, 15, 17, and 20 (Lakshman Guruswamy, ed. 2015).

[11] UN Women, *The 2030 Agenda for Sustainable Development,* http://www.unwomen.org/en/what-we-do/post–2015 (visited Dec. 10, 2015).

[12] Angelou, Nicolina; Elizondo Azuela, Gabriela; Banerjee, Sudeshna Ghosh; Bhatia, Mikul; Bushueva, Irina; Inon, Javier Gustavo; Jaques Goldenberg, Ivan; Portale, Elisa; Sarkar, Ashok. 2013. *Executive summary*. Sustainable energy for all. Washington DC; World Bank. http://documents.worldbank.org/curated/en/

Fourth, these energy needs, as well as cultural customs, gender norms, and community expectations vary widely among the Energy Poor. Preexisting cultural behaviors, norms, and traditions can inform whether and how an ASET will be accepted or rejected by a target community. One commentator perspicaciously points out how these cultural norms are critically important regarding gender roles.[13] To be aware of gender norms and behaviors of a community, particularly where cultural capital is concerned, can prove to be of critical advantage in the adoption of ASETs. There are also valuable opportunities, within ASET companies and organizations, to contribute to the empowerment and education of women, and these groups would be well advised to include women where feasible.

Fifth, active interaction and engagement with target communities can provide economic benefit, and subsequent improvement in quality of life to these communities. The experiences of both a nonprofit organization and a for-profit company, demonstrate how company interaction and engagement with their communities benefit both product distribution and provide economic opportunities for local entrepreneurs and agents.[14] In order for both of these benefits to be realized to their full potential, ASET companies must heavily engage with their target communities and make an effort to employ individuals familiar with the customs and people of the communities.

Sixth, it is necessary to offer practical and pragmatic examples of integration. One way of doing so is to promote collaboration among multiple stakeholders involved in the design, fabrication, funding, marketing, deployment, and adoption of ASETs. Such collaboration could be achieved within sectors and regions, through voluntary alliances, such as, solar bulbs in South Asia, or clean drinking water in East Africa.

One objective of such ventures should be to understand and flag the lifecycle of an ASET, from its conception through design and manufacture to marketing and service and its final disposal. Where possible, this requires tracking and tracing the supply and product

---

2013/01/17747194/global-tracking-framework-vol-1-3-global-tracking-framework-executive-summary (visited Feb. 27, 2015). International Energy Agency (IEA) and the World Bank. 2015. "Sustainable Energy for All 2015—Progress Toward Sustainable Energy" (2015).

[13] Margret Matinga et al, *Behavioral challenges and the adoption of appropriate sustainable energy technologies, in. International Energy and Poverty: The emerging contours* (Lakshman Guruswamy ed., 2015).

[14] Doug Vilsack, *Lessons learned from six years of selling solar in Africa,* Stephen Katsaros and Elizabeth Neville, *Globalization of Markets for ASETs, in* International Energy And Poverty: The emerging contours (Lakshman Guruswamy, ed. 2015).

chain of each ASET in a manner that will offer private and public investors a better understanding of every significant link.

Once established, an alliance faces the crucial question of how to promote viable business enterprises that design, manufacture, market, and deploy ASETs in developing countries. This calls for entrepreneurship. Entrepreneurs in developing countries, as well as those in developed countries who wish to set up their enterprises in developing countries, face a host of daunting economic, political, and regulatory risks not encountered in developed countries. These issues have been explored elsewhere.[15]

V. Justice and the Machinery of Law

It was argued in Chapter 3, and noted above, that the SDGs, and especially the primacy afforded to climate change, posed a threat to the Energy Poor. There are different estimates as to the actual costs of addressing climate change, but the expenditure will be enormous, and run into trillions of dollars. Chapter 3 also referred to the costs of the other GPGs, the predisposition of aid granting bodies to favor these GPGs, and the deficit in funding. It is, therefore, difficult to resist the conclusion that funding for access to energy faces a mottled, even daunting future. In light of the difficulties of advancing energy justice for the Energy Poor through the SDGs, this book posits that Model Laws, advancing ASETs, similar to those in Chapters 5 and 6, offer a significant, functional and practical way forward.

Chapters 5 and 6 deal with Model Laws as blueprints for the dissemination of cookstoves and lighting. These Model Laws would be publicly available and downloadable free of cost. These two chapters are examples of how to use law as an engine or mechanism for advancing the use of ASETs for cooking, lighting, sanitation, clean water, and motive power. The particular models illustrating how this might be done, focus on cookstoves and lighting. In each example, one model law applies to developing countries, and a different law applies to developed countries.

The introductions to Chapter 5 and 6 underscores that indoor air pollution, and lack of access to lighting, results in millions of premature deaths of women and children, and are international problems that call for international responses. The two introductions then discuss the formidable complexities and obstacles in drafting international treaties and looks for other ways of using laws, based on global energy justice and principles of sustainable development, common but differentiated responsibility, and SE4All, to reduce indoor air pollution. Model laws are presented as vehicles for doing

---

[15] Lakshman Guruswamy, *Conclusion*, in *International Energy and Poverty: The emerging contours*, Lakshman Guruswamy, ed. (2015).

so. The central idea is that both developed and developing countries should accept their common but differentiated responsibilities, predicated on global energy justice, by enacting Model Laws.

For their part, developing countries adopt legislation for the development and dissemination of cookstoves and lighting. The illustrative national laws on the dissemination of clean cookstoves and lighting contains a variety of legislative prescriptions that create a blueprint for adopting clean cookstoves and lighting. They include legislative findings about energy poverty and silent violence on women, policies articulating what actions need to be taken, National Minimum Standards and Certifications, Indoor Ambient Air Quality Standards, Interim Standards, Durability Standards, and Testing and Certification. The Model Laws recognize the need for administrative discretion and the establishment of an agency if necessary. The laws requires needs assessments, and specifications, in making cookstove and lighting selections.

They also provides for targeted installations and pilot projects, completions and review of pilot projects, and the implementation mechanisms and administration required. These include the strategic plans and the encouragement of market-based solutions. They also embodies sections dealing with monitoring and implementation and authorization and appropriations. In dealing with Research and Development (R & D), they deal with cooking and lighting technologies, health and safety, foreign aid, public information, education, and public health. Finally, there are provisions on enforcement by way of civil remedies, citizen enforcement, and criminal penalties

Developed countries would adopt a different law for the dissemination and development of clean cookstoves and lighting. They contain policies and provisions that encourage manufacturing industries for clean cookstoves and lighting in developing countries by supporting international partnerships and local entrepreneurs with financial, institutional, and technological assistance. The Model Laws also promote the distribution and maintenance of clean cookstoves and lighting by differing entities, including individuals in developing countries, and provides funding for research, development, and deployment of clean cookstoves and lighting and the necessary air quality monitoring systems for developing countries. They also deal with the support and dissemination of research and monitoring of the adverse human health and environmental effects associated with the black carbon and other pollutants emitted by inefficient cookstoves.

Toward these ends, each developed country will established within the ministry or agency for international aid a Clean Cookstove and Lighting Manufacturing and Distribution Program. The purpose of the program will be to provide international partnerships and local entrepreneurs with financial, institutional, and technological assistance to develop, manufacture, promote, distribute, and maintain clean cookstoves and lighting in developing countries. The program shall be funded.

If a significant number of developing and developed countries adopt and enact these model laws as national legislation, they will create a critical mass of laws addressing indoor air pollution and lack of lighting. These national laws will address the international problem of indoor air pollution by circumventing the intimidating and problem-ridden treaty making process.

The primary objective of this book is that societies the world over will re-discover the importance of global energy justice within their variegated philosophical traditions. Having done so, it is imperative they find practical ways of applying these principles to the burdened peoples of the world. Every step taken, however small, will create footprints leading to a better world.

INDEX

References are to Pages